COLLECTED POEMS

Literature of Canada

Poetry and Prose in Reprint

Douglas Lochhead, General Editor

Collected Poems

Isabella Valancy Crawford

Introduction by James Reaney

UNIVERSITY OF TORONTO PRESS

© University of Toronto Press 1972
Toronto and Buffalo
Printed in Canada
ISBN 0-8020-1936-6 (cloth)
ISBN 0-8020-6170-2 (paper)
ISBN Microfiche 0-8020-0275-7
LC 72-91689

Preface

Yes, there is a Canadian literature. It does exist. Part of the evidence to support these statements is presented in the form of reprints of the poetry and prose of the authors included in this series. Much of this literature has been long out of print. If the country's culture and traditions are to be sampled and measured, both in terms of past and present-day conditions, then the major works of both our well known and our lesser known writers should be available for all to buy and read. The Literature of Canada series aims to meet this need. It shares with its companion series, The Social History of Canada, the purpose of making the documents of the country's heritage accessible to an increasingly large national and international public, a public which is anxious to acquaint itself with Canadian literature — the writing itself — and also to become intimate with the times in which it grew.

DL

Isabella Valancy Crawford, 1850-87

James Reaney

Introduction

Since I have already written about the poetry of Isabella Valancy Crawford elsewhere I have been rather puzzled as to what I should do, especially when such a long hoped for and important event as this occurs – the reprinting of her *Collected Poems*, a volume long unobtainable but more and more searched for, particularly in the last twenty years when Canada has at last wanted eyes and prophets and ears and poets as well as the stomachs and politicians and bloodpumpers and doctors and toes and journalists it has, before now, been quite content with. Yes, where was that eye that tried to see for us in the 1880s? Well, you are holding it in your hands and it may be almost too late to see with it.

The answer to the above-mentioned puzzlement is the following attempt to construct an introduction which will bring together as many viewpoints and reactions as possible. For one thing I want to keep as much as I can of the prefatory material to the original edition: the 'Word from the Editor,' John W. Garvin, and the 'Introduction' by Ethelwyn Wetherald. Probably what I mean just here is that I want the reader to grasp the feeling this once gave me, and still does, of a past literary world in our country, in this case – Ontario – just a few years before Lawren Harris painted *Hurdy Gurdy* and those other very moving street scenes of the Ward in Toronto, not so far from the house on John Street in which Isabella Crawford died. Perhaps I shall want to bring together so many things, some of them almost of an objective and certainly documentary nature, that I might as well tell you now that what follows is really a collage (like those

Jackdaws that Clarke, Irwin prints on Riel and the Depression, etc.) out of which the reader may, if he likes, construct something.

A What is this? Through the gloom of a basement jungle in Peterborough-Hindoostan comes gliding a safari consisting of a large elephant, and behind it a much smaller one — baby? Perched on the larger elephant, three turbaned Hindoos — one the driver with stick, one with feather, and one steadying the sides of a still bright blue tasseled elephant howdah. An entourage of at least six high Brahmin types with long white beards are beating the ground before the elephant-emperor. Behind, astraddle the smaller beast come two children? back to back. Their Brahmin is larger than the others and carries a longer wand to beat back the cobras and panthers, or it might be Bombay riff-raff since it is also possible that the creator of this scene intended to show us one of the great squares of a Holy City; for just beneath us a pedlar-snake-charmer squats on a rug with a tray proffered of fruit? although his snake wriggles about a great deal too much. And needs a footnote I can't manage even with a magnifying glass.

This happens to be embroidery sculpture made by Miss Crawford to amuse a sick child eight years old; the whole tableau is about two feet high and wide, long etc. and the only one to survive of a whole series mentioned in Katherine Hale's 1923 volume in the 'Makers of Canadian Literature' series. If you should ever go to the Peterborough Centennial Museum, ask to see it; kept in the basement at present, it will one day I hope get upstairs where it belongs and where the sunshine brings out still the glitter of faded brocades and silks, and reinforces one's feeling even down in the basement that whoever made these marionettes

viii

knew how to make things that have swagger and strut and suggest a whole journey both before and behind them.

B   Central Ontario Medical Association
Peterborough Medical Society 1902-1922

Crawford, Dr

Dr Crawford lived in Peterborough, in the early sixties, and did an irregular practice, being in years when he came to the town. The family lived for a time in one of the first houses of the brick terrace on the east side of Water St opposite the market square.

The following narrative, related to the writer, by one who participated, is interesting. 'In the summer of 1864 my brother and I travelling for the Canada Land Company throughout Eastern Canada, happened to put up for the night at a village hotel, north of Kingston.

There we met Dr Crawford, at that time a man of nearly sixty years of age. His wife, a son and two daughters. The eldest of these daughters afterwards turned out to be that great poetess of Canada, Isabel Valancy Crawford.

They seemed to be very poorly off and we felt really sorry for them out here in Canada amidst such unsuitable surroundings. My brother, knowing that there was no resident physician in the village of Lakefield, made to them the following offer. That they move to Lakefield and make use of his home during the months in which he would be away from the village.'

His offer was accepted and presently Dr Crawford and family came to the village and he took up practice being the first resident practitioner that Lakefield acquired.

His practice was not very remunerative and afterwards the family removed to Peterborough, where Dr Crawford carried on for several years until his death. The date of which is not recorded.

This too was found in the above museum.[1] From Katherine Hale's book we learn that

the Crawfords were of Highland, and later of Irish, descent, and it was in Dublin, on Christmas Day, 1850, that there was born to Sydney Scott and Stephen Dennis Crawford, her husband, a daughter, whom they named for a maternal relative, Isabella Valancy. Dr Crawford was a man of wide experience and literary culture. ... In 1858 they migrated to Canada, and, of all places, to a little Ontario village just emerging from the bush, the village of Paisley upon the Saugeen River. Here, instead of golden guineas, ordinary farm produce was exchanged for medical service, and there was hardship for them all. But from the first the family lived true to its traditions, and even yet in Paisley one may hear echoes of the Crawfords' dignified hospitality.

For six years this village existence was continued, formative years of a child's life. The Crawfords were unlike the other young people of the settlement. The girls were not sent to the public school, but were carefully grounded in Latin and English by their parents, and in French, which they spoke fluently. Isabella Valancy was especially fond of reading, and attached to the kind of books that no young girl in an Ontario village in the early sixties had studied — translations of Horace and of Dante, for instance. But to offset all this education there was the splendid and primitive drama of the bush going on around them; the rush of its streams, the life of its trees, their death, too, as they fell crashing in the forest under the woodsman's axe. Even more than her sisters did Isabella love the forest; it was her mightiest book, and she possessed a vigorous young body which nature loved and called. Nature was unkind to the others. There were twelve children when they came to Paisley, and only three when, eight years later, the family removed to Lakefield.

The first document catches the family between Paisley in Grey County (western Ontario) and Lakefield on the borderland of the Kawartha Lakes district (and so in eastern Ontario) scene of Susanna Moodie's *Roughing it in the Bush* and also of her sister's much more loving *Studies of Plant Life in Canada*. Katherine Hale continues, 'There were several old English families living in or near [Lakefield] and hence congenial society.' Aside from the interesting fact that Isabella Crawford came to Canada at the same age as did Jay Macpherson, one thing that strikes me here is the probable magic collision of Canada West and all that means in the nineteenth century – farms, primeval forest, very fresh *new* villages, the slightly wild (not quite *pays d'en haut*) Grey County landscape so close to the limestone cliffs of the Bruce. Out of this collision between a new landscape and the cultivation of her family probably came some of her strongest imagery. It's important, I think, to remember the Horace and Dante; unlike others who came to Canada about the same time (I'm thinking of fellow Irishmen on the Roman Line in the Donnelly story) the Crawfords brought really cultivated minds, mirrors in which the Canadian forests, and animals and birds and men found an expression unavailable since petroglyph days. The Moodies, of course, were cultivated too; but the reflection there sometimes was ironic and evil. It is Mrs Moodie's sister Catharine Parr Traill who has the ability to love the strange newness that Isabella Crawford loved with even more intensity. When I speak of 'magic collision' I would like to emphasize *collision*, for I have just been looking at a drawing of Reydon Hall, Suffolk, the home of Mrs Traill's father, Thomas Strickland. *Country Life* (22 January 1970) opines that 'the log-house in Ontario was a far cry from this'; true, the drawing reeks of rootedness and civility. Would the Crawford family have come from some Georgian set-up in Dublin where every square inch of ground would be tiled or paved or cared for and then the shock (still there when you go from Europe to a Canadian airport) as you feel ground with your feet that is simply not used to you, and grass that is not used to being sheared as English and Irish grass and twigs have for centuries. Somewhat earlier, another Anglo-Irish girl (in 1827) came out to Pickering, Ontario, and expressed a 'collision' in what is known in folk-art circles as the Jane Reazon quilt; part of the quilt shows castle fireplaces, young lovers under a flower arbour with nearby chaperon, riding to hounds, balls, suddenly turning to: rough benches, pot-bellied stoves, hunters seriously hunting ducks for food and so on. In Crawford this becomes the gyres and circle of Dante turning into spirals of stampeding cattle and huge world-enclosing daffodils and pond lilies. However, I can only speculate. The reader needs the sort of definitive biography that is now being written for Major Richardson, the author of *Wacousta*; there the 'magic collision' is between his Indian self and his white father, I expect. I think nowadays we tend to imagine the pioneer period as being far behind us; but it is only *now* that we see what a strange meeting was back there and it is *now* that we need help in dealing with its after-effects. 'They seemed to be very poorly off and we felt really sorry for them, out here in Canada amidst such..."

C It may seem a bit soon to switch to the obituaries but perhaps what happened to Isabella Crawford *after* she left Lakefield and Peterborough is most simply presented this way.

The Evening Telegram, Toronto, Monday, 14 February 1887

'The Reporter's Diary'

...
— The death of Miss Isabella Valancy Crawford occurred at half-past eleven on Saturday night at 57 John Street, where she lived with her mother, widow of Dr Stephen Crawford, of Peterboro. Miss Crawford was one of the best known of Canadian writers, and furnished many stories for Frank Leslie's publications. Not long ago she published a book of poems, which were highly spoken of by the English and Canadian press. A week ago last Saturday one of the poems entitled 'The Rose of a Nation's Thanks,' written on the return of the volunteers from the Northwest, was republished by request in this paper, and a continued story entitled 'Married with an Opal; or, a Kingly Restitution,' is at present running through a serial published by the Toronto News Co. Miss Crawford was a young lady of marked ability and native wit, and had already made her mark in the world of literature, poetry as well as prose.

The Globe, Toronto, Monday, 14 February 1887

'Local News'

...

A TALENTED LADY DEAD

On Saturday evening Isabella Valancy Crawford, the last surviving daughter of the late Stephen Crawford of Peterborough, suddenly passed away at 57 John Street, in this city. She spent part of her life in France, and was an accomplished linguist. She was well known to the readers of THE GLOBE as the writer of 'The Little Bacchante,' together with several poems of extraordinary merit. For several years she has written for leading American and English newspapers, and published one volume of poems which received the highest commendation from first-class English literary journals.

Glancing over columns beside these items the reader sees the great Empire she was born into: 'Mr Gladstone's Vigorous Letter on Home Rule,' A SOCIALIST DEMONSTRATION IN GLASGOW and 'Falls Road Rioters.' As well, in the country she died in, there were outcries against 'mutilated scriptures' and announcements of DOMINION ELECTIONS and 'The Lynch Mowat Concordat'!

By 1895, some years later, an article by E.J. Hathaway with a perspective somewhat wider than the above obituaries appeared in *The Canadian Magazine*:

During the ten years previous to her death, in 1887, she contributed much, both of verse and prose to the local press and also to Frank Leslie's publications in New York, and had she lived she undoubtedly would have occupied a place in the world of letters with the very best of her time.

Miss Crawford was born in Ireland and spent her earlier years in France, but for many years her home had been in Canada, at first in the town of Peterborough and afterwards in Toronto.

From time to time, during several years, there appeared in the columns of *The Evening Telegram* verses of sentiment, of description and of heroics, and, although they attracted some attention, few of the many readers knew anything of the writer beyond the fact that her name was Isabella Valancy Crawford. These verses bore the stamp of genius and showed a true, poetic instinct. They were copied at times by the provincial press, and the name of their author soon became widely known as a writer of marked ability.

About the year 1885 a serial story by her, entitled 'A Little Bacchante, or Some Black Sheep,' appeared in the Toronto *Globe*. This was an honor which few local writers had ever received, and the success of the novel proved the wisdom of the selection. Short stories also appeared in the *Globe*'s columns at intervals, and at the time of her death she had almost completed another lengthy novel — 'Married with an Opal' — which subsequently appeared in the *Fireside Weekly*.

But it is as a poetess that Miss Crawford's name will be remembered. Among the first to recognize her ability was John Ross Robertson, of the Toronto *Evening Telegram*, and her published poems appeared only in the columns of that journal. In 1884 she issued a modest, blue card-board covered volume of poems called 'Old Spookses' Pass; Malcolm's Katie, and other poems.' This volume contained only pieces which had never yet been printed, and it came into the world without even the dignity of its publisher's imprint. But whether it was that its unfortunate name was against it, or no effort was made to push its sale, the fact is that it almost dropped from the press. Scarcely anybody but the critics noticed the little book, and when, some two years later, the authoress died, many attributed her early death to the neglect which her book had suffered. She was a passionate, high-spirited girl, and, though many kind expressions of appreciation were afterwards made, they arrived too late — the poor authoress had died, possibly of a broken heart.

Miss Crawford appeared to be about 30 years of age, somewhat stout and a little below the average height. Her dress was poor, at times almost shabby, and it was not until she spoke that one was at all impressed with her personality. Her features were not beautiful, but in conversation she lighted up and her eyes sparkled with vivacity to an unusual degree. She was a clever conversationalist and an accomplished linguist, and her animation and versatility made her a delightful companion.

Ungallant E.J. Hathaway no doubt was to write 'stout' and 'shabby,' but nevertheless someone to be thanked for giving us a note we needed; she was a *real* person. And the life after girlhood, then, seems to go like this: writes the important *narrative* poems in Toronto(?) as well as lyrics, novels, and short stories, all of which, since the family is poor, she is writing if at all possible for money. Her work is accepted by some of the same American magazines that L.M. Montgomery first wrote for; my impression is that they at least paid her something, while the Canadian magazines did not. An editorial in the *Varsity*, the University of Toronto student paper still with us, said on 23 January 1886 that 'The novel by Isabella Crawford in the *Globe* is vastly superior to the ordinary run of newspaper fiction.' This would be *The Little Bacchante*, apparently lost, since it appeared in the uncollected *Evening Globe*. Other prose MSS exist, and I shall be quoting from them in just a moment; but first of all it would not have been hard to write better than most of the newspaper novelists of that era. 'It is useless to ask it, Olive,' replied John, 'Lady Trewavas stays here herself, and Eleanor with her, and Hilton returns home with them to-morrow, if well enough. You see all your mad endeavours to separate these two, only endear them the more to each other' (8 October 1880, *True to the Last, The Listowel Banner*). The trick to be turned would be to curb the structures in Dante and the Bible learned so long ago as a natural imaginative tongue, and somehow adapt to pasteboard outworn romance conventions in order to help her family. When does Dr Crawford die; in the mid seventies? Her brother Stephen Crawford goes to Algoma. The Garvins knew him, and evidently received the MSS from him. What was he like? What about the mother and an invalid sister, Emma Naomi 'always busy with beautiful and intricate designs in embroidery. On one piece she had worked for a year, and sent it, in hopes of a sale or a prize, to the Centennial Exhibition at Philadelphia. It was lost in the mails. At the same time it was announced that Isabella had won a six-hundred dollar prize in a short story competition. This meant financial salvation. But on the heels of the first cheque for a hundred dollars came the news that the prize-giving corporation had failed and nothing more was to be expected from them. It is not improbable that this double blow, so tragic for the two sisters, should have hastened the heart disease which afflicted Emma Naomi, as it had the other ill-fated children, for she died, leaving Isabella and her mother alone.'

Katherine Hale continues: 'They left Peterborough and went to live in Toronto, taking lodgings over a grocery shop at the corner of King and John Streets, kept by Mrs Charles J. Stuart, who was a sincere friend to the young poet and her mother. The two were very lonely. The spirit which in Peterborough had been too proud to admit visitors because there was "no fire in the drawing-room to keep them warm" was not that which beckons those friends and acquaintances who pass on the legend of one's work. Single-handed, Isabella fought her battle for recognition. She would take her poems to the *Globe* and the *Telegram* and sell them for little or nothing. They gleamed there for a day in their strange foreign beauty and were forgotten. She made them of subjects far and near, sometimes of roses in Madrid, sometimes of a little French laundress, washing out her clothes on the bank of a river that she had never seen, sometimes of Toronto in September, and once when the soldiers were returning after the Battle of Batoche, in 1885, she made a beautiful song of welcome for them, which appeared in the Toronto *Telegram*, and is called "The Rose of a Nation's Thanks." ' '

'We hope that Canadian editors will endeavour to do their best to encourage native talent. They should also pay for it,' continued the *Varsity* editorial we have already quoted from. Of course, but what we worry about even more is that the mother, by the sound of things, survived her last daughter's death in Toronto. Out of twelve children, Mrs Crawford would have had only Stephen left, and although from our point of view the journey they took in 1858 was wonderful – gave poetry here an ancestress, a grandmother – the mother might have had a different opinion about a New World where winters must have been harder than Dublin's, where people must have seemed rougher, more wearing, especially to those with heart conditions. Also, the obituaries mention the poet's stay in France. The reader needs more information here as well as how much contact in Paisley and Lakefield there might have been with Indians. This woman — Isabella Valancy Crawford — is someone in our past everyone benefits from knowing more about; her life resembles a trial-run for the imagination in this country, and because the run was made and dared it has been much easier since.

D What is the experience of reading these collected poems like? I would like to take the reader through my personal copy and glance at the marginalia. The editor, J.W. Garvin, tells us that 'the contents have been divided into four books, the first containing forty-seven shorter and simpler poems of rarely beautiful quality...' When I first started to read this section I remember thinking that it was going to be some time before I reached the passages I couldn't forget in *Malcolm's Katie*. Many of the forty-seven 'shorter and simpler' poems are the sort that appear in Victorian gift book collections; collections by Lucy Larcom, Mary Howitt, John G. Whittier with Tennyson and Longfellow a great distance out in front: such titles as 'Fairy Toil,' 'Sylvanus to Chloris' and 'Said the Skylark' indicate the lukewarm temperature to be expected. But my pencil finds things to underline that I don't find in Whittier, Helen Hunt Jackson or Longfellow — or, sometimes, even Tennyson. Across the convention of the parlour gift book lyric will come a line such as 'This mighty Viking was the Night' ('A Harvest Song') or 'Outside, the convent maple stirs — /Her leafy playmate, plumed and tall' ('Fairy Toil') or '... love is a cord woven out of life,/And dyed in the red of the living heart;/And time is the hunter's rusty knife,/That cannot cut the red strands apart' ('The Carnage of Souls'). There is a shock, a bite here that we didn't expect in a poet who can also rhyme lawn, fawn, and dawn with the followers of Lord Alfred. 'The Inspiration of Song' is a Queen whose 'turret hung above a glassy lake'; in this poem I began to sense that Crawford had an imagination that was architectural — there were levels of meaning, a grammar of image, of various worlds she was constantly referring to. She was tough like Bach; not all moody and glimmery like late romantic Chopin. This structural strength of a hidden myth shows itself in 'The darkness built its wigwam walls/Close round the camp, and at its curtain/Pressed shapes...' ('Said the Canoe'); Night is a 'startled stag' hunted by the Sun; a true moon is accompanied by a 'false moon in the sea.' In the last lyric of this first section the epigraphs from not only First Corinthians but also the *Bhagavad Gita* and *Rig Veda* reveal the adventurousness of her mind. She had a mind that was no doubt daily thinking about an iconic backbone of Eden, Beulah, Fallen World, Hell: whether she got it from India or not doesn't matter. Its presence, and in the places I have pointed out, its successful presence, carry one past expendable poems about 'Roses in Madrid' (the sort of subject the London, Ontario, painter Paul Peel would be finding commercially profitable about the same time) and sailors' brides. After I found these 'iconic' passages I re-read in my mind the beginning of a long poem (*not* lyrical) she should have, could have, written, but never quite did. Readers who get to like her voice will probably construct this hidden sub-poem best by themselves. Before leaving this section I might add that I wish 'Thistle Down' had ended with the destruction of 'lilied chastity'; it almost does and in some of the erotic imagery elsewhere certainly does. Also as a lover of regional local colour I'm struck by 'a rugged bush of tansy,' but nothing else in a poem called 'Love in a Daisy.'

Book Two, in which Mr Garvin promises us 'fifteen poems of greater length and stronger fibre,' gives us just that: 'gyres' in 'Gisli, the Chieftain' seems a key word to me round which, since it means dynamic, restless interchange of opposites, easily cluster the drunken slave and Puritan Spartan of 'The Helot'; the River's iron lip versus the barky towers of the tree-souls in 'The Ghost of the Trees'; brother Evil and brother Good in 'Gisli, the Chieftain' and last of all, the 'cedar paddle, scented red' which is 'thrust down through the lily-bed' in a poem entitled with the last three words I have just quoted. Beside 'Till now he stood, in triumph's rest./His image painted in her breast' at the age of twenty I pencilled ♂ and ♀ : by this I don't just mean male and female, but Mars and Venus. Her universe has levels that reflect each other from the Queen of Heaven/Anima Mundi figure already mentioned to the red and white lovers hermaphroditically reflecting each other à la Phoenix and Turtle or Scudamour and Amoret. Right offhand I can't think of any nineteenth-century poet in our country who could write a poem where eros and cosmos so beautifully meet; except, as I've hinted before, Indian love chants (a West Coast chant collected by Kenneth Peacock about a girl making a basket for a coiled, woven whip). While speaking of our nineteenth-century poets I think of how Crawford might have handled Roberts' poem about the flaying of Marsyas. He can only, it seems to me, give you a two-dimensional handling – Marsyas made the bad mistake of thinking he could rival Apollo's music and so he has to be skinned. *She* would get at the other dimension lurking in the ritual origin of the myth in which Marsyas can only be renewed by singing and rivaling and sloughing off his *old* skin to joyfully grow a new one, even *become* Apollo. Crawford has that way of looking at things.

The other two books of Garvin's division contain the two long narrative poems I find representative of her very best work. I think that before I discuss these I would like to set before you some reactions contemporary to the first publication of *Old Spookses' Pass* and *Malcolm's Katie*.

E   A CANADIAN CONTRIBUTION

...

Here is a volume that comes from a Country as yet unfertile of literature. If the harvest is as good as the first fruits, it will be well, for Miss Crawford writes with a power of expression quite unusual among aspirants to poetic fame. The first poem is written in a dialectic which we commonly associate with the Western States, and tells in a vigorous fashion (though not without a curious, and we should think inappropriate sprinkling of ornate literary English), the story of a stampede of cattle in a pass of the Rocky Mountains. 'Malcolm's Katie' is a live story spoiled in a way by an immoderate use of rhetoric, witness Alfred's speech on pp. 66-7, (such a tirade as surely never was delivered over a camping fire in the woods), but still powerful. Miss Crawford's blank verse is indeed of no ordinary kind. Here is a passage which seems to us finely expressed, and which has besides the great merit of freshness; —

> I heard him tell
> How the first field upon his farm was ploughed.
> He and his brother Reuben, stalwart lads,
> Yoked themselves, side by side, to the new plough;

Their weaker father, in the grey of life —
But rather the wan age of poverty
Than many winters — in large, gnarlèd hands
The plunging handles held; with mighty strains
They drew the ripping beak through knotted sod,
Thro' tortuous lanes of blackened, smoking stumps,
And past great flaming brush-heaps, sending out
Fierce summers, beating on their swollen brows.
O such a battle! had we heard of serfs
Driven to the hot conflict with the soil,
Armies had marched and navies swiftly sailed
To burst their gyves. But here's the little point —
The polished-diamond pivot on which spins
The wheel of difference — they OWNED the soil,
And fought for love — dear love of wealth and power -
And honest ease and fair esteem of men.

The passage descriptive of forest scenery in Part II of the same poem is also noteworthy. There are other poems, also, which might be mentioned, did space permit; on the whole, this volume seems full of promise.
[*Spectator*, London, England, 18 October 1884]

POETRY

A very unpretentious-looking volume is OLD SPOOKSES' PASS, MALCOLM'S KATIE, AND OTHER POEMS: by Isabella Valancy Crawford (Toronto: James Bain and Son); and at the first glance, even after the first few stanzas, one is not disposed to think that to send it so many miles, so many thousand miles indeed, for the opinion of English readers, was a happy thought either for them or for the writer. But a different conclusion is soon drawn: the first piece, notwithstanding the unpoetical, slangy diction in which (after a questionable modern fashion) it is written, shows a depth of feeling and a power of description indicative of the real poetic faculty, and the second piece causes us to feel grateful to the author for giving us the opportunity of reading what is truly a beautiful, charming little poem, abounding in noble sentiments, picturesque narration, glowing language, and pathetic touches, combined with simple, impressive dignity. If this little volume be a fair specimen of our Canadian brethren's minor muse, their higher and more ambitious efforts must be very noteworthy indeed. The most striking blemishes in this extremely promising collection are faulty versification, and grammatical or orthographical errors; but the former can be easily remedied by care and study, and the latter are no doubt due, in many instances, to mistakes of the press. Indeed, the writer expressly states that there are at least a hundred and fifty such mistakes, which have been allowed to go uncorrected from considerations of expense. These matters, the versification and the errors that may be ascribed partly to the hurry of composition in two senses, are of comparatively little importance: that which is inborn, which cannot be acquired by any training or any amount of attention and application, which belongs to those only whose birth has watched by Melpomene with gentle smile, is the one thing needful; and that is exhibited in no small degree. That the pieces are unequal it can scarcely be necessary to state; this is always the case, and it should be sufficient for the writer's and the reader's satisfaction to know that the best are very good indeed. Such, at least, is the opinion of one who has derived much pleasure from them, and felt much admiration for them. The question whether poetry may not be considered to lose in height what it gains in breadth, to be degraded to some extent, by the adoption of that slangy phraseology which has been mentioned, and which, though it adds to the reality, detracts from the grace and delicacy of a poem, there is here neither space nor inclination to discuss.

[*Illustrated London News*, 3 April 1886]

THE WEEK, 24 February 1887

...

A Canadian book can be viewed in two ways: it can be regarded as simply a Canadian book, and valued accordingly for its treatment and choice of Canadian subjects, or it can be compared with books published in other countries with regard to conception, execution, style, and weight and value of thought. How many Canadian books can be reviewed under the latter heading? Possibly three or four certainly not more than half a dozen. The names of Heavysege, Sangster, Kirby, Prof. Roberts, Mrs Maclean, among our English-Canadian writers, occur to me. Two or three of these names are slightly, though favourably, known in England and in occasional circles in the States — I speak, of course, here only of *belles lettres* properly considered; that is, poetry and lighter prose. It would not hurt us if these names were a little more known amongst ourselves, and with them the name of Isabella Valancy Crawford, author of 'Old Spookses' Pass' and other poems. There can be no mistake about Miss Crawford's rank as a poet. Her work fulfils the most arduous conditions that the modern school can impose. There is scholarship in her book (a rare thing in Canada); there is that intimate knowledge of Nature and all natural processes which belongs so divinely to Tennyson, and which the more erotic poets show so much indifference to; there is a positive riot of imagery, warm, dazzling, and mostly correct; there is a wonderful command over various trying forms of verse, and there is a deep, spiritual vein under all the overlying charms of metre and rhetoric that proclaim the thinker as well as the versifier. The very highest qualities of the poet meet in her best work, notably, 'Malcolm's Katie,' a story in blank verse of about fifteen hundred lines; in 'The Helot,' a lurid picture of Spartan aggression, told in four hundred lines of simple but impressive quatrain and in one or two highly original shorter pieces, such as 'The Ghosts of the Trees' and 'March.' The subjects are mostly drawn from old-world sources, and exhibit a variety and degree of culture which entitle the book to the consideration of the world, and not one public alone. Here are 'Roses in Madrid' —

Roses, Senors, roses!
    Love is subtly hid
In the fragrant roses
    Blown in gay Madrid.

Catch the roses, Senors,
    Light on finger-tips;
He who buys red roses
    Dreams of crimson lips.

Tinkle! my fresh roses,
    With the rare dew wet;
Clink! my crisp, red roses,
    Like a castanet!

And here La Bouquetière sings in Paris while the guillotine
crashes down momentarily behind her:

> Buy my flowers, citizens —
>   Here's a Parma violet;
> Ah! why is my white rose red?
>   'Tis the blood of a grisette.
>
> She sold her flowers by the quay —
>   Brown her eyes and fair her hair;
> Sixteen summers old, I think —
>   With a quaint, Provincial air.
> *Vogue la galère!* she's gone the way
>   That flesh as well as flowers must stray.

And here the Roman rose-seller:

> Not from Paestum come my roses; Patrons, see
> My flowers are Roman-blown. Marcus Lucius, thou
> To-day dost wed; buy roses, roses, roses,
> To mingle with the nuptial myrtle...
>   ...Virginia.
>
> Here's a rose that has a canker in't, and yet
> It is most glorious dyed, and sweeter smells
> Than those death hath not touched. ...
>
>   ...Priestess, priestess,
> Thy ivory chariot stay. ...
>
>   Thus I make
> My roses Oracles. O hark! the cymbals beat
> In god-like silver bursts of sound; I go
> To see great Caesar leading Glory home
> From Campus Martius to the Capitol!

There are many more glimpses of Spain and Italy, all vivid, highly coloured, and correct. Very different in manner are the following extracts from the 'Helot':

> Day was at her high unrest,
>   Fevered with the wine of light;
> Loosing all her golden vest,
>   Reeled she toward the coming night
>   ...
> Neck-curved, serpent, silent, scaled,
>   With locked rainbows stole the sea
> On the sleek, long beaches; wail'd
>   Doves from column and from tree.

And different again these superb bits of blank verse:

> ...The lean, lank lion peals
> His midnight thunders over lone, red plains,
> Long-ridged, and crested on their dusty waves
> With fires from moons red-hearted as the sun.
>   ...
> O, am I breeding that false thing, a heart?
> Making my breast all tender for the fangs
> Of sharp remorse to plunge their hot fire in.
>   ...
> Between the last loud bugle of the Wind
> And the first silver coinage of the Rain
> Upon my flying hair, there came her kiss.

Of the passion of Love Miss Crawford is no stale exponent. What can be more original than this?

O Love! art thou a silver deer,
 Swift thy starred feet as wing of swallow,
 While we with rushing arrows follow;
And at the last shall we draw near,
 And over thy velvet neck cast thongs,
 Woven of roses, of stars, of songs?

In Nature there is nothing that escapes her, from the pines at sunrise, transformed into 'cressets of pure gold' (*vide* Ruskin, who asserts that only two English poets have noticed this, Shakespeare and Wordsworth), to the 'ice-pale blooms, firing all the bay with angel fires built up of snow and gold.'

But to multiply extracts would not be to give even an idea of the versatility and scope of her rare genius, and so I can only commend the book in its entirety to Canadian readers. Miss Crawford was not a Canadian by birth, and there is little, if any, direct Canadian inspiration in her verse, but by right of adoption her work is ours, and we should be proud of it. If it will not be putting last what should have come first, the worth of her work is, perhaps, best shown by her English notices. The *Athenaeum*, the *Spectator*, the *Literary World*, the *Graphic*, the *Illustrated London News*, the *Leisure Hour*, and the *Saturday Review* all contributed lengthy and enthusiastic notices of the book.

The cause of Miss Crawford's untimely death was heart disease. She was of a retiring disposition, and lived very quietly with her mother. Of her prose I have not spoken, though even in that uncommon talent is revealed, in spite of some offences against good taste.

SERANUS

I find it ominous that the first two British reviews are conscious of something unusual in her narrative power ('tells in a vigorous fashion' and 'depth of feeling') whereas the Canadian reviewer ultimately emphasizes, by quotation at least, the 'Roses in Madrid' aspect of her talent. Narrative poets are hard to present in readers and anthologies but the axle-epiphany moments in her story poems are superior to the 'O love builds on the azure sea' or 'Bite deep and wide, O Axe' lyrics which have been for generations the Crawford selections young readers get to see in this country. The native myopia about her abilities, despite the fact that this collection sold 600 copies in a few weeks when it first appeared in 1905, continued well on into the twentieth century with refusals to anthologize the 'one great daffodil' passage from *Malcolm's Katie*, statements about her being too undisciplined or 'pseudo-Indian' or 'clumsily florid' and, one suspects, men's suspicions about what one reviewer called the 'virility' of 'Miss Crawford's writings' (*Canadian Magazine*, October 1895). Fortunately, the power and the primitive directness found admirers in such critics as Frye, Daniells and younger critics such as the late Frank Bessai and John Ower.

But if one reads the two story poems mentioned above with an open mind, as stories, not as lyrics where every sound counts; as flowing narrative filled with symbolic turns and psychological landscape, then the following is the result:

In the beginning there was a huge daffodil which contained all reality, was all reality — its centre was everywhere and its circumference nowhere. It was both inside out and outside in at the same time. What upheld this huge daffodil? It was caused, like the reality that existed before God created the angels, by a Trinity of the 'one beloved, the lover and sweet love.' In the world of the daffodil there was neither day nor night — the stars, moon, and sun shone all at once, not spelling each other off as they do in our fallen world or drowning each other out either. Crawford suggests that this daffodil apocalypse is possible whenever two human beings love each other.

But for some unaccountable reason the daffodil shattered — broke apart, divided. Perhaps, as the theosophist Jacob Boehme puts it, the unity of God wanted to show forth its wonders. One of these wonders is pain and another is evil and another is good; sometimes when one has experienced all three of these one wishes that God would stop showing forth his wonders and tuck Himself back into daffodil unity again. At any rate Crawford's daffodil breaks up, breaks up into tree and lake, eagle and dove, eagle and swan, the queen of heaven looking at herself in a glassy lake, wind and ship, cloud and caged skylark, whip and stampeding herd, good brother and evil brother, paddle and lily bed, smouldering darkness and prickly starlight, aristocratic Spartan and beaten Helot, Isabella Valancy Crawford and King Street, Toronto.

This division can produce the greatest agonies, the most fearful dread, even a disastrous swing into an abyss — in 'Old Spookses' Pass' it is referred to as a gulch — which might as well be called the black daffodil world, a world of complete opposition to all return of the golden daffodil unity with which we began our Crawford Bible. This black daffodil might in turn be called complete nothingness and seems to be a sort of necessary condition of return to the first daffodil. Both the strictly moral and the atheistic live here, but horrible as they are they serve a purpose.

In between the black daffodil and the glorious one we have the divided pairs already mentioned. The evil brother is sometimes clever enough to see that he is as much a child of the daffodil as his good brother and that they are really working at the same reconstruction of Eternity. Only if the good brother is extremely stupid will the evil brother become a completely black daffodil abyss type, but then of course he becomes so extremely horrible that the tension of dread arouses the good brother's intelligence and he rights a lopsided dangerous situation. The stampeding herd of cattle rocket on straight towards nothingness; eventually a mysterious whip descends from the darkness which turns their flowing shapelessness into a revolving circle that mills about and mills about until it stands still.

Out of this still dark circle flares up the great daffodil vision again. This vision does not return from a fleeing away from evil and chaos; in several of her poems Crawford is quite insistent that the daffodil springs from stepping back into chaos and disorder and stilling it with the imagination within oneself. In connection with the good brother aspect of things she twice mentions gyres, and so I assume that just as evil may be seen as a line that spins itself up into a circle so the world of good is also a revolving spiralling shape of some sort whose narrow part gives you a vision of Eternity but not the actuality of it. This can only come from descending back towards the black spinning chaos of stampeding cattle again. So the daffodil at the beginning breaks up into a spinning black whirlpool and a spinning white whirlpool.

The volume you are about to read then has to be *read* into the *other* epic I am excited by. In a less specialist age, back in more primitive times, Crawford's book would have been re-told this way because re-telling like water smooths away the things the artist doesn't really need. Perhaps some contemporary painter or engraver might accomplish the same task by illuminating the passages he finds *tactile*.

F In the most cursory fashion I have recently tried to glance at the prose MSS collected at Queen's University Library. My collage is almost ended but I would like to point out how the following sentences relate to the power structure I have been discussing. Among such titles as *From Yule to Yule*, *The Halton Boys*, *A Hereditary Prince*, *Pillows of Stone*, and 'Tudor Tramp' one finds from this last, a short story:

> '...it don't pay to beat rides on the old G.T.R., you bet. Let her go-o-o!'
> She went — five or six freight cars with cabalistic marks on them like written spells on [casks?] of treasure, and then a long line of long cars, crammed to suffocation with eager travellers gasping for the free air of holiday time in summer. She went twisting eel wise round a curve and plunging into a narrow ravine black with pine, like some dragon into his hole.

So, even in the prose with its obviously more bread and butter intentions the imaginative architect is still at work, hammering even a Grand Trunk train shunting out of Toronto into a 'cabalistic' dragon, a symbol the mind can soar with. Part IV of *Malcolm's Katie* begins:

> From his far wigwam sprang the strong North Wind
> And rushed with war-cry down the steep ravine,
> And wrestled with the giants of the woods;

And with his ice-club beat the swelling crests
Of the deep water courses into death.

If you now ask why the book within the book, the sub-poem I
have hitherto spoken of, never fully rose to the surface, my
answer is that we never asked her to use her talents that way.
Where was the audience? Where the critics? in 1887, even in the
early twentieth century. But this has changed now. Whether they
know it or not, Crawford has followers who are raising the be-
neath, the submerged architecture of icons and identities to
visible articulation. The reader is invited to assist with all the
energy he might find hard to match in the description above, so
typical of Isabella Crawford's best work, of a wind at work.

NOTES

1 I am indebted to Mrs Catherine Ross for knowledge of this docu-
   ment and photographs of the previously mentioned embroidery.

Collected Poems

Isabella Valancy Crawford

ISABELLA VALANCY CRAWFORD

The Collected Poems

of

Isabella Valancy Crawford

Edited by

J. W. GARVIN, B.A.

꙳

With Introduction by

ETHELWYN WETHERALD

Author of "The House of the Trees,"
"Tangled in Stars," "The Radiant Road,"
etc., etc.

꙳

TORONTO

WILLIAM BRIGGS

1905

A WORD FROM THE EDITOR.

A GREAT poet dwelt among us and we scarce knew
her. Hers was a master muse which illumined with
imagination, emotion and originality the noblest and
most profound thoughts of her time, and wove them
with the skill of an artist into divine melodies.

Isabella Valancy Crawford had barely completed her
thirty-sixth year when she suddenly and prematurely
passed away, yet the spirit of her brilliant genius must
ever remain.

The more we study these children of her brain the
more we marvel at what she accomplished. What other
poem in the language more powerfully and nobly ex-
presses the divine right of man to freedom from slavery
than " The Helot " ? What other dialect poem surpasses
in conception, in humour, and in heart-reaching philo-
sophy, " Old Spookses' Pass " ? What other epic of
its kind excels " Malcolm's Katie " in picturesque de-
scription, in brave-hearted purpose, and in tender,
constant passion ? What other Canadian patriotic poem
exceeds in nobility and grandeur of expression " Canada
to England " ? As for Miss Crawford's shorter rhyming
verse, such poems as " Love's Forget-me-not," " Said

the Daisy," " A Harvest Song," " A Perfect Strain," " The Rose," " The King's Kiss," " The Rose of a Nation's Thanks," " Fairy Toil," " The Camp of Souls," " The City Tree," " Said the Skylark," etc., are exquisitely beautiful.

This volume contains eighty-six poems of superior merit, of which fifty-two appear for the first time in book form; the remainder appeared originally in a collection entitled " Old Spookses' Pass, Malcolm's Katie, and Other Poems," published by James Bain & Son, Toronto, in 1884. This unassuming volume, issued at the author's special request in cheap paper covers, attracted but little general interest, and, strange as it seems in view of the worth of its contents, had so meagre a sale as to entail financial loss. And yet the unpretentious little book won praise in high quarters. The London *Athenæum* compared certain of the poems with the work of standard English poets; the *Spectator* referred to Miss Crawford's blank verse as " indeed of no ordinary kind—vigorous, powerful "; the *Illustrated London News* described her verse as " abounding in noble sentiments, picturesque narration, glowing language and pathetic touches, combined with simple, impressive dignity "; the *Graphic* declared the humorous poems " equal to anything Colonel Hay had ever published," and characterized the book as " throughout a delightful one." Lord Dufferin's kindly tribute, in a letter written from the British Embassy at Constantinople, is reproduced in facsimile in the present volume.

A WORD FROM THE EDITOR

Miss Crawford preserved few of her poetic compositions in the original manuscript. Most of the poems in this volume, other than those printed in the early collection, were preserved in the form of clippings from the newspapers in which they originally appeared, and with few corrections, even of obvious errors, by the author's hand. Some of the finest poems herein contained, such as " The Rose of a Nation's Thanks," " Peace," " His Clay," " The Rose," " Fairy Toil," and " The Christmas Baby," were discovered in files of the Toronto *Evening Telegram* of the years 1884 to 1887.

The task of collecting and editing the poems of this gifted Canadian singer was undertaken with the desire that her work should be given that place in literature to which, by its high merit, it is amply entitled. While the Editor has sought throughout to present the poems as he conceived their author intended —his principal labour being to correct the errors of the printers in punctuation, etc.—he is profoundly conscious that much would have been gained had she herself lived to revise them.

For the convenience of the reader, the contents have been divided into four books, the first containing forty-seven shorter and simpler poems of rarely beautiful quality; the second, fifteen poems of greater length and stronger fibre; the third, fifteen poems in blank verse of remarkable range, power and originality; and the fourth, nine poems of dialect verse—philosophic, humorous and pathetic. Throughout, the poetry is characterized by vital strength and splendid spontaneity.

3

A WORD FROM THE EDITOR

Miss Crawford left behind her much manuscript in prose (fiction), which may be published subsequently in book form.

Miss Wetherald, whose Introduction is worthy of her distinguished reputation, has referred to Miss Crawford as " Canada's first woman poet." This tribute and a careful study of her verse suggest the inquiry whether she may not with equal truth be called the first poet of Canada.

To Mrs. Charles J. Stuart, of Toronto, with whom Miss Crawford and her mother spent the closing years of their lives, and to Mr. Stephen Walter Crawford, the surviving brother, the Editor is much indebted for interesting information concerning the poet and her work.

J. W. Garvin

PETERBOROUGH, ONTARIO,
November, 1905.

British Embassy.
Constantinople
June 21: '84

My dear Miss Crawford

This really too good
of you to have thought
of sending me your
book. It has just
arrived, and I have
already read several
of the beautiful poems
it contains with very
great pleasure. You.

5

are quite right in supposing
that I still take the
deepest interest in
everything that concerns
the welfare of Canada.
It is time now that
Canada should have a
literature of its own,
and I am glad to
think that you should
have so nobly shown the
way.

Believe me, my dear
Miss Crawford, with

received thanks, and with
my best wishes for your
future fame,

Ever yours sincerely

Dufferin

CONTENTS

CONTENTS

CONTENTS

CONTENTS

BOOK IV.

(DIALECT VERSE.)

"Faith, Hope and Charity"

—.1.—
A star lean'd down and laid a clear hand
    On the pale brow of Death—
Before it roll'd bleak shadows from the land
    The star was Faith

—.2.—
Across wild storms that hid the mountains far
    In fun'ral cope;
Piercing the black there sail'd a throbbing star,
    The red star Hope!

—.3.—
From God's vast palm a large Sun grandly roll'd
    O'er land and sea
Its core pure fire, its stretching hands of gold
    Great Charity!

Isabella Valancy Crawford Aug 27th 83

INTRODUCTION.

THE chief incidents of Miss Crawford's life have been dwelt on so frequently in print that by this time the Canadian public are well acquainted with the arid facts in the career of Canada's first woman poet. Her birth in Dublin on the day before Christmas, 1850; the coming of the family to Canada in 1858, where they settled in the village of Paisley, on the Saugeen River, and where her father, a physician of wide reading and culture, waged an unsuccessful war with poverty; the deaths of successive members of a numerous family; the removal, when the twelve children had dwindled to three, to Lakefield, near the Kawartha Lakes, where for eight years the struggle with poverty was intensified; the death of the father and of the idolized younger sister, the disappointments that came in the almost total absence of recognition accorded to the poet's literary ventures, and her own death at the age of thirty-six—all this is an old, hard story sufficiently familiar.

It is a slight outline of seemingly one of the most unfortunate of superbly gifted lives; and yet we who realize that it is the greatest good fortune to be born courageous, and the rarest good fortune to be born a poet, must hesitate to believe that misfortune was the fate of Isabella Valancy Crawford. She was affluent in the possession of a high heart, an intrepid spirit, and that unfailing joy in the music and beauty of nature to which so many of us are mole blind and stone deaf.

INTRODUCTION

If Wordsworth spoke truth when he said that we live by admiration, hope and love, then Miss Crawford was enviably fortunate, for she abundantly admired, hoped and loved; but if, on the contrary, we live by recognition, wealth and ease, then indeed does the passion of pity poured out upon this poet's grave seem a just and fitting tribute.

In these easy latter days, when adulation falls like sunlight alike upon mediocre and less mediocre, one is tempted to envy this haughty young poet, the motions of whose spirit were so unclouded by the fumes of praise that they shine forth on our slow vision with almost startling distinctness. The sure reward that comes to all "enamoured architects of airy rhyme" is that they *are* enamoured. To be interested is to be in an earthly heaven, and Miss Crawford was prodigiously interested in existence as she saw and felt it. Rather should we say that to be a poet is to find in life the ecstasy of living, and in obscurity not a featherweight of cause for beating the breast.

So it is not with pity that we should approach Isabella Valancy Crawford. In her lifetime she would not allow herself to be compassionated. She proudly and persistently refused to admit that she was poor and needy, sorely neglected and tragically disappointed. Are we justified in taking advantage of her absence to talk over her private affairs, as it were, behind her back? She had the decent old-world pride that effectually bars the door upon the discussion of unpleasant personalities, and probably the most becoming attitude we can take toward her is to ignore her difficulties as beautifully as she ignored them.

If the big, crude, gossip-loving public could only realize that a poet's hardships and bereavements are entirely a poet's own affair, and that all it has to concern itself with is the value of the poetic work put forth—but the age of miracles is past.

Let us to the work of this divinely dowered Isabella —this angelic mendicant, craving nothing of life but its finer gifts—this blessed gypsy of Canadian woods and streams. What a royal life she led! No pose to take, no reputation to sustain, no poetic attitudes studied from those of other poets, no tendency to routine thinking or lassitude of the imaginative faculty to be struggled with, no half-penny worth of sack to an intolerable deal of bread, not a single syllable outbreathing the " vulgar luxury of despair." Happy, happy poet! She, like every other genius, found in the ecstasy of expression at the full height of her nature a compensation that turned all outward trials into details not worth speaking of.

The high gifts of her spirit are of the quality which thrive best when strongly separated from " the forms and shows of worldly respectabilities." She is purely a genius, not a craftswoman, and a genius who has patience enough to be an artist. She has in abundant measure that power of youth which persists in poets of every age—that capacity of seeing things for the first time, and with the rose and pearl of dawn upon them—and, as a part of this endowment, the poet's essential lightheartedness and good sense. Perhaps the most satisfying allurement in her poetry is its directness. It is as if she spoke to us face to face, and we gain the instant impression of a vigorous and striking personality, arresting our attention and " crying into us with a mighty directness and distinctness, in words that could not be more forcibly ordered," the athletic imagery that crowded her brain.

In " Old Spookses' Pass " her grasp on character and situation is passionately firm and strong. The verses are built up of cowboy language, through which her wit plays lambently, and the sense of her vividly wild, free spirit, showing in every line, brings the conviction that she must have been an eye-witness of the scene so glowingly thrown before us. The breadth of her religious belief is shown by her cowboy soliloquizing among the stars and mountains, with a crinkling and twinkling creek to arouse the sleeping memories in his heart:

> "It ain't no matter wharever ye be,—
> I'll 'low it's a cur'us sort uv case—
> Whar thar's runnin' water, it's sure tew speak
> Uv folks tew home an' the old home place.
>
> "An' yer bound tew listen an' hear it talk,
> Es yer mustang crunches the dry, bald sod ;
> Fur I reckon the hills an' stars an' crick
> Are all uv 'em preachers sent by God.
> An' them mountains talk tew a chap this way :
> 'Climb, if ye can, ye degenerate cuss !'
> An' the stars smile down on a man an' say,
> 'Cum higher, poor critter, cum up tew us.'
>
> "An' I reckon, pard, thar is One above
> The highest old star thet a chap can see,
> An' He says, in a solid, etarnal way,
> 'Ye never can stop till ye git tew *Me !*'
> Good fur Him, tew ! fur I calculate
> He ain't the One tew dodge an' tew shirk,
> Or waste a mite uv the things He's made,
> Or knock off till He's finished His great day's work.
>
> "We've got tew labour an' strain an' snort
> Along thet road thet He's planned an' made ;
> Don't matter a mite He's cut His line
> Tew run over a 'tarnal tough up-grade.
> An' if some poor sinner ain't built tew hold
> Es big a head uv steam es the next,
> An' keeps slippin' an' slidin' 'way down hill,
> Why, He don't make out thet He's awful vext ;
>
> "Fur He knows He made him in thet thar way,
> Sumwhars tew fit in His own great plan ;
> An' He ain't the Bein' tew pour His wrath
> On the head uv thet slimpsy an' slippery man ;

18

INTRODUCTION

An' He sez tew the feller, ' Look here, My son,
    You're the worst hard case thet ever I see,
But be thet it takes ye a million y'ars,
    Ye never can stop till ye git tew *Me!* ' "

This is large, forcible verse, direct and simple and vividly picturesque. Everything Miss Crawford has written is alive with her own personality, but in " Old Spookses' Pass " virility and sincerity are the clearest notes. In it, as in all her work, one is made to feel that behind the rich colouring, and what one is occasionally tempted to call the dashing and splendid verbal display, there are enduring forces of character.

The extent to which our poet's environment concerns us is that in which it is bodied forth in her writings. With her life and literature were one. When we read of

    " The hollow hearts of brakes,
Yet warm from sides of does and stags,"

or gaze with her at

    " The slaughtered deer,
His eyes like dead stars cold and drear.
. . . . .
And the sharp splendour of his branches,"

or hear the strong north wind,

" That rushed with war-cry down the steep ravines,
And wrestled with the giants of the wood ; "

or feel the atmosphere of a certain day,

    " All set about with roses and with fire,—
One of three days of heat which frequent slip,
Like triple rubies, in between the sweet,
Mild emerald days of summer ; "

or follow the motion of the shadow-grey swift that, from the airy eave,

19

> " Smites the blue pond, and speeds her glancing wing
>   Close to the daffodils ; "

or enter into the lives of her fellow-adventurers in the
New World, braced by poverty and " happy in new
honeymoons of hope," we recognize the inmates and
furnishings of her forest surroundings. It is true her
imagination travelled far,—but not into regions of super-
refinement. She knows the faith of the cowboy and the
loyal heart of the backwoodsman, and her sense of
humour is entertained by the rugged eccentricities of
Old Spense and Farmer Stebbins. Her Muse, like
Max's soul, shows a virile front, full-muscled and large-
statured.

In " The Helot," which is perhaps the most magnifi-
cent expression of Miss Crawford's genius, there occur
these searching lines, in which the innate divinity of
" The Man with the Hoe," or the slave besotted with
the fumes of the bowl, is triumphantly vindicated. Who
can read with unquickened breath the words that follow,
in which the poet's heart of flame comes up to white
heat, as in verse after verse she finds intenser utterance
of the same thought :

> " Who may quench the god-born fire
>   Pulsing at the soul's deep root ?
> Tyrant, grind it in the mire,
>   Lo, it vivifies the brute !

> " Stings the chain-embruted clay,
>   Senseless to his yoke-bound shame ;
> Goads him on to rend and slay,
>   Knowing not the spurring flame !

> " Tyrant, changeless stand the gods,
>   Nor their calm might yielded thee ;
> Not beneath thy chains and rods
>   Dies man's god-gift, Liberty !

" Bruteward lash thy Helots, hold
Brain and soul and clay in gyves,
Coin their blood and sweat in gold,
Build thy cities on their lives, —

" Comes a day the spark divine
Answers to the gods who gave ;
Fierce the hot flames pant and shine
In the bruised breast of the slave.

" Changeless stand the gods !—nor he
Knows he answers their behest,
Feels the might of their decree
In the blind rage of his breast.

" Tyrant, tremble when ye tread
Down the servile Helot clods !
Under despot heel is bred
The white anger of the gods.

" Thro' the shackle-cankered dust,
Thro' the gyved soul, foul and dark,
Force they, changeless gods and just,
Up the bright, eternal spark,

" Till, like lightnings vast and fierce,
On the land its terror smites ;
Till its flames the tyrant pierce,
Till the dust the despot bites."

Scarcely less powerful than " The Helot " is " The King's Garments," one of those extraordinarily rare moral poems in which the poetry is as great as the morality. A few bold lines place the picture before us —the careless monarch wearying of lute and harp, of wine and revelry, demanding out of the indolence of satiety that his seer shall prophesy what garments wait on kings in paradise. The seer describes an awful loom and One who weaves thereat:

" Whence come the warp, the woof ? Behold, O King !
From every deed of thine I see arise

21

Long filaments, dusk as the raven's wing
  That blots the melting azure of the skies ;
Thy battles, murders, wine-red blasphemy
  Yield warp and woof of which I prophesy.

  .   .   .   .   .   .

" For Law immutable hath one decree,
  ' No deed of good, no deed of ill can die ;
All must ascend unto my loom and be
  Woven for man in lasting tapestry,
Each soul his own.'   Now, tyrant, dare to die
  And claim thy robes of which I prophesy ! "

Miss Crawford's idea of Peace is of no limp negation, but of a being who is blest in proportion as she is strong. It is an heroic figure that she sets before us :

" Peace stands within the city wall ;
  Most like a god she towers tall,
  And bugle-like she cries to all.

" In place of sounds of nether hell,
  In place of serpent-hiss of shell,
  Sounds sweet her powerful 'All's well ! '

" Is she a willow by a stream ?
  The spirit of a dreamer's dream ?
  The pale moon's meek and phantom beam ?

" The mere desire of panting soul ?
  Water, not wine, within the bowl ?
  Rides she, a ghost, upon the roll

" Of spectral seas ? Nay, see her rise,
  Strong flesh against the flushing skies,
  Large calm within her watchful eyes."

Of the poems which have hitherto not appeared in book form, there are in some an Oriental prodigality of colours and images which almost affright the everyday imagination. Such is " The Inspiration of Song," which at first glance appears to be an inspired medley of starry distances, fine-flamed diamonds, immortal roses, banks of violets, the heavy wings of slow centuries, rarest gems of every hue, flowering walls and "a tawny lion with a mane that tossed in golden tempests round his awful eyes." But the fundamental design beneath this wealth of decoration is strong and sufficient. Miss Crawford ornaments with a lavish hand, but she demands immense structures to work upon.

Another sort—and a most enticing sort—is the rippling idyll of "La Blanchisseuse." How sweetly the stream speaks:

> " Blanchisseuse, Blanchisseuse,
>   Here I come from Picardy !
> Hurry off thy wooden shoes,
>   I will wash thy clothes with thee."

And how pretty the picture when—

> " Margaton her linen wrings,
>   White between her ruddy hands ;
> O'er her feet the rillet sings,
>   Dimpling all its golden sands ;
> Hawthorn blushes touch her hair."

Even fairer is this vision of God's bud-time in "Said the Daisy":

> " O never came so glad a morn before !
>   So rosy-dimpling burst the infant light,
> So crystal pure the air the meadows o'er,
>   The lark with such young rapture took his flight,
> The round world seemed not older by an hour
>   Than mine own daisy self."

One longs to quote the entire poem, with its felicitous reference to the daisy's "dew-sealed sleep," the "gay small wind, arch as a ruddy fox," and "the purple trumpets of the clover."

But who could excel our Isabella when she brings her royal imagination to bear upon the small, exquisite things of the outdoor world? Here are two verses from

" The Legend of the Mistletoe " that are a positive luxury to the artistic sense :

> " What time fierce Winter, like a wolf all lean,
>   With sharp, white fangs bit at weak woodland things,
>   Pierced furry breasts and broke small painted wings,
> And from dim homes all interlocked and green

> " Drove little spirits—those who love glossed leaves
>   And glimmer in tall grasses—those who ride
>   Glossed bubbles on the woodland's sheltered tide,
> And make blue hyacinths their household eaves."

But she is, perhaps, even more at home in larger scenes —in such a poem, for instance, as " A Battle," where, on the solemn field of night, the armoured warriors of the moon are trying great issues with the blind old king, the Titan Darkness. Here is room for truly Crawfordian work, and most characteristically is it executed :

> " The starry hosts with silver lances prick
>   The scarlet fringes of the tents of Day,
>   And turn their crystal shields upon their breasts,
>   And point their radiant lances, and so wait
>   The stirring of the giant in his caves."

" The Rose of a Nation's Thanks "—one of the most spirited poems ever inspired by love of country—was printed in a Toronto newspaper twenty years ago, where it has remained unhonoured and, in a completely literal sense, unsung. And yet every Canadian heart to-day must beat in time to music such as this :

> " A welcome ? There is not a babe at the breast won't
>   spring at the roll of the drum
> That heralds them home—the keen long cry in the air of
>   "They come ! They come !"
> And what of it all if ye bade them wade knee-deep in a
>   wave of wine,
> And tossed tall torches, and arched the town in garlands
>   of maple and pine ?

24

All dust in the wind of a woman's cry as she snatches
        from the ranks
Her boy who bears on his bold young breast the Rose of
        a Nation's Thanks."

In the presence of death the poet finds scope for some
of her most memorable utterances. Here again the
aptness of her metaphors compels admiration. In " The
Camp of Souls " she tells us that

" Love is a cord woven out of life,
    And dyed in the red of the living heart ;
And time is the hunter's rusty knife,
    That cannot cut the red strands apart."

In that touchingly beautiful poem of " The Mother's
Soul "

" The Sun set his loom to weave the day,
    The frost bit sharp like a silent cur."

The theme is that of the dead mother who

" Saw her child by the grave alone,
    With the sods and snow and wind at play,"

and whose undying love, stronger than death, draws
him closer to her breast, until

" The child's head drooped to the brown, sere mold,
    On the crackling cones his white breast lay ;
The butterfly touched the locks of gold,
    The soul of the child sprang from its clay.
The moon to the pine-tree stole,
And, silver-lipped, said to its bole :
' How strong is the mother's soul ! ' "

In " Life " Miss Crawford speaks from the heart of
bereaved humanity, standing stunned and desolate by
the beloved clay, " dumb in its shroud." Here is the
universal appeal that has at one time or another burst
from the lips of all earth's suffering children :

> " Cried then my soul of souls :
>   ' Answer, O clay !
> Shall those fond eyes of thine
>   Slumber alway ?
> That brow in noisome dust
>   Vanish away ?
>
> " ' Those tender hands of thine,
>   Gracious and kind,
> Turned into clay and ash,
>   Drift on the wind ?
> Sealed ever thy pure lips,
>   And thine eyes blind ?
>
> " ' Shall that sweet heart of thine,
>   Noble and true,
> Moulder to feed the sap
>   Of the weird yew ?
> Or the small graveside bud
>   Wet with death's dew ?
>
> " ' Answer my groaning soul,
>   O thou dear clay !
> Shall that brave soul of thine
>   Tremble away
> Into dark nothingness ?
>   Answer and say ! ' "

The attentive reader of our Isabella will find that she voices the universal heart, not only in its deepest pangs, but in its highest happiness—the happiness of assured love. The poem, " Love's Forget-me-not," is that rare combination of absolute simplicity with complete freedom from the least taint of the commonplace which is the final achievement of poetic souls. Every verse in it appeals for quotation. It is a mutilation to give part of this exquisite whole, and yet—let us read the concluding verses, and then turn the pages and read it all:

> " When Autumn raised the purple fruit
>   In clusters to his bearded lips,
> I laid a heartsease on the lute
>   That sang beneath her finger-tips.

'O Love,' she said—and fair her eyes
 Smiled thro' the dusk upon the lea—
'No heartsease glows beneath the skies
 But this thou givest me !'

" When Winter wept at shaking doors,
 And holly trimmed his ermine vest,
And wild winds maddened on the moors,
 I laid a flower upon her breast.
'Dear Heart,' I whispered to the clay,
 Which stilly smiled yet answered not,
'Bear thou to Heaven itself away
 True love's Forget-me-not.'"

And when we have read " Love's Forget-me-not " let us look for " The Rose," a poem that matches in perfection of finish the flower of which it speaks. Every stanza is a rose-leaf:

"The Rose was given to man for this:
 He, sudden seeing it in later years,
Should swift remember Love's first lingering kiss
 And Grief's last lingering tears ;

" Or, being blind, should feel its yearning soul
 Knit all its piercing perfume round his own,
Till he should see on memory's ample scroll
 All roses he had known."

There are five verses of this penetratingly beautiful quality.

" Malcolm's Katie," Miss Crawford's longest poem, is peculiarly rich in descriptive passages. Here we find in profusion the qualities and powers she has taught us to expect in her work—strong and coherent thought, imagery unhackneyed and unstrained, with a diction as concise, ringing and effective as the blows of its hero's axe. Here are lines that glow like veritable colours on a canvas:

" The Land had put his ruddy gauntlet on,
 Of harvest gold, to dash in Famine's face ;

And like a vintage wain deep dyed with juice
The great moon faltered up the ripe, blue sky,
Drawn by silver stars—like oxen white,
And horned with rays of light.   Down the rich land
Malcolm's small valleys, filled with grain lip high,
Lay round a lonely hill that faced the moon
And caught the wine-kiss of its ruddy light.
A cusped, dark wood caught in its black embrace
The valleys and the hill, and from its wilds,
Spiced with dark cedars, cried the whippoorwill.
A crane, belated, sailed across the moon."

And here is a rapier thrust, in which the false lover, Alfred, fetters down the unholy fires within his soul,

" To that mere pink, poetic, nameless glow
That need not fright a flake of snow away,
But, if unloosed, could melt an adverse rock,
Marrowed with iron."

When this poet of happiness speaks of grief it is not of her private woes. No effeminate or sentimental wail breaks from her, but she regards what she calls the Helper of the Universe in this broad impersonal style:

" Who curseth Sorrow knows her not at all.
Dark matrix she, from which the human soul
Has its last birth ; whence it, with misty thews
Close knitted in her blackness, issues out
Strong for immortal toil up such great heights
As crown o'er crown rise through eternity.
Without the loud deep clamour of her wail,
The iron of her hands, the biting brine
Of her black tears, the soul, but lightly built
Of indeterminate spirit, like a mist
Would lapse to chaos in soft, gilded dreams,
As mists fade in the gazing of the sun."

But it is the splendour of Miss Crawford's descriptions—the report she gives of visual feasts—that most profoundly holds her reader. Canadian poets have been accused of " treating Nature as if she had been

28

born and brought up in Canada," so authentically does the dew of first-hand observation lie upon their lines. Our Isabella, in the grace of her country-nurtured girl-hood, found a pulse and living colour in every natural object. Among the timbered hills of "hiding fern and hanging fir" she passed her days making pictures that differ from those of most word-painters in that they are at once vivid and intelligible. Always she has stuff of thought to express, and if the stream of her utterance is at times a little impeded, like that of a leaf-choked brook in October, it is because of an excess of riches. It is this that ensures her against shallowness—that bane of the poet who writes because he chooses and not because he must. Strong, ardent, self-sufficing, finding in her hard life a challenge to which her spirit heroically responded, and in her solitary environment the right and true atmosphere of her bright-winged muse, Isabella Valancy Crawford is a brilliant and fadeless figure in the annals of Canadian literary history.

Ethelwyn Wetherald

CHANTLER, ONTARIO,
   November, 1905.

29

Book 1

Poems by Isabella Valancy Crawford

LOVE'S FORGET-ME-NOT.

When Spring in sunny woodland lay,
  And gilded buds were sparely set
On oak tree and the thorny may,
  I gave my love a violet.
" O Love," she said, and kissed my mouth
  With one light, tender maiden kiss,
" There are no rich blooms in the south
  So fair to me as this!"

When Summer reared her haughty crest,
  We paused beneath the ruddy stars;
I placed a rose upon her breast,
  Plucked from the modest casement bars.
" O Love," she said, and kissed my mouth—
  Heart, heart, rememb'rest thou the bliss?—
" In east or west, in north or south,
  I know no rose but this!"

When Autumn raised the purple fruit
  In clusters to his bearded lips,
I laid a heartsease on the lute
  That sang beneath her finger-tips.

"O Love," she said—and fair her eyes
  Smiled thro' the dusk upon the lea—
"No heartsease glows beneath the skies
  But this thou givest me!"

When Winter wept at shaking doors,
  And holly trimmed his ermine vest,
And wild winds maddened on the moors,
  I laid a flower upon her breast.
"Dear Heart," I whispered to the clay,
  Which stilly smiled yet answered not,
"Bear thou to Heaven itself away
  True love's Forget-me-not!"

SAID THE DAISY.

THERE ne'er was blown out of the yellow east
  So fresh, so fair, so sweet a morn as this.
The dear earth decked herself as for a feast;
  And, as for me, I trembled with my bliss.
The young grass round me was so rich with dew,
  And sang me such sweet, tender strains, as low
The breath of dawn among its tall spikes blew;
  But what it sang none but myself can know!

O never came so glad a morn before!
  So rosy dimpling burst the infant light,
So crystal pure the air the meadows o'er,
  The lark with such young rapture took his flight,
The round world seemed not older by an hour
  Than mine own daisy self! I laughed to see
How, when her first red roses paled and died,
  The blue sky smiled, and decked her azure lea
With daisy clouds, white, pink-fringed, just like me!

SAID THE DAISY

" This is a morn for song," sang out the lark,
    " O silver-tressed beloved !"   My golden eye
Watched his brown wing blot out the last star-spark
    Amidst the daisy cloudlets of the sky.
" No morn so sweet as this, so pure, so fair—
    God's bud time," so the oldest white thorn said,
And she has lived so long ; yet here and there
    Such fresh white buds begem her ancient head.

And from her thorny bosom all last night
    Deep in my dew-sealed sleep I heard a note—
So sweet a voice of anguish and delight
    I dreamed a red star had a bird-like throat
And that its rays were music which had crept
    'Mid the white-scented blossoms of the thorn,
And that to hear her sing the still night wept
    With mists and dew until the yellow morn.

I wonder, wonder what the song he sang,
    That seemed to drown in melody the vales !
I knew my lark's song as he skyward sprang,
    But only roses know the nightingale's.
The yellow cowslip bent her honeyed lips
    And whispered :   " Daisy, wert thou but as high
As I am, thou couldst see the merry ships
    On yon blue wondrous field blown gaily by."

A gay, small wind, arch as a ruddy fox,
    Crept round my slender, green and dainty stem,
And piped :   " Let me but shake thy silver locks
    And free thy bent head from its diadem
Of diamond dew, and thou shalt rise and gaze,
    Like the tall cowslips, o'er the rustling grass,
On proud, high cliffs, bright strands and sparkling bays,
    And watch the white ships as they gaily pass."

" Oh, while thou mayst keep thou thy crystal dew!"
  Said the aged thorn, where sang the heart of night,
The nightingale. " The sea is very blue,
  The sails of ships are wondrous swift and white.
Soon, soon enough thy dew will sparkling die,
  And thou, with burning brow and thirsty lips,
Wilt turn the golden circle of thine eye,
  Nor joy in them, on ocean and her ships!"

There never flew across the violet hills
  A morn so like a dove with jewelled eyes,
With soft wings fluttering like the sound of rills,
  And gentle breast of rose and azure dyes.
The purple trumpets of the clover sent
  Such rich, dew-loosened perfume, and the bee
Hung like a gold drop in the woodbine's tent.
  What care I for the gay ships and the sea!

A HARVEST SONG.

THE noon was as a crystal bowl
  The red wine mantled through;
Around it like a Viking's beard
  The red-gold hazes blew,
As tho' he quaffed the ruddy draught
  While swift his galley flew.

This mighty Viking was the Night;
  He sailed about the earth,
And called the merry harvest-time
  To sing him songs of mirth;
And all on earth or in the sea
  To melody gave birth.

A HARVEST SONG

The valleys of the earth were full
  To rocky lip and brim
With golden grain that shone and sang
  When woods were still and dim,
A little song from sheaf to sheaf—
  Sweet Plenty's cradle-hymn.

O gallant were the high tree-tops,
  And gay the strain they sang!
And cheerfully the moon-lit hills
  Their echo-music rang!
And what so proud and what so loud
  As was the ocean's clang!

But O the little humming song
  That sang among the sheaves!
'Twas grander than the airy march
  That rattled thro' the leaves,
And prouder, louder, than the deep,
  Bold clanging of the waves:

" The lives of men, the lives of men
  With every sheaf are bound!
We are the blessing which annuls
  The curse upon the ground!
And he who reaps the Golden Grain
  The Golden Love hath found."

A PERFECT STRAIN.

O BID the minstrel tune his harp,
　And bid the minstrel sing;
And let it be a perfect strain
　That round the hall shall ring:
A strain to throb in lady's heart,
　To brim the warrior's soul,
As dew fills up the summer rose
　And wine the lordly bowl!

O let the minstrel's voice ring clear,
　His touch sweep gay and light;
Nor let his glittering tresses know
　One streak of wintry white.
And let the light of ruddy June
　Shine in his joyous eyes,
If he would wake the only strain
　That never fully dies!

O what the strain that woos the knight
　To turn from steed and lance,
The page to turn from hound and hawk,
　The maid from lute and dance;
The potent strain, that nigh would draw
　The hermit from his cave,
The dryad from the leafy oak,
　The mermaid from the wave;
That almost might still charm the hawk
　To drop the trembling dove?
O ruddy minstrel, tune thy harp,
　And sing of Youthful Love!

THE ROSE.

THE Rose was given to man for this:
    He, sudden seeing it in later years,
Should swift remember Love's first lingering kiss
    And Grief's last lingering tears;

Or, being blind, should feel its yearning soul
    Knit all its piercing perfume round his own,
Till he should see on memory's ample scroll
    All roses he had known;

Or, being hard, perchance his finger-tips
    Careless might touch the satin of its cup,
And he should feel a dead babe's budding lips
    To his lips lifted up;

Or, being deaf and smitten with its star,
    Should, on a sudden, almost hear a lark
Rush singing up—the nightingale afar
    Sing thro' the dew-bright dark;

Or, sorrow-lost in paths that round and round
    Circle old graves, its keen and vital breath
Should call to him within the yew's bleak bound
    Of Life, and not of Death.

WHERE, LOVE, ART HID?

"Love like a shadow flies."
—*Merry Wives of Windsor.*

At brightest dawn I'll rise and take
  Long, ruddy lances from the sun,
And search with them each shady brake
  To see where Love hath gone.
    Love, Love, where liest thou?
    " Thou shalt not find me so."

I'll filch the brightest star on high
  And tie it to my pilgrim's staff;
And by its rays I'll onward hie
  To see where Love doth laugh.
    Love, Love, where dost thou lie?
    " Oh, not in shadows by!"

I'll climb the rainbow's rosy bridge,
  And peep the pearlèd clouds above;
I'll cling to Luna's diamond edge,
  Or I will find thee, Love!
    Love, Love, beware my net!
    " Thou shalt not find me yet."

I'll take the dandelion's crown
  And blow its silver plumes to rout;
And wheresoe'er they flutter down
  I'll seek for Love about.
    Love, shall I find thee, say?
    " Not thro' a summer's day."

LA BLANCHISSEUSE

I'll shake the oxlip's freckled bell,
　And toss thee from it like a bee;
The small white daisy in the dell,
　Love, shall not shelter thee.
　　Love, wilt thou to me yield?
　　" Nay, thou art far a-field."

I'll search the hearts of pearls down deep,
　A hundred fathoms, in the south;
Beneath a monarch's lashes peep,
　Kiss wide the rose's mouth.
　　Ho! Gossip Love, I'll capture thee!
　　" Nay, nay, that cannot be;
　　Seek Love, and Love will flee!"

LA BLANCHISSEUSE.

MARGATON at early dawn
　Thro' the vineyard takes her way,
With her basket piled with lawn
　And with kerchiefs red and gay,
To the stream which babbles past
　Grove, chateau, and clanking mill.
As it runs it chatters fast
　Like a woman with a will:
　　" Blanchisseuse, Blanchisseuse,
　　　Here I come from Picardy!
　　Hurry off thy wooden shoes,
　　　I will wash thy clothes with thee!"

Margaton's a shapely maid;
　Laughter haunts her large, soft eye;
When she trips by vineyard shade
　Trips the sun with her, say I.

41

Wooden shoes she lays aside,
  Puts her linen in the rill;
And the stream, in gossip's pride,
  Chatters to her with a will:
    " Blanchisseuse, Blanchisseuse,
      I—I know a thing or two!
    Thus, this is the latest news,
      Some one dreams of eyes of blue!"

Margaton her linen wrings,
  White between her ruddy hands;
O'er her feet the rillet sings,
  Dimpling all its golden sands;
Hawthorn blushes touch her hair,
  Birdlings twitter sweet and shrill,
Sunbeams seek her everywhere;
  Gossips on the wordy rill:
    " Blanchisseuse, Blanchisseuse,
      He who dreams has lands and flocks!
    Margaton may idly choose
      Pebbles in the place of rocks!"

Margaton her linen treads,
  Ankle-dimple deep her feet;
Nod the stately green fern-heads,
  Nod the violets damp and sweet;
Dewy places in the wood
  With the ruddy morning fill;
Silenter the downy brood,
  Chatters on the gossip rill:
    " Blanchisseuse, Blanchisseuse,
      He who dreams is rich and great!
    Margaton may idly choose
      Golden sorrow for a mate!"

42

THE KING'S KISS

Margaton her linen wrings;
  Day's gold goblet overflows;
Leaves are stirred with glancing wings;
  One can smell the distant rose.
" Silly stream, the Curè said
  Just such warning yesterday!"
Rippling o'er its pebbly bed,
  Still the stream would have its say:
    " Blanchisseuse, Blanchisseuse,
      Yet another tale I know,—
    Some one dreams of, runs my news,
      Golden heart in bosom's snow!"

Margaton her linen spreads
  On the violet bank to dry;
Droop the willows low their heads,
  Curious, for her low reply:
" Dearest stream, but yesternight
  Whispered Jean those words to me!"
And the rillet in its flight
  Buzzed and murmured like a bee:
    " Blanchisseuse, Blanchisseuse,
      He who dreams is good and true!
    How can Margaton refuse?
      Blanchisseuse, adieu, adieu!"

THE KING'S KISS.

A KING rode hunting in the wood;
  His bugle sounded on the lawn;
He rode in merry hunter's mood
  Till ripe day mellowed from the dawn,
Nor met in green-leafed solitude
  With antlered stag, sleek doe, or fawn.

But when his good steed neighed to smell
　Thro' sultry noon the longed-for wave,
And leaped adown a ferny dell
　Where burst a brooklet from a cave,
'Twas there he met, as legends tell,
　A damsel willow-slim and grave.

She showed so bright his courser gazed,
　Forgetful of his thirst, across
The rippling brook; the hound, amazed,
　Paused dewlap deep in fern and moss,
Won from his scent; where jewels blazed,
　The monarch touched his dagger's cross:

" If thou art thing of spell and charm,
　Avaunt, sweet eyes, and locks of gold!
A Christian knight thou canst not harm.
　But, an thou be of mortal mould,
I swear by sword and good right arm
　I'll kiss those red lips' witching fold."

" What wilt thou give to grace the kiss?"
　She asked, with such sweet majesty,
He answered swift, " For such a bliss
　I'd share my kingly crown with thee!"
" That guerdon still would prove amiss;
　No crown can buy dear love," quoth she.

" Then would I give my pleasant land,
　My kingdom, fallow-field and wood,
High spirèd cities, to thy hand
　My falcon with her jewelled hood."
" And all might not dear love command,"
　She said.　Blew round the monarch's mood
44

From sun to storm. " It is not thine,
    Disdainful damsel, to refuse
To me those lips of ruddy wine—
    A king shall kiss where he may choose!"
She tranquil said, " And leave still mine
    The love that coward kiss must lose!"

'Twas sun again. The monarch stood
    Beside her, clasped her willow waist;
The noontide sunbeams smote the wood,
    The brooklet by sweet winds was chased:
" My heart for thine, for by the Rood
    By love alone can love be graced!"

THE ROSE OF A NATION'S THANKS.

A WELCOME? Oh, yes, 'tis a kindly word, but why will
    they plan and prate
Of feasting and speeches and such small things, while
    the wives and mothers wait?
Plan as ye will, and do as ye will, but think of the
    hunger and thirst
In the hearts that wait; and do as ye will, but lend us
    our laddies first!
Why, what would ye have? There is not a lad that
    treads in the gallant ranks
Who does not already bear on his breast the Rose of a
    Nation's Thanks!

A welcome? Why, what do you mean by that, when the
    very stones must sing
As our men march over them home again; the walls of
    the city ring

45

With the thunder of throats and the tramp and tread of
    feet that rush and run?—
I think in my heart that the very trees must shout for
    the bold work done!
Why, what would ye have? There is not a lad that
    treads in the gallant ranks
Who does not already bear on his breast the Rose of a
    Nation's Thanks!

A welcome? There is not a babe at the breast won't
    spring at the roll of the drum
That heralds them home—the keen, long cry in the air
    of " They come! They come!"
And what of it all if ye bade them wade knee-deep in a
    wave of wine,
And tossed tall torches, and arched the town in garlands
    of maple and pine?
All dust in the wind of a woman's cry as she snatches
    from the ranks
Her boy who bears on his bold young breast the Rose of
    a Nation's Thanks!

A welcome? There's a doubt if the lads would stand
    like stone in their steady line
When a babe held high on a dear wife's hand or the
    stars that swim and shine
In a sweetheart's eyes, or a mother's smile, flashed far
    in the welded crowd,
Or a father's proud voice, half-sob and half-cheer, cried
    on a son aloud.
O the billows of waiting hearts that swelled would sweep
    from the martial ranks
The gallant boys who bear on their breasts the Rose of
    a Nation's Thanks!

GOOD-BYE'S THE WORD

A welcome? O Joy, can they stay your feet, or measure
    the wine of your bliss?
O Joy, let them have you alone to-day—a day with a
    pulse like this!
A welcome? Yes, 'tis a tender thought, a green laurel
    that laps the sword—
But Joy has the wing of a wild white swan, and the song
    of a free wild bird!
She must beat the air with her wing at will, at will must
    her song be driven
From her heaving heart and tremulous throat through
    the awful arch of heaven.
And what would ye have? There isn't a lad will burst
    from the shouting ranks
But bears like a star on his faded coat the Rose of a
    Nation's Thanks!

GOOD-BYE'S THE WORD!

HEAVE up the anchor, heave ye ho!
    And swing her head about;
The blue flag flies, the breezes blow,
    Let all her canvas out!
Blue eyes and black upon the quay
    Are smiling tears away;
And sweethearts blush at parting kiss,
    And wives and mothers pray.

The babe upon my Polly's breast will toddle down the
    strand,
And pipe a welcome when again our good ship sails to
    land;

47

And Tom will reach my elbow then, and Ned be shoulder
    high—
Avast! avast! I sail too fast—good-bye's the word,
    good-bye!

> Heave up the anchor, heave ye ho!
>   And speed us on our way;
> A stiff breeze, sweet with rose and thyme,
>   Blows fast along the bay;
> The sails round out, the rattling shrouds
>   Are loud with noisy glee;
> The staunch craft trembles as she hears
>   The footsteps of the sea.

Belike, my mates, 'tis just the way a lass's heart will
    beat
When sounds upon the shingly strand her tar's returning
    feet;
Or Poll will tremble when she hears my footsteps
    drawing nigh—
Avast! avast! I sail too fast—good-bye's the word,
    good-bye!

> Heave up the anchor, heave ye ho!
>   God bless the dear brown hands
> That wave " good-bye " when Jack sets sail
>   To steer for other strands;
> And tho' our ship her anchor heaves
>   When she would sail afar,
> My eyes! she don't resemble there
>   The ways of true Jack tar.

For when Jack casts life's anchor down—his heart, be-
    like, you know—
He never hauls it up again, whatever squalls may blow:

LAUGHTER

Mine's grappled safe in Polly's breast until the day I
    die—
Avast! avast! the wind blows fast—good-bye's the
    word, good-bye!

LAUGHTER.

Laughter wears a lilied gown—
    She is but a simple thing;
Laughter's eyes are water-brown,
Ever glancing up and down
    Like a woodbird's restless wing.

Laughter slender is and round—
    She is but a simple thing;
And her tresses fly unbound,
And about her brow are found
    Buds that blossom by Mirth's spring.

Laughter loves to praise and play—
    She is but a simple thing—
With the children small who stray
Under hedges, where the May
    Scents and blossoms richly fling.

Laughter coyly peeps and flits—
    She is but a simple thing—
Round the flower-clad door, where sits
Maid who dimples as she knits,
    Dreaming in the rosy spring.

Laughter hath light-tripping feet—
    She is but a simple thing;

Ye may often Laughter meet
In the hayfield, gilt and sweet,
    Where the mowers jest and sing.

Laughter shakes the bounteous leaves—
    She is but a simple thing—
On the village ale-house eaves,
While the angered swallow grieves
    And the rustic revellers sing.

Laughter never comes a-nigh—
    She's a wise though simple thing—
Where men lay them down to die;
Nor will under stormy sky
    Laughter's airy music ring.

FAIRY TOIL.

BENEATH grave Sister Claudia's eyes
    She droops the dimple of her chin,
Drops frolic glances from far skies
    Upon her fairy rolling-pin.

Outside, the convent maple stirs—
    Her leafy playmate, plumed and tall;
The sweet, far organ swells and birrs
    And shakes the green vine on the wall.

The golden shuttle of her years
    Across the loom of life has fled
In light, gay flashes—all her tears
    Have rounded for her dear dove, dead.

SYLVIUS TO CHLORIS

Her laugh—a zigzag butterfly
  Of silver sound that hardly knows
Against what joyous blossom's dye
  Mirth's breath its fairy fluttering blows.

The rose-rays on her finger-tips
  Kiss satin rose to ripening mold;
She purses up her rose-bright lips,
  She twines the thread of glittering gold.

A snowflake fair her soul might soil,
  A lily-cup hold all her sin
And stainless stay.   O fairy toil,
  The decking of the rolling-pin!

SYLVIUS TO CHLORIS.

CHLORIS, if the swain be true,
  As his heart is fondly warm,
Thy fair cheek and eye of blue
  Do save him still from harm;
    Tho' many fair he see,
    Yet his delight will be
    To live, to breathe, alone for thee!

Could he step from star to star,
  Making gold-rimmed worlds a bridge,
Could he cling to Phœbus' car,
  And whirl by Space's edge,
    Still his delight would be
    Beneath a bowery tree
    To lingering bide, O fair, with thee!

Could the gods the hues combine
  Of each rarest flower that grows,
Mingle all their perfumes fine
  In one consummate rose,
    Still his delight would be
    To wander o'er the lea
    And pluck the daffodil with thee!

Did the clear-browed Dian tall
  Smile him to the joyous chase
T' hear her hounds' melodious call,
  To match her beauteous face,
    His joyance yet would be
    Thy milk-white ewes to see
    And tend thy snowy lambs with thee!

If from purple-bosomed seas
  Aphrodite should arise,
Wiling—seeking him to please
  With her sun-glossed eyes,
    Still Sylvius would be free,
    For he would fainer be
    Beside the rippling brook with thee!

THE CAMP OF SOULS.

MY white canoe, like the silvery air
  O'er the River of Death that darkly rolls
When the moons of the world are round and fair,
  I paddle back from the " Camp of Souls."
When the wishton-wish in the low swamp grieves
Come the dark plumes of red " Singing Leaves."

THE CAMP OF SOULS

Two hundred times have the moons of spring
   Rolled over the bright bay's azure breath
Since they decked me with plumes of an eagle's wing,
   And painted my face with the " paint of death,"
And from their pipes o'er my corpse there broke
The solemn rings of the blue " last smoke."

Two hundred times have the wintry moons
   Wrapped the dead earth in a blanket white;
Two hundred times have the wild sky loons
   Shrieked in the flush of the golden light
Of the first sweet dawn, when the summer weaves
Her dusky wigwam of perfect leaves.

Two hundred moons of the falling leaf
   Since they laid my bow in my dead right hand
And chanted above me the " song of grief "
   As I took my way to the spirit land;
Yet when the swallow the blue air cleaves
Come the dark plumes of red " Singing Leaves."

White are the wigwams in that far camp,
   And the star-eyed deer on the plains are found;
No bitter marshes or tangled swamp
   In the Manitou's happy hunting-ground!
And the moon of summer forever rolls
Above the red men in their " Camp of Souls."

Blue are its lakes as the wild dove's breast,
   And their murmurs soft as her gentle note;
As the calm, large stars in the deep sky rest,
   The yellow lilies upon them float;
And canoes, like flakes of the silvery snow,
Thro' the tall, rustling rice-beds come and go.

Green are its forests; no warrior wind
  Rushes on war trail the dusk grove through,
With leaf-scalps of tall trees mourning behind;
  But South Wind, heart friend of Great Manitou,
When ferns and leaves with cool dews are wet,
Blows flowery breaths from his red calumet.

Never upon them the white frosts lie,
  Nor glow their green boughs with the " paint of
    death ";
Manitou smiles in the crystal sky,
  Close breathing above them His life-strong breath:
And He speaks no more in fierce thunder sound,
So near is His happy hunting-ground.

Yet often I love, in my white canoe,
  To come to the forests and camps of earth:
'Twas there death's black arrow pierced me through;
  'Twas there my red-browed mother gave me birth;
There I, in the light of a young man's dawn,
Won the lily heart of dusk " Springing Fawn."

And love is a cord woven out of life,
  And dyed in the red of the living heart;
And time is the hunter's rusty knife,
  That cannot cut the red strands apart:
And I sail from the spirit shore to scan
Where the weaving of that strong cord began.

But I may not come with a giftless hand,
  So richly I pile, in my white canoe,
Flowers that bloom in the spirit land,
  Immortal smiles of Great Manitou.
When I paddle back to the shores of earth
I scatter them over the white man's hearth.

For love is the breath of the soul set free;
  So I cross the river that darkly rolls,
That my spirit may whisper soft to thee
  Of *thine* who wait in the " Camp of Souls."
When the bright day laughs, or the wan night grieves,
Come the dusky plumes of red " Singing Leaves."

THE MOTHER'S SOUL.

WHEN the moon was horned the mother died,
  And the child pulled at her hand and knee,
And he rubbed her cheek and loudly cried:
  " O mother, arise, give bread to me!"
    But the pine tree bent its head,
    And the wind at the door-post said:
    " O child, thy mother is dead!"

The sun set his loom to weave the day;
  The frost bit sharp like a silent cur;
The child by her pillow paused in his play:
  " Mother, build up the sweet fire of fir!"
    But the fir tree shook its cones,
    And loud cried the pitiful stones:
    " Wolf Death has thy mother's bones!"

They bore the mother out on her bier;
  Their tears made warm her breast and shroud;
The smiling child at her head stood near;
  And the long, white tapers shook and bowed,
    And said with their tongues of gold,
    To the ice lumps of the grave mold:
    " How heavy are ye and cold!"

55

ISABELLA VALANCY CRAWFORD

They buried the mother; to the feast
  They flocked with the beaks of unclean crows.
The wind came up from the red-eyed east
  And bore in its arms the chill, soft snows.
    They said to each other: " Sere
    Are the hearts the mother held dear;
    Forgotten, her babe plays here!"

The child with the tender snowflakes played,
  And the wind on its fingers twined his hair;
And still by the tall, brown grave he stayed,
  Alone in the churchyard lean and bare.
    The sods on the high grave cried
    To the mother's white breast inside:
    " Lie still; in thy deep rest bide!"

Her breast lay still like a long-chilled stone,
  Her soul was out on the bleak, grey day;
She saw her child by the grave alone,
  With the sods and snow and wind at play.
    Said the sharp lips of the rush,
    " Red as thy roses, O bush,
    With anger the dead can blush!"

A butterfly to the child's breast flew,*
  Fluttered its wings on his sweet, round cheek,
Danced by his fingers, small, cold and blue.
    The sun strode down past the mountain peak.
    The butterfly whispered low
    To the child: " Babe, follow me; know,
    Cold is the earth here below."

* In Eastern Europe the soul of the deceased is said to hover,
in the shape of a bird or butterfly, close to the body until after the
burial.

56

THE MOTHER'S SOUL

The butterfly flew; followed the child,
  Lured by the snowy torch of its wings;
The wind sighed after them soft and wild
  Till the stars wedded night with golden rings;
    Till the frost upreared its head,
    And the ground to it groaned and said:
    " The feet of the child are lead!"

The child's head drooped to the brown, sere mold,
  On the crackling cones his white breast lay;
The butterfly touched the locks of gold,
  The soul of the child sprang from its clay.
    The moon to the pine tree stole,
    And, silver-lipped, said to its bole:
    " How strong is the mother's soul!"

The wings of the butterfly grew out
  To the mother's arms, long, soft and white;
She folded them warm her babe about,
  She kissed his lips into berries bright,
    She warmed his soul on her breast;
    And the east called out to the west:
    " Now the mother's soul will rest!"

Under the roof where the burial feast
  Was heavy with meat and red with wine,
Each crossed himself as out of the east
  A strange wind swept over oak and pine.
    The trees to the home-roof said:
    " 'Tis but the airy rush and tread
    Of angels greeting thy dead."

THE INSPIRATION OF SONG.

Her turret hung above a glassy lake,
  And in all ages changeless thus had stood;
About its foot, dark laurels and a brake
  Of gleaming bay eternal zephyrs wooed.
Up by the battlements there climbed a vine
  Gemmed with great roses that the eye of morn
Looked on the birth of, but there came no time
  That saw them die or one bright petal shorn.

Centuries that on the world breathed but decay
  Wheeled their slow flight, and from their heavy wings
Smote on its walls a light that paled the day,
  A light such as illumined diamond flings.
Sheer from a bank of violets sprang the walls,
  And climbed from thence above the lordliest trees,
Until their hoary foreheads caught the rose
  And gold of far-off Heaven; and the breeze

Swept from the Spirit city harmonies,
  Faint voiced thro' starry distances, that fell
In stronger echoes from the rocky walls
  And swept abroad o'er city, moor and dell.
And by a casement brightening in the wall,
  With fine-flamed diamonds latticed, sat the Queen,
From age to age more beautiful, and looked
  To where a road the bay trees wound between.

Whiter than whitest dove her flowing robe
  Of precious samite, and the border round
Glowed with all rarest gems of every hue;
  And at her feet, crouched on the pearly ground,

58

THE INSPIRATION OF SONG

A tawny lion, with a mane that tossed
  In golden tempests round his awful eyes,
Lay placid, as her pointed fingers struck
  From her tall lyre a sound of Paradise.

Her deep and lambent eyes were ever fixed
  On the white road that glimmered far below;
The immortal roses glowed about her head;
  A starry radiance shook above her brow.
Along the road, that was no common way,
  But led to heights where fanes, all bathed in light,
Held thrones for those that won, pilgrims there passed
  In humblest weed or gorgeously bedight.

As passed each one beneath the towering wall,
  And raised his dazzled gaze to woo her eyes
That at the casement sat, she brake a rose
  And breathed upon it till its crimson dyes
Leaped into warmer fire. " Take it," she sang, and cast
  It, meteor-glancing, to the outstretched hand
Of him below; and so content he passed
  And journeyed to the distant-lying land.

And each one bore a lyre, and some that caught
  The Queen's fair flower placed it on the breast;
Then warbling strains breathed from the lyre and sang
  Of Love, of sweet-eyed Love, fair Joy and Rest.
And some there were that twined the flower amid
  Cold gems that twinkled on the high, pale brow;
Then burst the lyre to trumpet tones and sang
  Of power, high deeds, and Fame's eternal glow.

And some there were that crushed the flower between
  Gross palms that burned and sapped its charmèd
     life;

Then fire-eyed Madness struck the clanging strings,
  Charmed Vice to fairer form, more vivid life.
And rife the world became with demons masked
  In seraph brightness; and so toward the fanes
That held the thrones the pilgrims, singing, passed
  Across the mighty glories of the plains.

BABY'S DREAMS.

WHAT doth the Moon, so lily white,
Busily weave this summer night?
" Silver ropes and diamond strands
For Baby's pink and dimpled hands;
Cords for her rosy palms to hold
    While she floats, she flies,
To Dreamland, set with its shores of gold,
With its buds like stars shaken out of the skies,
Where the trees have tongues and the flowers have lips
    To coax, to kiss
    The velvet cheek of the Babe who slips
    Thro' the Dream-gate up to a land like this."

What is the mild Sea whispering clear
In the rosy shell of Baby's ear?
See! she laughs in her dimpled sleep.
What does she hear from the shining deep?
" Thy father comes a-sailing, a-sailing, a-sailing,
Safely comes a-sailing from islands fair and far.
O Baby, bid thy mother cease her tears and bitter
    wailing:
The sailor's wife's his only port, his babe his beacon
    star!"

BABY'S DREAMS

Softly the Wind doth blow;
What say its murmurs low?
What doth it bring
On the wide, soft plume of its dewy wing?
" Only scented blisses
Of innocent, sweet kisses
For such a cheek as this is,
Of Baby in her nest,
From all the dreaming flowers,
A-nodding in their bowers,
Or bright on leafy towers,
Where the fairy monarchs rest.
But chiefly I bring,
On my fresh, sweet mouth,
Her father's kiss,
As he sails from the south.
He hitherward blew it at break of day;
I lay it, Babe, on thy tender lip;
I'll steal another and hie away,
And kiss it to him on his wave-rocked ship.

" I saw a fairy twine,
Of star-white jessamine,
A dainty seat, shaped like an airy swing,
With two round yellow stars
Against the misty bars
Of night; she nailed it high
In the pansy-purple sky,
With four taps of her little rainbow wing.
To and fro
That swing I'll blow.
" The baby moon in the amethyst sky
Will laugh at us as we float and fly,
And stretch her silver arms and try
To catch the earth-babe swinging by."

61

SAID THE SKYLARK.

O SOFT, small Cloud, the dim, sweet dawn adorning,
Swan-like a-sailing on its tender grey,
  Why dost thou, dost thou float
  So high the winged, wild note
Of silvery lamentation from my dark and pulsing throat
  May never reach thee,
  Tho' every note beseech thee
To bend thy white wings downward thro' the smiling of
  the morning,
And by the black wires of my prison lightly stray?

O dear, small Cloud, when all blue morn is ringing
With sweet notes piped from other throats than mine,
  If those glad singers please
  The tall and nodding trees,
If to them dance the pennants of the swaying columbine,
  If to their songs are set
The dance of daffodil and trembling violet,
  Will they pursue thee
With tireless wings as free and bold as thine?
  And will they woo thee
With love-throbs in the music of their singing?
  Ah, nay! fair Cloud, ah, nay!
  Their hearts and wings will stay
With yellow bud of primrose and soft blush of the may;
  Their songs will thrill and die
Tranced in the perfume of the rose's breast,
  While I must see thee fly
With white, broad, lonely pinions down the sky.

SAID THE SKYLARK

O fair, small Cloud, unheeding o'er me straying,
Jewelled with topaz light of fading stars,
  Thy downy edges red,
As the great eagle of the dawn sails high
  And sets his fire-bright head
And wind-blown pinions toward thy snowy breast!
  And thou canst blush while I
  Must pierce myself with song and die
On the bald sod behind my prison bars,
  Nor feel upon my crest
Thy soft-sunned touches delicately playing!

O fair, small Cloud, grown small as lily flower,
Even while I smite the bars to see thee fade,
  The wind shall bring thee
  The strain I sing thee—
I, in wirèd prison stayed,
Worse than the breathless primrose glade
  That in my morn
  I shrilly sang to scorn.
I'll burst my heart up to thee in this hour!

O fair, small Cloud, float nearer yet and hear me!
A prisoned lark once loved a snowy cloud,
  Nor did the Day
  With sapphire lips and kiss
  Of summery bliss
Draw all her soul away;
  Vainly the fervent East
Decked her with roses for their bridal feast;
  She would not rest

In his red arms, but slipped adown the air,
  And, wan and fair,
Her light foot touched a purple mountain crest,
  And, touching, turned
Into swift rain, that like to jewels burned
In the great, wondering azure of the sky.
  And while a rainbow spread
Its mighty arms above, she, singing, fled
  To the lone feathered slave
  In his sad, weird grave,
Whose heart upon his silvery song had sped
  To her in days of old,
  In dawns of gold,
And murmuring to him, said:
" O Love, I come!   O Love, I come to cheer thee!
  Love, to be near thee!"

SAID THE WIND.

  " Come with me," said the Wind
  To the Ship within the dock,
  " Or dost thou fear the shock
  Of the ocean-hidden rock,
When tempests strike thee full and leave thee blind;
  When low the inky clouds
  Blackly tangle in thy shrouds,
  And every strainèd cord
  Finds a voice and shrills a word—
That word of doom so thundrously upflung
  From the tongue
  Of every forkèd wave,
  Lamenting o'er a grave
  64

SAID THE WIND

Deep hidden at its base,
Where the dead whom it has slain
Lie in the strict embrace
Of secret weird tendrils?   But the pain
Of the ocean's strong remorse
Doth fiercely force
The tale of murder from its bosom out
In a mighty tempest clangour; and its shout,
In the threat'ning and lamenting of the swell,
Is as the voice of Hell!
Yet all the word it saith
Is ' Death.'

" Come with me !" sang the Wind.
" Why art thou, love, unkind?
Thou art too fair, O Ship,
To kiss the slimy lip
Of the cold and dismal shore; and, prithee, mark
How chill and dark
Shew the vast and rusty linkings of the chain,
Hoarse grating as with pain,
Which moors thee
And secures thee
From the transports of the soft wind and the main!
Ay, strain thou and pull,
Thy sails are dull
And dim from long close furling on thy spars;
But come thou forth with me,
And full and free
I'll kiss them, kiss them, kiss them, till they be
White as the arctic stars,
Or as the salt-white pinions of the gull!

" Come with me," sang the Wind,
" O Ship beloved, and find

How golden-glossed and blue
Is the sea;
How thrush-sweet is my voice; how dearly true
I'll keep my nuptial promises to thee!
Oh, mine to guide thy sails
By the kisses of my mouth,
Soft as blow the gales
On the roses in the south!
Oh, mine to guide thee far
From ruddy coral bar!
From horizon to horizon thou shalt glimmer like a star.
Thou shalt lean upon my breast,
And I shall rest,
And murmur in thy sails
Such fond tales
That thy finest cords
Will, siren-like, chant back my mellow words
With such renewed enchantment unto me
That I shall be,
By mine own singing, closer bound to thee!

" Come with me," sang the Wind;
" Thou knowest, love, my mind;
No more I'll try to woo thee,
Persuade thee or pursue thee,
For thou art mine
Since first thy mast, a tall and stately pine,
Beneath Norwegian skies
Sang to my sighs.
Thou, thou wert built for me,
Strong lily of the sea!
Thou canst not choose
The calling of my low voice to refuse;
And if Death
Were the sole, sad, wailing burthen of my breath,

SAID THE CANOE

Thy timbers at my call
Would shudder in their thrall,
Thy sails outburst to touch my stormy lip;
Like a giant in a grave
Quick thy anchor heave,
And close upon my thunder-pulsing breast, O Ship,
Thou wouldst tremble; nor repine
That, being mine,
Thy spars,
Like long pale lights of falling stars,
Plunged in the Stygian blackness of the sea;
And, to billowy ruin cast,
Thy tall and taper mast
Rushed shrieking headlong down to an abyss.
O Ship! O love! if death
Were such sure portion, thou couldst not refuse,
But thou wouldst choose
As mine to die, and call such choosing bliss;
For thou for me
Wert planned from all eternity!"

SAID THE CANOE.

My masters twain made me a bed
Of pine-boughs resinous, and cedar;
Of moss, a soft and gentle breeder
Of dreams of rest; and me they spread
With furry skins and, laughing, said:
"Now she shall lay her polished sides
As queens do rest, or dainty brides,
Our slender lady of the tides!"

My masters twain their camp-soul lit;
Streamed incense from the hissing cones;

67

Large crimson flashes grew and whirled;
Thin golden nerves of sly light curled
Round the dun camp; and rose faint zones,
Half way about each grim bole knit,
Like a shy child that would bedeck
With its soft clasp a Brave's red neck,
Yet sees the rough shield on his breast,
The awful plumes shake on his crest,
And, fearful, drops his timid face,
Nor dares complete the sweet embrace.

Into the hollow hearts of brakes—
Yet warm from sides of does and stags
Passed to the crisp, dark river-flags—
Sinuous, red as copper-snakes,
Sharp-headed serpents, made of light,
Glided and hid themselves in night.

My masters twain the slaughtered deer
Hung on forked boughs with thongs of leather:
Bound were his stiff, slim feet together,
His eyes like dead stars cold and drear.
The wandering firelight drew near
And laid its wide palm, red and anxious,
On the sharp splendour of his branches,
On the white foam grown hard and sere
    On flank and shoulder.
Death—hard as breast of granite boulder—
    Under his lashes
Peered thro' his eves at his life's grey ashes.

My masters twain sang songs that wove—
As they burnished hunting-blade and rifle—
A golden thread with a cobweb trifle,
Loud of the chase and low of love:

SAIL THE CANOE

" O Love! art thou a silver fish,
   Shy of the line and shy of gaffing,
   Which we do follow, fierce, yet laughing,
   Casting at thee the light-winged wish?
   And at the last shall we bring thee up
   From the crystal darkness, under the cup
         Of lily folden
         On broad leaves golden?

" O Love! art thou a silver deer
   With feet as swift as wing of swallow,
   While we with rushing arrows follow?
   And at the last shall we draw near
   And o'er thy velvet neck cast thongs
   Woven of roses, stars and songs—
         New chains all moulden
         Of rare gems olden?"

They hung the slaughtered fish like swords
   On saplings slender; like scimitars,
   Bright, and ruddied from new-dead wars,
Blazed in the light the scaly hordes.

They piled up boughs beneath the trees,
   Of cedar web and green fir tassel.
   Low did the pointed pine tops rustle,
The camp-fire blushed to the tender breeze.

The hounds laid dewlaps on the ground
   With needles of pine, sweet, soft and rusty,
   Dreamed of the dead stag stout and lusty;
A bat by the red flames wove its round.

69

The darkness built its wigwam walls
    Close round the camp, and at its curtain
    Pressed shapes, thin, woven and uncertain
As white locks of tall waterfalls.

SONGS FOR THE SOLDIERS.

IF songs be sung let minstrels strike their harps
To large and joyous strains, all thunder-winged
To beat along vast shores. Ay, let their notes
Wild into eagles soaring toward the sun,
And voiced like bugles bursting thro' the dawn
When armies leap to life! Give them such breasts
As hold immortal fires, and they shall fly,
Swept with our little sphere thro' all the change
That waits a whirling world.

                        Joy's an immortal;
She hath a fiery fibre in her flesh
That will not droop or die; so let her chant
The pæans of the dead, where holy Grief
Hath, trembling, thrust the feeble mist aside
That veils her dead, and in the wondrous clasp
Of re-possession ceases to be Grief.
Joy's ample voice shall still roll over all,
And chronicle the heroes to young hearts
Who knew them not. Beside their hoary urns
Shall leap the laugh of babes, and men shall pause,
Lifting their little lads to gaze, and say:
" Come, now, my son, spell the three names aloud—
Brown, Moor, and Fitch. Ay, right, my lad! Be proud
Of them! It was a joyous day for us,

The day they made that bold burst at Batoche,
And with their dead flesh built a wall about
Our riving land."

                      There's glory on the sword
That keeps its scabbard-sleep, unless the foe
Beat at the wall, then freely leaps to light
And thrusts to keep the sacred towers of Home
And the dear lines that map the nation out upon the
    world.

HIS MOTHER.

In the first dawn she lifted from her bed
The holy silver of her noble head,
And listened, listened, listened for his tread.

"Too soon, too soon!" she murmured, "yet I'll keep
My vigil longer—thou, O tender Sleep,
Art but the joy of those who wake and weep!

"Joy's self hath keen, wide eyes. O flesh of mine,
And mine own blood and bone, the very wine
Of my aged heart, I see thy dear eyes shine!

"I hear thy tread; thy light, loved footsteps run
Along the way, eager for that 'Well done!'
We'll weep and kiss to thee, my soldier son!

"Blest mother I—he lives! Yet had he died
Blest were I still,—I sent him on the tide
Of my full heart to save his nation's pride!"

" O God, if that I tremble so to-day,
  Bowed with such blessings that I cannot pray
  By speech—a mother prays, dear Lord, alway

" In some far fibre of her trembling mind!
  I'll up—I thought I heard a bugle bind
  Its silver with the silver of the wind."

HIS WIFE AND BABY.

In the lone place of the leaves,
  Where they touch the hanging eaves,
There sprang a spray of joyous song that sounded sweet
        and sturdy;
  And the baby in the bed
  Raised the shining of his head,
And pulled the mother's lids apart to wake and watch
        the birdie.

She kissed lip-dimples sweet,
  The red soles of his feet,
The waving palms that patted hers as wind-blown
        blossoms wander;
  He twined her tresses silk
  Round his neck as white as milk—
" Now, baby, say what birdie sings upon his green spray
        yonder."

" He sings a plenty things—
  Just watch him wash his wings!
He says Papa will march to-day with drums home thro'
        the city.

Here, birdie, here's my cup,
  You drink the milk all up;
I'll kiss you, birdie, now you're washed like baby clean
    and pretty."

She rose; she sought the skies
  With the twin joys of her eyes;
She sent the strong dove of her soul up thro' the dawn-
    ing's glory;
  She kissed upon her hand
  The glowing golden band
That bound the fine scroll of her life and clasped her
    simple story.

HIS SWEETHEART.

Sylvia's lattices were dark—
  Roses made them narrow.
In the dawn there came a Spark,
  Armèd with an arrow:
Blithe he burst by dewy spray,
  Winged by bud and blossom,
All undaunted urged his way
  Straight to Sylvia's bosom.
" Sylvia! Sylvia! Sylvia!" he
  Like a bee kept humming,
" Wake, my sweeting; waken thee,
  For thy Soldier's coming!"

Sylvia, sleeping in the dawn,
  Dreams that Cupid's trill is
Roses singing on the lawn,
  Courting crested lilies.

73

Sylvia smiles and Sylvia sleeps,
  Sylvia weeps and slumbers;
Cupid to her pink ear creeps,
  Pipes his pretty numbers.
Sylvia dreams that bugles play,
  Hears a martial drumming;
Sylvia springs to meet the day
  With her Soldier coming.

Happy Sylvia, on thee wait
  All the gracious graces!
Venus mild her cestus plait
  Round thy lawns and laces!
Flora fling a flower most fair,
  Hope a rainbow lend thee!
All the nymphs to Cupid dear
  On this day befriend thee!
"Sylvia! Sylvia! Sylvia!" hear
  How he keeps a-humming,
Laughing in her jewelled ear,
  "Sweet, thy Soldier's coming!"

WHO SEES A VISION.

WHO sees a vision bright and bold
Hath found a treasure of pure gold;
  For say it vanisheth
  When Morning banisheth
Sleep, mother of all dreams,
Before his comely beams,
Thou didst not wis, before sleep showed to thee,
That things so nobly fair might ever be;

WHO SEES A VISION

But now that thou dost know,
Waking shall make it so;
So here is treasure hid
Beneath a closed eyelid.

Who dreams a dream both sweet and bright
Hath found true nectar of delight;
    For say with pain and smart
    It fadeth out apart,
Thy gallèd heart did never,
In waking sad endeavour,
Bend back the veil of murky tapestry
And show such things of light and joy to thee;
    But now that thou dost know,
    Hope builds her skyward bow;
    There cannot be a shade
    But for it form is made.

Who sees a vision foul and dim
Hath seen the naked shade of sin;
    And say its grim masque closeth
    When Morn himself discloseth,
Thy soul hath seen the colour,
The anguish and the dolor,
Of her whom thou hast haply only seen
In fair attire and feasted as a queen;
    But now thou dost her know,
    She may not fool thee so;
    Sin may not ever be
    Again a queen to thee.

MAVOURNEEN.

DARK are the waters of sorrow, Mavourneen,
  Bleak the grey rocks that surround the cold wave;
Pale are the small silver daisies that borrow
  Life from the green sod that's laid on a grave.

Cheerless the songs of the thrushes, Mavourneen,
  Scentless the blossom of each hawthorn tree;
Salt is the hot tear that bitterly rushes,
  Kneeling by green altar sacred to thee.

Blue is the low, misty mountain, Mavourneen,
  We lived on, loved on, and toiled on of yore;
Clear the bright torrent that runs from its fountain,
  Bursting in glee by our own lowly door.

Green stretch the dew-brightened meadows, Mavourneen,
  Bees haunt the lilac and white blooming hedge,
Swallows dart still thro' the sunshine and shadows,
  Sings the brook, fairy-like, under its sedge.

Still on the roof of our dwelling, Mavourneen,
  Wall flowers swing to the soft mountain breeze;
Still in the white cloud the lark's song is swelling;
  Still nod to hill-tops the tall valley trees.

Green is the thatch still with mosses, Mavourneen,
  Golden the sunbeam that strikes on the door;
Bright the great wing of the rainbow that crosses
  Hill-top to hill-top above the dark moor.

Golden the mists of the morning, Mavourneen,
  Silver the star-daisies bloom in the sky;

MAVOURNEEN

Red on the wild sea the storm lights its warning,
   Still wheel the eagles to greet it on high.

Still blooms the brier-rose brightly, Mavourneen,
   By the old settle that stands by the door;
Hollyhocks nod to the fresh wind as lightly
   As when amid them you knitted, asthore.

Cowslips are bright in the grasses, Mavourneen,
   As when our baby cried out for their gold;
Daisies are white as his pure cheek that presses
   To thy still breast its snow under the mold.

What ails the sunshine and blossoms, Mavourneen,
   Stars and the birds and the green waving tree?
Still God gives sunshine to eyes and to bosoms,—
   Thou wert the sunlight that God gave to me.

Brave was thy heart, and thy glances, Mavourneen,
   Gave their blue heaven to dwell in my breast,
Shone in their glory on Want's cold expanses,
   Clung to my soul as fond doves to their nest.

Strong was thy weak hand and tender, Mavourneen,
   Braced it my sinews afresh for my toil—
Toil, hopeless, drear as dark skies in November—
   Sweat of a freeborn, but serf of the soil.

Sunshine may flame with its brightness, Mavourneen,
   Rayless the dark heart when, under the sod,
Clasped in the lily of death's silent whiteness,
   Sunlight that smote on the bosom from God.

Sunlight! my sunlight! no weeping, Mavourneen,
   Melts the strong arrow that bites the heart's core;

77

Darker the shadows that on me are sweeping,
  Blood of my heart! O my Moyna, asthore!

Waters of sorrow are soundless, Mavourneen,
  Black as the depths of the deeply hewn grave;
Heaven above me, so blue, bright and boundless,
  Smiles from the breast of the motionless wave.

And from its black, sullen bosom, Mavourneen,
  Slips up a lily, all snowy to see;
On sorrow's waters lies star-like the blossom
  Of hope and mem'ry, my Moyna, of thee.

THE DARK STAG.

A STARTLED stag, the blue-grey Night,
  Leaps down beyond black pines.
Behind—a length of yellow light—
  The hunter's arrow shines:
His moccasins are stained with red,
  He bends upon his knee,
From covering peaks his shafts are sped,
The blue mists plume his mighty head,—
  Well may the swift Night flee!

The pale, pale Moon, a snow-white doe,
  Bounds by his dappled flank:
They beat the stars down as they go,
  Like wood-bells growing rank.
The winds lift dewlaps from the ground,
  Leap from the quaking reeds;
Their hoarse bays shake the forests round,
With keen cries on the track they bound,—
  Swift, swift the dark stag speeds!

78

THE DARK STAG

Away! his white doe, far behind,
  Lies wounded on the plain;
Yells at his flank the nimblest wind,
  His large tears fall in rain;
Like lily-pads, small clouds grow white
  About his darkling way;
From his bald nest upon the height
The red-eyed eagle sees his flight;
He falters, turns, the antlered Night,—
  The dark stag stands at bay!

His feet are in the waves of space;
  His antlers broad and dun
He lowers; he turns his velvet face
  To front the hunter, Sun;
He stamps the lilied clouds, and high
  His branches fill the west.
The lean stork sails across the sky,
The shy loon shrieks to see him die,
  The winds leap at his breast.

Roar the rent lakes as thro' the wave
  Their silver warriors plunge,
As vaults from core of crystal cave
  The strong, fierce muskallunge;
Red torches of the sumach glare,
  Fall's council-fires are lit;
The bittern, squaw-like, scolds the air;
The wild duck splashes loudly where
  The rustling rice-spears knit.

Shaft after shaft the red Sun speeds:
  Rent the stag's dappled side,
His breast, fanged by the shrill winds, bleeds,
  He staggers on the tide;

He feels the hungry waves of space
    Rush at him high and blue;
Their white spray smites his dusky face,
Swifter the Sun's fierce arrows race
    And pierce his stout heart thro'.

His antlers fall; once more he spurns
    The hoarse hounds of the day;
His blood upon the crisp blue burns,
    Reddens the mounting spray;
His branches smite the wave—with cries
    The loud winds pause and flag—
He sinks in space—red glow the skies,
The brown earth crimsons as he dies,
    The strong and dusky stag.

ERIN'S WARNING.

ERIN, lift thy bending head,
Rise majestic by the sea;
Say, in soul-compelling voice:
Sons, who fain would have me free,
Have a care, lest when ye rend
From my limbs the biting chain,
Ye, my sons, around my brow
Bind the fiery crown of shame!

Sons, for ages I have sat
Sackcloth-girded on the ground,
Glory-widowed, captive queen,
Shackled, dethroned and discrowned;
Mute my harp, ingloriously
Dumb its old heroic strains;

But its loosened strings wailed low,
Vibrant to my clanking chains.

At my knee my starvelings lay,
Jewels crowned my captive head—
Hearken, God, I might not sell
One to buy my children bread!
Beauty, fresh, immortal, dwelt
On my bent and hapless brow;
Conquered but unshamed I sat—
Sons, why would ye shame me now?

Children of my troubled breast,
When, as Glory's spouse, on high
Throned with him, I sat and saw
Golden days pass grandly by,
In my kings', my warriors' souls
Valour lit his purest flame,—
Would ye, O my sons, replace
Such a light with blackest shame?

Would ye, valiant sons of mine,
Play the traitor's loathly part?
Bow my proud head in the dust?
Sell my honour in the mart?
If ye may not break my chains,
Fearless-fronted, true and brave,
Spotless as thy sires were,
Then let Erin live a slave!

Could I mount my throne again,
Sun-like placed in freedom's air,
Hearkening as the nations say:
" Midnight murders placed her there"?

Could my sunburst proudly float
Glorious o'er my ancient land,
Were its mighty folds let loose
By the dark assassin's hand?

How could Glory's star arise,
Set its pure light on my head,
In the lurid glare of flames
By the secret torches spread?
O my sons, take heed and see,
If ye break my chafing chain,
That ye bind not round my brow
Fiery crown of lasting shame!

BESIDE THE SEA.

ONE time he dreamed beside a sea
   That laid a mane of mimic stars
In fondling quiet on the knee
   Of one tall, pearlèd cliff; the bars
Of golden beaches upward swept;
Pine-scented shadows seaward crept.

The full moon swung her ripened sphere
   As from a vine; and clouds, as small
As vine leaves in the opening year,
   Kissed the large circle of her ball.
The stars gleamed thro' them as one sees
Thro' vine leaves drift the golden bees.

He dreamed beside this purple sea;
   Low sang its trancéd voice, and he—
He knew not if the wordless strain
   Made prophecy of joy or pain;

82

BESIDE THE SEA

He only knew far stretched that sea,
He knew its name—Eternity.

A shallop with a rainbow sail
   On the bright pulses of the tide
Throbbed airily; a fluting gale
   Kissed the rich gilding of its side;
By chain of rose and myrtle fast
A light sail touched the slender mast.

" A flower-bright rainbow thing," he said
   To one beside him, " far too frail
To brave dark storms that lurk ahead,
   To dare sharp talons of the gale.
Beloved, thou wouldst not forth with me
In such a bark on such a sea?"

" First tell me of its name." She bent
   Her eyes divine and innocent
On his. He raised his hand above
   Its prow and answering swore, " 'Tis Love!"
" Now tell," she asked, " how is it built—
Of gold, or worthless timber gilt?"

" Of gold," he said. " Whence named?" asked she,
   The roses of her lips apart;
She paused—a lily by the sea.
   Came his swift answer, " From my heart!"
She laid her light palm in his hand:
" Let loose the shallop from the strand!"

THE SAILOR AND HIS BRIDE.

" Let out the wet dun sail, my lads,
    The foam is flying fast;
It whistles on the fav'ring gale,
    To-night we'll anchor cast.
What though the storm be loud, my lads,
    And danger on the blast;
Though bursting sail swell round and proud,
    And groan the straining mast;
The storm has wide, strong wings, my lads,
    On them our craft shall ride,
And dear the tempest swift that brings
    The sailor to his bride."

" Fear not the tempest shrill, my heart,
    The tall, white breakers' wrath;
I would not have the wild winds still
    Along the good ship's path.
The ship is staunch and strong, my heart,
    The wind blows to the strand;
Why tremble? for its fiercest song
    But drives the ship to land.
Be still, nor throb so fast, my heart,
    The storm but brings, betide
What may to ship and straining mast,
    My sailor to his bride."

Blow soft and low, and sigh, O gale!
    Sob, sea, upon the bar!
No more o'er thee the ship shall fly
    White-winged as vesper star.
Roll up the shattered mast, O gale!
    Upon the yellow strand,

WEALTH

A dead man's form cast, gently cast,
  Upon the waiting land.
And when again thy breath, O gale!
  Wails o'er the vaulting tide,
Bear not on hurtling wings of death
  A sailor to his bride.

WEALTH.

WEALTH, doff thy jewelled crown of gold,
  Thy sceptre strong, nor rave;
I tell thee, Wealth, on Christian mold
  Thou canst not buy a slave.
Nay, tyrant, seek some other sod
For slaves to tremble at thy nod!

Hence, despot, with thy clanking chains!
  Thou canst not purchase here.
Seek brutal hinds on savage plains;
  We hold our poor men dear.
They shall not bend beneath thy yoke,
Nor cringe before thy sceptre's stroke.

God spake—we listened—loud His voice,
  High o'er the noise of waves.
Arose our answer: " Laud, rejoice,
  No more shall blood of slaves
Enrich our soil!"   From sea to sea
Rolled God's grand watchword, " Liberty."

What! tyrant, dost thou linger yet
  With sceptre and with crown?
Can it be thy mighty foot is set
  On necks of men bowed down?

And dost thou smile with fierce lips locked?
Is God by despot Wealth still mocked?

Look down, O God! whence comes this train
   Yoked to the tyrant's wheel?
Hark! dost Thou hear that clanking chain?
   See yon gaunt wretches reel?
Art Thou not mocked, eternal God?
Are these not serfs on freedom's sod?

Out, fool! this is a Christian land,
   And they but idly rave
Who clamour that yon grisly band
   Contains a single slave;
Not one was bought in any mart,
None captive to the sword or dart.

Wealth is no despot, owns no slave;
   No wretch must take his dole—
He hath a choice, the yawning grave—
   Then answer, foolish soul,
Is Wealth a tyrant if he thrives
When famine strikes at lowly lives?

THE HIDDEN ROOM.

   I MARVEL if my heart
   Hath any room apart,
Built secretly its mystic walls within,
   With subtly warded key
   Ne'er yielded unto me,
Where even I have surely never been.

THE HIDDEN ROOM

Ah, surely I know all
  The bright and cheerful hall,
With the fire ever red upon its hearth;
  My friends dwell with me there,
  Nor comes the step of Care
To sadden down its music and its mirth.

Full well I know as mine
  The little cloistered shrine
No foot but mine alone hath ever trod;
  There come the shining wings,
  The face of One who brings
The prayers of men before the throne of God.

And many know full well
  The busy, busy cell
Where I toil at the work I have to do;
  Nor is the portal fast
  Where stand phantoms of the past,
Or grow the bitter plants of darksome rue.

I know the dainty spot
  (Ah, who doth know it not?)
Where pure young Love his lily-cradle made,
  And nestled some sweet springs
  With lily-spangled wings—
Forget-me-nots upon his bier I laid.

Yet marvel I, my soul,
  Know I thy very whole,
Or dost thou hide a chamber still from me?
  Is it built upon the wall?
  Is it spacious? Is it small?
Is it God, or man, or I who hold the key?

TRUE AND FALSE.

OH! spring was in his shining eyes
  And summer in his happy soul;
He bounded o'er the misty rise
  And saw the purple ocean roll.

With stars above and stars below,
  The lovely eve was fair as noon;
He saw above him richly glow
  The white shores of the sailing moon,

Her vales of jet, her pearly peaks,
  The lustre on her shining sands;
Leaped eager roses to his cheeks,—
  He cried, " I seek her silver strands!"

There rose a siren where the foam
  Of ocean sparkled most with stars:
She combed gold locks with golden comb;
  She floated past the murmuring bars.

She sang so loud, so silvery clear,
  The trees in far woods seemed to stir,
And seaward lean; from lake and mere
  Rushed eager rivers down to her.

She swept in mist of far blown hair,
  Star-white, from glittering steep to steep;
She loved his gay and dauntless air—
  Rose loftier from the purple deep,

TRUE AND FALSE

Till, whiter than white coral rocks,
   She glimmered high against the moon.
And oh, she loved his raven locks!
   And oh, she sang him to his doom!

" O boy, why dost thou upward turn
   The crystal of thy youthful eyes?
The true moon in the sea doth burn;
   Far 'neath my silver feet she lies.

" Look down, look down, and thou shalt see
   A fairer moon and mellower stars;
A shadow pale and wan is she
   That floats o'er heaven's azure bars.

" Look down, look down—the true moon lies
   Deep in mid-ocean's fairest part;
Nor let that wan shade on the skies
   Draw all the tides of thy young heart.

" O let mine arms thy neck entwine!
   O boy, come down to me, to me!
I'll bring thee where the moon doth shine,
   The round moon in the silver sea."

He heard the song, he felt the spell,
   He saw her white hand beckon on,
Believed the tale she sang so well,
   Beheld the moon that falsely shone.

The true moon wheeled her silver isle
   Serene in heaven's blue mystery;
He sank in those white arms of guile
   To seek the false moon in the sea.

LOVE AND REASON.

ONCE Reason, calm, majestic maid,—
Thro' bosky gloom of garden strayed—
A garden planned in every part
To please the mind yet scarce the heart.
'Tis true the level walks, the bowers,
Were gemmed with all the fairest flowers
That royal Nature's bounteous hand
Had flung upon that radiant land,
Where Summer kisses Summer's lips,
And all the year the brown bee sips
His nectar from the chain of flowers
That stretches o'er those sunny hours,
And finds no missing link of bloom
To cloud his busy life with gloom.

'Tis true the fountains sprang their height,
And frolicked in the upper light;
The peacock strutted on the lawn,
And gambolled there the graceful fawn;
And thro' the laurel, bay and myrtle
There glanced the sheen of many a kirtle
Of nymphs who'd chosen this retreat
To come and sit at Reason's feet,
To pensive con her starry page
And fly the follies of the age.

'Tis true such beauties all were there,
And yet lacked much of being fair:
The blossoms bloomed in formal pride,
The fountains played in measured tide;
That which alone the soul can warm,
Sweet Nature's wild, enchanting charm,

LOVE AND REASON

From that fair spot had fled and vanished,
By cold-eyed Reason sternly banished;
And in that cold and formal school
No flower dare bloom except by rule.
Love, too, 'twas firmly there decreed,
Fair Nature's loveliest child, should bleed
If found amidst those bowers astray,
Sacred to Reason's lofty sway.

But to my tale.   While Reason strayed
All pensive thro' the formal glade,
She saw, couched lightly on a rose,
Arch Cupid in profound repose;
For o'er her walls of marble white
In some mad hour he'd winged his flight.
With horrent brow and dark'ning frown
Reason on Love stood looking down;
She raised her hand to crush the fay,
When loud a rolling voice cried, " Stay!"

Imperial thunders in the tone;
And looking up, upon a throne
Upborne by eagles, eyed with flame,
Great Jove to Reason's vision came:
" Thy hand restrain, great nymph divine;
As thou henceforth to men would shine
In all thy beauties known and blest,
Take Love and bear him in thy breast;
With thy sage counsel him restrain,
And so let Love with Reason reign!"
With mellowed thunders rolled the clouds,
Great Jove withdrew behind their shrouds.
The mandate Reason quick obeyed,
And joyous Love securely played,
And brightened that once formal spot
Where Reason dwelt but Love was not.

ISABELLA VALANCY CRAWFORD

LOVE AMONGST THE ROSES.

When swing the morning-glory bells,
  By marble pillar wreathing;
When o'er the perfumed violet dells
  The morning zephyr's breathing,
That time I wander down a way
  That myrtle sweet encloses,
And all about I pry and peep
  For Love amongst the Roses.

A rosy brake I see ahead,
  In golden vapour flushing;
My steps are winged, and on I speed,
  The fragrant fortress crushing.
The dewy petals flutter fast—
  The gap to me discloses,
Asleep upon the damask blooms,
  Sweet Love amongst the Roses.

I stand entranced.   O beauteous sight!
  He looks so sweet and simple—
The infant curls of golden hair,
  The crimson cheek and dimple.
His golden quiver empty lies;
  His chubby hand encloses
A crimson heart, and thus I find
  Arch Love amongst the Roses.

ROSES IN MADRID.

ROSES, Senors, roses!
　Love is subtly hid
In the fragrant roses,
　Blown in gay Madrid.
Roses, Senors, roses!
　Look, look, look, and see
Love hanging in the roses
　Like a golden bee!
Ha! ha! shake the roses—
　Hold a palm below;
Shake him from the roses,
　Catch the vagrant—so!

High I toss the roses
　From my brown palm up,
Like the wine that bubbles
　From a golden cup.
Catch the roses, Senors,
　Light on finger-tips;
He who buys red roses
　Dreams of crimson lips.
Tinkle my fresh roses,
　With the rare dews wet;
Clink my crisp, red roses
　Like a castanet.

Roses, Senors, roses!
　Come, Hidalgo, buy!
Proudly wait my roses
　For thy Rose's eye.
93

Be thy Rose as stately
    As a pacing deer,
Worthy are my roses
    To burn behind her ear.
Ha! ha! I can see thee,
    Where the fountains foam,
Twining my red roses
    In her golden comb!

Roses, Donnas, roses!
    None so fresh as mine,
Plucked at rose of morning
    By our Lady's shrine.
Those that first I gathered
    Laid I at her feet,
That is why my roses
    Still are fresh and sweet.
Roses, Donnas, roses,
    Roses waxen fair!
Acolytes my roses,
    'Censing ladies' prayer!

Roses, roses, roses!
    Hear the tawny bull
Thund'ring in the circus—
    Buy your arms full.
Roses by the dozen!
    Roses by the score!
Pelt the victor with them—
    Bull or toreador!

MARY'S TRYST.

Young Mary stole along the vale
    To keep her tryst with Ulnor's lord.
A warrior clad in coat of mail
    Stood darkling by the brawling ford.

" O let me pass, O let me pass,
    Dark falls the night on hill and lea;
Flies, flies the bright day swift and fast
    From lordly bower and greenwood tree!

" The small birds twitter as they fly
    To dewy bough and leaf-hid nest;
Dark fold the black clouds on the sky,
    And maiden terrors throng my breast!"

" And thou shalt pass, thou bonnie maid,
    If thou wilt only tell to me
Why hiest thou forth in lonesome shade,
    And where thy wished-for bourne may be?"

" O let me by, O let me by,
    My grandam dwells by Ulnor's shore;
She strains for me her failing eye
    Beside her lowly ivied door!"

" I rode by Ulnor's shore at dawn,
    I saw no ancient dame and cot;
I saw but startled doe and fawn—
    Thy bourne thou yet hast told me not."

95

" O let me pass—my father lies
    Long-stretched in coffin and in shroud,
Where Ulnor's turrets climb the skies,
    Where Ulnor's battlements are proud!"

" I rode by Ulnor's walls at noon,
    I heard not bell for passing sprite,
And saw no henchman straiked for tomb—
    Thou hast not told thy bourne aright."

" O let me pass—a monk doth dwell
    In lowly hut by Ulnor's shrine;
I seek the holy friar's cell
    That he may shrive this soul of mine!"

" I rode by Ulnor's shrine this day,
    I saw no hut, no friar's cowl;
I heard no holy hermit pray—
    I heard but hooting of the owl."

" O let me pass—time flies apace—
    And since thou wilt not let me be,
I tryst with chief of Ulnor's race
    Beneath the spreading hawthorn tree!"

" I rode beside the bonnie thorn
    When this day's sun was sinking low;
I saw a damsel like the morn,
    I saw a knight with hound and bow.

" The chief was chief of Ulnor's name,
    The maid was of a high degree;
I saw him kiss the lovely dame,
    I saw him bend the suitor's knee.

96

THE CITY TREE

" I saw the fond glance of his eye
  To her red cheek red roses bring;
Between them, as my steed flew by,
  I saw them break a golden ring."

" O wouldst thou know, thou curious knight,
  Where Mary's bourne to-night shall be,
Since thou hast seen such traitor sight
  Beneath the blooming hawthorn tree?"

Fair shone the yellow of her locks,
  Her cheek and bosom's drifted snow;
She leaped adown the sharp, grey rocks,
  She sought the sullen pool below.

The knight his iron vizard raised,
  He caught young Mary to his heart;
She lifted up her head and gazed,
  She drew her yellow locks apart.

The roses touched her lovely face,
  The lilies white did faint and flee;
The knight was chief of Ulnor's race,
  His only true love still was she.

THE CITY TREE.

I STAND within the stony, arid town,
  I gaze forever on the narrow street,
I hear forever passing up and down
  The ceaseless tramp of feet.

I know no brotherhood with far-locked woods,
    Where branches bourgeon from a kindred sap,
Where o'er mossed roots, in cool, green solitudes,
    Small silver brooklets lap.

No emerald vines creep wistfully to me
    And lay their tender fingers on my bark;
High may I toss my boughs, yet never see
    Dawn's first most glorious spark.

When to and fro my branches wave and sway,
    Answ'ring the feeble wind that faintly calls,
They kiss no kindred boughs, but touch alway
    The stones of climbing walls.

My heart is never pierced with song of bird;
    My leaves know nothing of that glad unrest
Which makes a flutter in the still woods heard
    When wild birds build a nest.

There never glance the eyes of violets up,
    Blue, into the deep splendour of my green;
Nor falls the sunlight to the primrose cup
    My quivering leaves between.

Not mine, not mine to turn from soft delight
    Of woodbine breathings, honey sweet and warm;
With kin embattled rear my glorious height
    To greet the coming storm!

Not mine to watch across the free, broad plains
    The whirl of stormy cohorts sweeping fast,
The level silver lances of great rains
    Blown onward by the blast!

THE CITY TREE

Not mine the clamouring tempest to defy,
  Tossing the proud crest of my dusky leaves—
Defender of small flowers that trembling lie
  Against my barky greaves!

Not mine to watch the wild swan drift above,
  Balanced on wings that could not choose between
The wooing sky, blue as the eye of love,
  And my own tender green!

And yet my branches spread, a kingly sight,
  In the close prison of the drooping air:
When sun-vexed noons are at their fiery height
  My shade is broad, and there

Come city toilers, who their hour of ease
  Weave out to precious seconds as they lie
Pillowed on horny hands, to hear the breeze
  Through my great branches die.

I see no flowers, but as the children race
  With noise and clamour through the dusty street,
I see the bud of many an angel face,
  I hear their merry feet.

No violets look up, but, shy and grave,
  The children pause and lift their crystal eyes
To where my emerald branches call and wave
  As to the mystic skies.

LATE LOVED—WELL LOVED.

HE stood beside her in the dawn—
　And she his Dawn and she his Spring.
From her bright palm she fed her fawn,
　Her swift eyes chased the swallow's wing;
Her restless lips, smile-haunted, cast
　Shrill silver calls to hound and dove;
Her young locks wove them with the blast.
　To the flushed azure shrine above
The light boughs o'er her golden head
　Tossed emerald arm and blossom palm;
The perfume of their prayer was spread
　On the sweet wind in breath of balm.

" Dawn of my heart," he said, " O child,
　Knit thy pure eyes a space with mine:
O crystal child eyes, undefiled,
　Let fair love leap from mine to thine!"
" The Dawn is young," she, smiling, said,
　" Too young for Love's dear joy and woe;
Too young to crown her careless head
　With his ripe roses. Let me go
Unquestioned for a longer space;
　Perchance when day is at the flood
In thy true palm I'll gladly place
　Love's flower in its rounding bud.
But now the day is all too young,
　The Dawn and I are playmates still."
She slipped the blossomed boughs among,
　He strode beyond the violet hill.

Again they stand—Imperial Noon
　Lays her red sceptre on the earth—

LATE LOVED—WELL LOVED

Where golden hangings make a gloom,
  And far-off lutes sing dreamy mirth.
The peacocks cry to lily cloud
  From the white gloss of balustrade;
Tall urns of gold the gloom make proud;
  Tall statues whitely strike the shade
And pulse in the dim quivering light
  Until, most Galatea-wise,
Each looks from base of malachite
  With mystic life in limbs and eyes.

Her robe—a golden wave that rose,
  And burst, and clung as water clings
To her long curves—about her flows.
  Each jewel on her white breast sings
Its silent song of sun and fire.
  No wheeling swallows smite the skies
And upward draw the faint desire,
  Weaving its mystery in her eyes.
In the white kisses of the lips
  Of her long fingers lies a rose:
Snow-pale beside her curving lips,
  Red by her snowy breast it glows.

"Noon of my soul," said he, "behold
  The day is ripe, the rose full blown!
Love stands in panoply of gold,
  To Jovian height and strength now grown;
No infant he—a king he stands,
  And pleads with thee for love again!"
"Ah, yes!" she said, "in all known lands
  He kings it—lord of subtlest pain!
The moon is full, the rose is fair—
  Too fair! 'tis neither white nor red!

I know the rose that love should wear
   Must redden as the heart hath bled!
The moon is mellow bright, and I
   Am happy in its perfect glow.
The slanting sun the rose may dye,
   But for the sweet noon—let me go."

She parted—shimmering thro' the shade,
   Bent the fair splendour of her head.
" Would the rich noon were past," he said;
   " Would the pale rose were flushed to red!"

Again. The noon is past and Night
   Binds on his brow the blood-red Mars;
Down dusky vineyards dies the fight,
   And blazing hamlets slay the stars.
Shriek the shrill shells; the heated throats
   Of thundrous cannon burst; and high
Scales the fierce joy of bugle notes
   The flame-dimmed splendours of the sky.
He, dying, lies beside his blade,
   Clear smiling as a warrior blest
With victory smiles; thro' sinister shade
   Gleams the White Cross upon her breast.

" Soul of my soul, or is it night,
   Or is it dawn, or is it day?
I see no more nor dark nor light,
   I hear no more the distant fray."
" 'Tis Dawn," she whispers, " Dawn at last,
   Bright flushed with love's immortal glow.
For me as thee all earth is past!
   Late loved—well loved—now let us go!"

JOY'S CITY.

Joy's city hath high battlements of gold;
  Joy's city hath her streets of gem-wrought flowers;
She hath her palaces high reared and bold,
  And tender shades of perfumed lily bowers;
But ever day by day, and ever night by night,
An Angel measures still our City of Delight.

He hath a rule of gold, and never stays,
  But ceaseless round the burnished ramparts glides;
He measures minutes of her joyous days,
  Her walls, her trees, the music of her tides,
The roundness of her buds. Joy's own fair city lies
Known to its heart-core by his stern and thoughtful eyes.

Above the sounds of timbrel and of song,
  Of greeting friends, of lovers 'mid the flowers,
The Angel's voice arises clear and strong:
  " O City, by so many leagues thy bowers
Stretch o'er the plains, and in the fair, high lifted blue
So many cubits rise thy towers beyond the view."

Why dost thou, Angel, measure Joy's fair walls,
  Unceasing gliding by their burnished stones?
Go, rather measure Sorrow's gloomy halls,
  Her cypress bowers, her charnel-house of bones,
Her groans, her tears, the rue in her jet chalices;
But leave unmeasured more Joy's fairy palaces.

The Angel spake: " Joy hath her limits set,
  But Sorrow hath no bounds; Joy is a guest
Perchance may enter, but no heart pulsed yet
  Where Sorrow did not lay her down to rest;
She hath no city by so many leagues confined;
I cannot measure bounds where there are none to find."

103

BOUCHE-MIGNONNE.

Bouche-Mignonne lived in the mill,
    Past the vineyards shady,
Where the sun shone on a rill
    Jewelled like a lady.

Proud the stream with lily-bud,
    Gay with glancing swallow;
Swift its trillion-footed flood
    Winding ways to follow;

Coy and still when flying wheel
    Rested from its labour;
Singing when it ground the meal,
    Gay as lute or tabor.

" Bouche-Mignonne," it called, when red
    In the dawn were glowing
Eaves and mill-wheel, " leave thy bed;
    Hark to me a-flowing !"

Bouche-Mignonne awoke, and quick
    Glossy tresses braided.
Curious sunbeams clustered thick;
    Vines her casement shaded

Deep with leaves and blossoms white
    Of the morning-glory,
Shaking all their banners bright
    From the mill-eaves hoary.

BOUCHE-MIGNONNE

Swallows turned their glossy throats,
   Timorous, uncertain,
When, to hear their matin notes,
   Peeped she thro' her curtain.

Shook the mill-stream sweet and clear
   With its silvery laughter;
Shook the mill, from flooring sere
   Up to oaken rafter.

" Bouche-Mignonne!" it cried, " come down;
   Other flowers are stirring:
Pierre, with fingers strong and brown,
   Sets the wheel a-birring."

Bouche-Mignonne her distaff plies
   Where the willows shiver;
Round the mossy mill-wheel flies;
   Dragon-flies, a-quiver,

Flash athwart the lily-beds,
   Pierce the dry reeds' thicket;
Where the yellow sunlight treads,
   Chants the friendly cricket.

Butterflies about her skim—
   Pouf! their simple fancies
In the willow shadows dim
   Take her eyes for pansies.

Buzzing comes a velvet bee;
   Sagely it supposes
Those red lips beneath the tree
   Are two crimson roses.

Laughs the mill-stream wise and bright—
   It is not so simple;
Knew it, since she first saw light,
   Every blush and dimple.

" Bouche-Mignonne !" it laughing cries,
   " Pierre as bee is silly;
Thinks two morning stars thine eyes,
   And thy neck a lily."

Bouche-Mignonne, when shadows crept
   From the vine-dark hollows,
When the mossy mill-wheel slept,
   Curved the airy swallows,

When the lilies closed white lids
   Over golden fancies,
Homeward drove her goats and kids.
   Bright the gay moon dances

With her light and silver feet,
   On the mill-stream flowing;
Come a thousand perfumes sweet,
   Dewy buds are blowing;

Comes an owl and greyly flits,
   Jewel-eyed and hooting,
Past the green tree where she sits;
   Nightingales are fluting;

Soft the wind as rustling silk
   On a courtly lady;
Tinkles down the flowing milk;
   Huge and still and shady

Stands the mill-wheel, resting still
  From its loving labour.
Dances on the tireless rill,
  Gay as lute or tabor;

" Bouche-Mignonne!" it laughing cries,
  " Do not blush and tremble;
If the night has ears and eyes,
  I'll for thee dissemble;

" Loud and clear and sweet I'll sing
  On my far way straying;
I will hide the whispered thing
  Pierre to thee is saying.

" Bouche-Mignonne, good night, good night!
  Every silver hour
I will toss my lilies white
  'Gainst thy maiden bower."

FAITH, HOPE AND CHARITY.

A STAR leaned down and laid a silver hand
      On the pale brow of Death;
Before it rolled bleak shadows from the land—
      The star was Faith!

Across wild storms that hid the mountains far
      In funeral cope,
Piercing the black, there sailed a throbbing star—
      The red star, Hope!

From God's vast palm a large sun grandly rolled
      O'er land and sea;
Its core pure fire, its stretching hands of gold—
      Great Charity!

THE POET OF THE SPRING.

COME, thou dainty, joyous Spring,
Spread, O spread thy swallow wing,
Wheel and waver, weave thy flight!
Frolic farewell bid this night
To the land which would thee hold
Bound in summer's sultry gold!

Come, thou Ariel of the year,
I would cleave a maple here;
In the cleft, sweet cheater, close
Daintily thy breast of rose:
In its honeyed wood, wild Spring,
Catch and keep thy wayward wing.
Thou shouldst suck like any bee
Sugar from the sappy tree.
Potent, thou, as Prospero;
At thy lute green leaves shall glow,
And the tall trees hide their plinths
Deep in grass and hyacinths.

South, swing wide thy sapphire gate!
Come, Spring-Ariel delicate,
Play thy lute along the strands,
Then shall bend the willow wands.
As men followed Ariel
With his shell invisible,

THE BURGOMEISTER'S WELL

Flowers shall frolic after thee,
Bursting from the barren lea;
Softer stars steal up and down
In thy train by field and town—
Nay, the sun for thee shall dance
Like a courtier of old France.

Come, Spring-Spirit, quit thy quips!
At the laughing of thy lips,
Shakespeare, leaning from his sphere,
Draws thy music to his ear:
Leaves the ambrosial daffodils,
Temples on supernal hills;
Wanders down by sunset bars,
Hears the rush of Avon's strain,
And loves the earth he lit again.

The poet thrills! On Spring's sweet blast
He feels the mighty soul glide past:
Its mantle sweeps him like a wing,
And this is why he needs must sing—
The gentle poet of the Spring!

THE BURGOMEISTER'S WELL.

A PEACEFUL spot, a little street,
    So still between the double roar
Of sea and city that it seemed
    A rest in music, set before
Some clashing chords, vibrating yet
    With hurried measures fast and sweet;
For so the harsh chords of the town,
    And so the ocean's rhythmic beat.

A little street, with linden trees
   So thickly set the belfry's face
Was leaf-veiled, while above them pierced
   Four slender spires' flamboyant grace;
Old porches carven when the trees
   Were seedlings, yellow in the sun
Five hundred years ago that bright
   Upon the quaint old city shone.

A fountain prim, and richly cut
   In ruddy granite, carved to tell
How a good burgomeister reared
   The stone above the people's well.
A sea-horse from his nostrils blew
   Two silver threads; a dragon's lip
Dropped diamonds, and a giant hand
   Held high an urn on finger-tip.

'Twas there I met my little maid,
   There saw her flaxen tresses first;
She filled the cup for one who leaned
   (A soldier, crippled and athirst)
Against the basin's carven rim;
   Her dear small hand's white loveliness
Was pinkly flushed, the gay bright drops
   Plashed on her brow and silken dress.

I took the flagon from her hand,—
   Too small, dear hand, for such a weight;
From cobweb warp and woof is spun
   The tapestry of Life and Fate!
The linden trees had gilded buds,
   The dove wheeled high on joyous wing,

SAID THE THISTLE-DOWN

When on that slender hand of hers
    I slipped the glimmer of a ring.
Ah, golden heart and golden locks,
    Ye wove so sweet, so sure a spell,
That quiet day I saw her first
    Beside the Burgomeister's Well!

SAID THE THISTLE-DOWN.

" IF thou wilt hold my silver hair,
    O lady sweet and bright,
I'll bring thee, maiden darling, where
    Thy lover is to-night!
Lay down thy robe of cloth of gold—
    Gold weigheth heavily—
Thy necklace wind in jewelled fold,
    And hie thee forth with me."

" O Thistle-down, dear Thistle-down!
    I've laid my robe aside,
My necklace and my jewelled crown,
    And yet I cannot glide
Along the silver crests of night
    With thee, light thing, with thee!
Fain would I try the airy flight,
    What sayest thou to me?"

" If thou wilt hold my silver hair,
    O maiden fair and proud,
We'll float upon the purple air
    High as yon lilied cloud!
There is a jewel weighs thy heart;
    If thou with me wouldst glide
111

That cold, cold jewel place apart—
   The jewel of thy pride."

" O Thistle-down, dear Thistle-down!
   That jewel apart I've set
With golden robe and shining crown,
   And cannot follow yet.
Fain would I clasp thy silver tress
   And float on high with thee,
Yet somewhat me to earth doth press—
   What sayest thou to me?"

" If thou wilt hold my silver hair,
   O lady sweet and chaste,
We'll dance upon the sparkling air
   And to thy lover haste!
A lily lies upon thy breast,
   Snow-white as it can be;
It holds thee strong—Sweet, with the rest
   Yield lilied chastity!"

" O Thistle-down, false Thistle-down!
   I've parted Pride and Gold,
Laid past my jewels and my crown,
   My golden robings' fold.
I will not lay my lily past—
   Love's light as vanity
When to the mocking wind is cast
   The lily, Chastity."

"LOVE ME, LOVE MY DOG."

He had a falcon on his wrist,
  A hound beside his knee,
A jewelled rapier at his thigh;
  Quoth he: "Which may she be?
My chieftain cried: 'Bear forth, my page,
  This ring to Lady Clare;
Thou'lt know her by her sunny eyes
  And golden lengths of hair.'
But here are lovely damsels three,
  In glittering coif and veil,
And all have sunny locks and eyes,—
  To which unfold the tale?"

Out spake the first: "O pretty page,
  Thou hast a wealthy lord;
I love to see the jewels rare
  Which deck thy slender sword!"
She smiled, she waved her yellow locks,
  Rich damask glowed her cheek;
He bent his supple knee and thought:
  "Not this the maid I seek."

The second had a cheek of rose,
  A throat as white as milk,
A jewelled tire upon her brow,
  A robe and veil of silk.
"O pretty page, hold back the hound;
  Uncouth is he and bold;
His rough caress will tear my veil,
  My fringe of glittering gold!"
She frowned, she pouted ruby lips—
  The page he did not speak;

8   **113**

He bent his curly head and thought:
  " Not this the maid I seek."

The third, with cobweb locks of light
  And cheeks like summer dawn,
Dropped on her knee beside the hound
  Upon the shaven lawn.
She kissed his sinewy throat, she stroked
  His bristly rings of hair;
" Ho!" thought the page, " she loves his hound,
  So this is Lady Clare!"

THE SHELL.

O LITTLE whispering, murmuring shell, say, canst thou
    tell to me
Good news of any stately ship that sails upon the sea?
I press my ear, O little shell, against thy rosy lips!
Canst tell me tales of those who go down to the sea in
    ships?

What, not a word? Ah, hearken, shell! I've shut the
    cottage door;
There's scarce a sound to drown thy voice, so silent is
    the moor;
A bell may tinkle far away upon its purple rise,
A bee may buzz among the heath, a lavrock cleave the
    skies,

But, if you only breathe the name I name upon my
    knees,
Ah, surely I shall catch the word above such sounds as
    these!

114

THE SHELL

And Grannie's needles click no more, the ball of yarn is
    done,
And she's asleep outside the door where shines the merry
    sun.

One night while Grannie slept I dreamed he came across
    the moor
And stood, so handsome, brown and tall, beside the open
    door;
I thought I turned to pick a rose that by the sill had
    blown,
(He liked a rose) and when I looked, O shell, I was
    alone!

Across the moor there dwells a wife; she spaed my for-
    tune true,
And said I'd plight my troth with one who wore a jacket
    blue.
That morn before my Grannie woke, just when the lap-
    wing stirred,
I sped across the misty rise and sought the old wife's
    word.

With her it was the milking time, and while she milked
    the goat
I asked her then to spae my dream—my heart was in my
    throat,
But that was just because the way had been so steep and
    long,
And not because I had the fear that anything was wrong.

"Ye'll meet, ye'll meet," was all she said, "ye'll meet
    when it is mirk."
I gave her tippance that I meant for Sabbath-day and
    kirk,

And then I hastened back again; it seemed that never
  sure
The happy sun delayed so long to gild the purple moor.

That's six months back, and every night I sit beside the
  door,
And while I knit I keep my gaze upon the mirky moor;
I keep old Collie by my side—he's sure to spring and
  bark
When Ronald comes across the moor to meet me in the
  dark.

I *know* the old wife spaed me true, for did she not fore-
  tell
I'd break a ring with Ronald Grey beside the Hidden
  Well?
It came to pass at shearing-time, before he went to sea,—
(We're neighbours' bairns) how *could* she know that
  Ronald cared for me?

So night by night I watch for him,—by day I sing and
  work
And try to never mind the latch—he's coming in the
  dark!
Yet as the days and weeks and months go slipping
  slowly thro',
I wonder if the wise old wife has spaed my fortune true.

Ah, not a word about his ship? Well, well, I'll lay thee
  by.
I see a heron from the marsh go sailing in the sky;
The purple moor is like a dream, a star is twinkling
  clear—
Perhaps the meeting that she spaed is drawing very
  near!

116

LOVE IN A DAIRY.

Of all the spots for making love,
  Give me a shady dairy,
With crimson tiles, and blushing smiles
  From its presiding fairy;
The jolly sunbeams peeping in
  Thro' vine leaves all a-flutter,
Like greetings sent from Phœbus to
  The Goddess of Fresh Butter.

The swallows twittering in the eaves,
  The air of Summer blowing
Thro' open door from where a score
  Of tall rose-trees are growing,
A distant file of hollyhocks,
  A rugged bush of tansy,
And nearer yet beside the steps
  A gorgeous purple pansy;

Suggestive scents of new-mown hay,
  From lowland meadows coming;
The distant ripple of a stream,
  And drowsy sounds of humming
From able-bodied bees that bevy
  About the morning-glory,
Or dawdle pleasantly around
  The apple-blossoms hoary.

A rosy bloom pervades the spot;
  And where the shadows darkle,
In glittering rows the shining pans
  Show many a brilliant sparkle.

117

As snowy as my lady's throat,
  Or classic marble urn,
In central floor there proudly stands
  The scourèd white-wood churn.

And she who reigns o'er churn and pan—
  In truth, my friend, between us,
My dimpled Chloe is more fair
  Than Milo's famous Venus.
Mark, mark those eyes so arch and dark,
  Those lips like crimson clover,
And ask yourself, as well you may,
  How I could prove a rover.

Talk not to me of moonlit groves,
  Of empress, belle, or fairy;
To me the fairest love of loves
  Is Chloe of the Dairy.

THE CHRISTMAS BABY.

How did the new baby get into the house?
There isn't a cranny for cricket or mouse
To squeeze thro', I'm certain; yet when my eyes
Got open this morning, O what a surprise!
There lay the new baby in long, snowy clothes;
And oh, such a lot of dear little pink toes.
I count them all over every time when
Nurse says I may—he has deal more than ten!
I'll give him my top and my pretty new sleigh,—
And Aunt, do you think I've a long time to wait
Before the new baby can learn how to skate?
Will a week be enough? Auntie, I say,

THE CHRISTMAS BABY

Do you think he'll be able against New Year's Day?
How did he get there? Do you think he will stay?
I wish he would keep his eyes wider, because
He could see the things brought me by good Santa Claus.

Santa Claus rose when the stars were clear,
And brought from their stalls his two reindeer;
And round the edge of his quaint old sledge
All manner of toys that were quaint and queer,
And delicate, dainty, marvellous things,
He nailed with tacks and he tied with strings.
He tied the dolls' hoods under their chins,
And fastened their cloaks with buttons and pins:
"Keep warm, my dears, if you can, because
We've a long way to go over ice and snow,"
Said, cheerily laughing, old Santa Claus.

The wax doll nodded her dainty head;
The wooden one laughed till her cheeks were red;
The little drums rattled, tin trumpets blew,
As the reindeer off thro' the starlight flew;
And the beasts in the ark set up such a roar
As never was heard in the world before;
The grey felt donkey sent out such a bray
That it lasted, I've heard, all Christmas day;
The flannel elephant waved his paws,
And the wooden soldiers, snugly hid
In the long white box, poked up the lid
And shouted, "Hooray for Christmas day,
And a sleigh-ride with jolly old Santa Claus!"

Do you think that Santa Claus meant to go
With his reindeer over the crisp, white snow?
Not he, indeed; for greater speed
He drew up his sledge on the whistling edge

Of a merry young wind that was taking a stroll
From his home on the top of the far North Pole,
Close to the lair of the great white bear,
Who wears white stockings over his toes,
And a greatcoat up to his pointed nose.

O 'twas a merry and wonderful sight,
The drive that Santa Claus took that night!
How the maples swayed, and the pine trees bent
And shouted and rocked as the gay wind went
Over their tall tops, away, away,
With Santa Claus, reindeer, and wonderful sleigh.
And the stars stretched out their hands of light,
And touched each other that wonderful night,
And whispered, "Brothers and sisters, shine
Ten times brighter this Christmas time,
Nor suffer a cloud on our brows to pause,
To darken the path of good Santa Claus."

Speed on, speed on!   Hullo! Hullo!
There never was such a mad wind to blow.
While Santa Claus slipped down chimneys wide,
Wind, sledge and reindeer waited outside;
And the wind laughed out with so loud a shout,
That up from the pillows of warm, small beds
Half rose many thousands of bright curly heads.
Round eyes went a-winking, half awake, half asleep,
And some of the bolder from blankets would creep;
And against every rule, all orders and laws,
('Twas really shocking!) would peep in the stocking
Hung up by the chimney for good Santa Claus.

Speed on, speed on, over forest and street!
The bold wind was nimble, the reindeer were fleet;
The sledge was near empty and daylight was nigh,

THE CHRISTMAS BABY

When a-sailing, a-sailing across the pink sky,
Dropping down thro' the bars of the vanishing stars,
A white stork came wearily flying the way
Old Santa Claus journeyed with reindeer and sleigh.
Said the jolly old Santa Claus: "Dear Mistress Stork,
What brings you abroad must be wonderful work;
And hullo! let me see—of all marvellous things,
What's that snuggled close in the down of your wings?
And what is that cuddled, dear Stork, on your breast,
Close, close as a birdling deep hid in its nest—
A doll, or a blossom-bud? Dear neighbor Stork, pause,
And show me your treasures!" cried good Santa Claus.

Said the Stork, "Dear friend, I just have come
    From that land close to Heaven,
Where babies are brought by angels down
    And to the wise Storks given,
That on their wings so warm and white
They may carry them down thro' the stars so bright,
And lay them in the cradles set,
    By many a glowing hearth,
In palace tall or cottage small,
    Upon the merry earth.
And I am tired, and well I may be,
For the dear, good angels gave to me
Three little baby buds—Santa Claus, see!"

She ruffled her feathers, warm and deep,
    To let the good saint see
    How cosily and rosily,
Like stars in snowy clouds asleep,
    There lay the babies three!
Pink smiles upon their dimpled lips,
    Like lily buds their hands;

Their heads still shining from the touch
  Of snowy angel bands.
" The dear, dimpled babies !" said good Santa Claus,
And took one of them up in his fur-mittened hands.
" Let me help you to finish your Christmastide work,
Your wings must be tired, my dear Mistress Stork.
There's yet one wide chimney I have to slip down
Before I can turn my sledge from the town.
I'll carry the dear little baby down, too,
And take some of the trouble, good neighbour, from you ;
And I'll wrap it close in my long beard, because
It's a very cold morning," said good Santa Claus.

The wise Stork said, " Thanks, I've a long way to fly ;
Take care of the baby, dear Santa ; good-bye !"
Away went the Stork, her legs flying like strings,
And the two other babies asleep on her wings.

So it happened, my dear, in this wonderful way,
Santa Claus brought the baby on bright Christmas day.
And when you roused up, in your stocking to peep,
Lo ! there in his crib lay the baby asleep.
And you'll love the old Santa, I'm certain, because
He brought the new baby—the good Santa Claus !

LIFE.

"O death, where is thy sting? O grave, where is thy victory?"
1 Cor. xv. 55.
"There is another invisible, eternal existence, superior to this
visible one, which does not perish when all things perish."—
Bhagavad Gîtâ.
"Go, give to the waters and the plants thy body, which belongs
to them, but there is an immortal portion—transport it to the
world of the Holy."—*Rig Veda.*

SHINING so gloriously,
  What dost thou here?
Only last evensong
  Spread we thy bier,
Lit the tall tapers white,
  Ghastly and drear.

Two stood at side and foot,
  Two at thy head;
Over thee, full and wide,
  Black the pall spread;
Slow tolled the mellow bell,
  For—thou wert dead.

Lilies lay on thy breast,
  I placed them there;
None, priest or kin or earl,
  Guessed my despair
As I wreathed bud and bloom
  In thy dark hair.

Have thy white feet, O Love,
  Spotless which trod
Over the mire and clay
  Of the earth's sod,
No brighter paths to tread
  Nearer to God?

123

Thus cried my soul last night,
   Fearful and loud.
Glanced out the silver moon
   From a swift cloud,
Laid all her light on thee
   Dumb in thy shroud.

Never came smile or frown
   Over thy face;
No whisper answered me
   In that still place;
White shone the tapers tall
   On thy dead grace.

On thy fringed pall I lay,
   Prone by thy bier,
While the night-watches passed
   Fearful and drear.
Oh! could mere icy dust
   Still be so dear?

But when the dawn arose,
   Golden and grey,
Bier, pall and tapers high
   Vanished away;
Nor looked my anguished eyes
   On thy dead clay.

Shining so gloriously,
   I saw thee stand
With our dead children three
   Clasped by the hand;
And round thy brows were set
   Stars in a band.

Cried then my soul of souls:
  " Answer, O clay!
Shall those fond eyes of thine
  Slumber alway?
That brow in noisome dust
  Vanish away?

" Those tender hands of thine,
  Gracious and kind,
Turned into clay and ash,
  Drift on the wind?
Sealed ever thy pure lips,
  And thine eyes blind?

" Shall that sweet heart of thine,
  Noble and true,
Moulder to feed the sap
  Of the weird yew?
Or the small graveside bud
  Wet with death's dew?

" Answer my groaning soul,
  O thou dear clay!
Shall that brave soul of thine
  Tremble away
Into dark nothingness?
  Answer, and say

" Shall all the gracious deeds
  Hands, heart and soul
Nobly have joined to work
  Win thee no dole?
Hast thy fair, beauteous life
  Won its last goal?"

125

Book II.

THE HELOT.

Low the sun beat on the land,
  Red on vine and plain and wood;
With the wine-cup in his hand,
  Vast the Helot herdsman stood.

Quenched the fierce Achean gaze
  Dorian foeman paused before,
Where cold Sparta snatched her bays
  At Achea's stubborn door.

Still with thews of iron bound,
  Vastly the Achean rose
Godward from the brazen ground,
  High before his Spartan foes.

Still the strength his fathers knew
  (Dauntless when the foe they faced)
Vein and muscle bounded through,
  Tense his Helot sinews braced.

Still the constant womb of Earth
  Blindly moulded all her part,
As when to a lordly birth
  Achean freeman left her heart.

Still insensate mother bore
  Goodly sons for Helot graves;
Iron necks that meekly wore
  Sparta's yoke as Sparta's slaves.

Still, O god-mocked mother! she
   Smiled upon her sons of clay,
Nursed them on her breast and knee,
   Shameless in the shameful day;

Knew not old Achea's fires
   Burnt no more in souls or veins,
Godlike hosts of high desires
   Died to clank of Spartan chains.

Low the sun beat on the land,
   Purple slope and olive wood;
With the wine-cup in his hand,
   Vast the Helot herdsman stood.

As long, gnarlèd roots enclasp
   Some red boulder, fierce entwine
His strong fingers in their grasp
   Bowl of bright Caecuban wine.

From far Marsh of Amyclae,
   Sentried by lank poplars tall,
Thro' the red slant of the day
   Shrill pipes did lament and call.

Pierced the swaying air sharp pines
   Thyrsi-like; the gilded ground
Clasped black shadows of brown vines;
   Swallows beat their mystic round.

Day was at her high unrest:
   Fevered with the wine of light,
Loosing all her golden vest,
   Reeled she toward the coming night.

THE HELOT

Fierce and full her pulses beat:
   Bacchic throbs the dry earth shook,
Stirred the hot air wild and sweet,
   Maddened every vine-dark brook.

Had the red grape never burst
   All its heart of fire out
To the red vat all athirst,
   To the treader's song and shout;

Had the red grape died a grape,
   Nor, sleek daughter of the vine,
Found her unknown soul take shape
   In the wild flow of the wine,

Still had reeled the yellow haze,
   Still had pulsed the sun-pierced sod,
Still had throbbed the vine-clad days
   To the pulses of their god.

Fierce the dry lips of the Earth
   Quaffed the subtle Bacchic soul,
Felt its rage and felt its mirth,
   Wreathed as for the banquet bowl.

Sapphire-breasted Bacchic priest
   Stood the Sky above the lands,
Sun and moon, at west and east,
   Brazen cymbals in his hands.

Temples, altars smote no more
   Sharply white as brows of god,
From the long, sleek, yellow shore,
   Olived hill or dusky sod.

131

Gazed the angered gods while he,
  Bacchus, made their temples his;
Flushed their marble silently
  With the red light of his kiss.

Red, the arches of his feet
  Spanned grape-gleaming vales; the Earth
Reeled from grove to marble street,
  Mad with echoes of his mirth.

Nostrils widened to the air,
  As, above the wine-brimmed bowl,
Men and women everywhere
  Breathed the fierce, sweet Bacchic soul.

Flowed the vat and roared the beam,
  Laughed the must; while far and shrill,
Sweet as notes in Pan-born dream,
  Loud pipes sang by vale and hill.

Earth was full of mad unrest,
  While red Bacchus held his state;
And her brown vine-girdled breast
  Shook to his wild joy and hate.

Strife crouched red-eyed in the vine,
  In its tendrils Eros strayed;
Anger rode upon the wine,
  Laughter on the cup-lip played.

Day was at her chief unrest;
  Red the light on plain and wood;
Slavish-eyed and still of breast,
  Vast the Helot herdsman stood.

THE HELOT

Wide his hairy nostrils blew,
  Maddening incense breathing up;
Oak to iron sinews grew
  Round the rich Caecuban cup.

"Drink, dull slave," the Spartan said;
  "Drink, until the Helot clod
Feels within him subtly bred
  Kinship to the drunken god;

"Drink, until the leaden blood
  Stirs and beats about thy brain,
Till the hot Caecuban flood
  Drowns the iron of thy chain;

"Drink, till even madness flies
  At the nimble wine's pursuit,
Till the god within thee lies
  Trampled by the earth-born brute;

"Helot, drink, nor spare the wine;
  Drain the deep, the maddening bowl;
Flesh and sinews, slave, are mine,
  Now I claim thy Helot soul!

"Gods, ye love our Sparta! Ye
  Gave, with vine that leaps and runs
O'er her slopes, these slaves to be
  Mocks and warnings to her sons.

"Thou, my Hermos, turn thine eyes"
  (God-touched still their frank, bold blue)
"On the Helot; mark the rise
  Of the Bacchic riot through

133

" Knotted vein and surging breast;
  Mark the wild, insensate mirth,
Godward boast, the drivelling jest,
  Till he grovel to the earth!

" Drink, dull slave!" the Spartan cried.
  Meek the Helot touched the brim,
Scented all the purple tide,
  Drew the Bacchic soul to him.

Cold the thin-lipped Spartan smiled.
  Couched beneath the weighted vine,
Large-eyed gazed the Spartan child
  On the Helot and the wine.

Rose pale Doric shafts behind,
  Stern and strong; and thro' and thro',
Weaving with the grape-breathed wind,
  Restless swallows called and flew.

Dropped the rose-flushed doves and hung
  On the fountains' murmuring brims.
To the bronzed vine Hermos clung,
  Silver-like his naked limbs.

Flashed and flushed rich coppered leaves;
  Whitened by his ruddy hair,
Pallid as the marble eaves,
  Awed, he met the Helot's stare.

Clanged the brazen goblet down;
  Marble-bred loud echoes stirred.
With fixed fingers, knotted, brown,
  Dumb the Helot grasped his beard;

134

THE HELOT

Heard the far pipes, mad and sweet,
    All the ruddy hazes thrill;
Heard the loud beam crash and beat
    In the red vat on the hill.

Wide his nostrils as a stag's
    Drew the hot wind's fiery bliss;
Red his lips as river flags
    From the strong Caecuban kiss.

On his swarthy temples grew
    Purple veins, like clustered grapes;
Past his rolling pupils blew
    Wine-born, fierce, lascivious shapes.

Cold the haughty Spartan smiled—
    His the power to knit that day
Bacchic fires, insensate, wild,
    To the grand Achean clay;

His the might—hence his the right.
    Who should bid him pause? Nor Fate,
Warning, passed before his sight,
    Dark-robed and articulate;

Nor black omens on his eyes,
    Sinister, god-sent, darkly broke;
Nor from ruddy earth or skies
    Portents to him mutely spoke.

" Lo!" he said, " he maddens now;
    Flames divine do scathe the clod;
Round his reeling Helot brow
    Stings the garland of the god."

" Mark, my Hermos, turn to steel
    The soft tendons of thy soul;
Watch the god beneath the heel
    Of the strong brute swooning roll!

" Shame, my Hermos! Honey-dew
    Breeds not on the Spartan spear;
Steel thy mother-eyes of blue,
    Blush to death that weakling tear.

" Nay, behold! breed Spartan scorn
    Of the red lust of the wine;
Watch the god himself down borne
    By the brutish rush of swine.

" Lo, the magic of the drink!
    At the nimble wine's pursuit,
See the man-halfed satyr sink
    All the human in the brute.

" Lo, the magic of the cup!
    Watch the frothing Helot rave!
As great buildings labour up
    From the corpse of slaughtered slave,

" Build the Spartan virtue high
    From the Helot's wine-dead soul;
Scorn the wild, hot flames that fly
    From the purple-hearted bowl.

" Helot clay! Gods, what its worth,
    Balanced with proud Sparta's rock!
Ours its force to till the earth;
    Ours its soul to gyve and mock.

THE HELOT

" Ours its sullen might. Ye Gods,
    Vastly build the Achean clay,
Iron-breast the slavish clods,—
    Ours their Helot souls to slay.

" Knit great thews; smite sinews vast
    Into steel; build Helot bones
Iron-marrowed: such will last,
    Ground by ruthless Sparta's stones.

" Crown the strong brute satyr-wise,
    Narrow-wall his Helot brain,
Dash the soul from breast and eyes,
    Lash him toward the earth again.

" Gods, recall, your spark at birth
    Lit his soul with high desire;
Blend him, grind him with the earth,
    Tread out old Achea's fire.

" Lo! my Hermos, laugh and mark;
    See the swift mock of the wine;
Faints the primal, god-born spark,
    Trodden by the rush of swine.

" Gods, ye love our Sparta! Ye
    Gave, with vine that leaps and runs
O'er her slopes, these slaves to be
    Mocks and warnings to her sons."

Cold the haughty Spartan smiled;
    Maddening from the purple hills
Sang the far pipes, sweet and wild.
    Red as sun-pierced daffodils,

ISABELLA VALANCY CRAWFORD

Neck-curved serpent, silent, scaled
   With locked rainbows, stole the sea
On the sleek, long beaches; wailed
   Doves from column and from tree.

Reeled the mote-swarmed haze, and thick
   Beat the hot pulse of the air;
In the Helot, fierce and quick,
   All his soul sprang from its lair.

As the drowsing tiger, deep
   In the dim cell, hears the shout
From the arena—from his sleep
   Launches to its thunders out—

So to fierce calls of the wine
   (Strong the red Caecuban bowl!)
From its slumber, deep, supine,
   Panted up the Helot soul,

At his blood-flushed eyeballs reared.
   (Mad and sweet came pipes and songs!)
Roused at last, the wild soul glared,
   Spear-thrust with a million wrongs.

Past—the primal, senseless bliss;
   Past—red laughter of the grapes;
Past—the wine's first honeyed kiss;
   Past—the wine-born, wanton shapes!

Still the Helot stands, his feet
   Set like oak-roots; in his gaze
Black clouds roll and lightnings meet,
   Flames from old Achean days.

THE HELOT

Who may quench the god-born fire
  Pulsing at the soul's deep root?
Tyrant, grind it in the mire,
  Lo, it vivifies the brute!

Stings the chain-embruted clay,
  Senseless to his yoke-bound shame;
Goads him on to rend and slay,
  Knowing not the spurring flame!

Tyrant, changeless stand the gods,
  Nor their calm might yielded thee;
Not beneath thy chains and rods
  Dies man's god-gift, Liberty!

Bruteward lash the Helots, hold
  Brain and soul and clay in gyves,
Coin their blood and sweat in gold,
  Build thy cities on their lives,—

Comes a day the spark divine
  Answers to the gods who gave;
Fierce the hot flames pant and shine
  In the bruised breast of the slave.

Changeless stand the gods!—nor he
  Knows he answers their behest,
Feels the might of their decree
  In the blind rage of his breast.

Tyrant, tremble when ye tread
  Down the servile Helot clods!
Under despot heel is bred
  The white anger of the gods.

Thro' the shackle-cankered dust,
  Thro' the gyved soul, foul and dark,
Force they, changeless gods and just,
  Up the bright, eternal spark,

Till, like lightnings vast and fierce,
  On the land its terror smites;
Till its flames the tyrant pierce,
  Till the dust the despot bites.

Day was at its chief unrest.
  Stone from stone the Helot rose;
Fixed his eyes; his naked breast
  Iron-walled his inner throes.

Rose-white in the dusky leaves
  Shone the frank-eyed Spartan child.
Low the pale doves on the eaves
  Made their soft moan, sweet and wild.

Wandering winds, fire-throated, stole,
  Sybils whispering from their books.
With the rush of wine from bowl
  Leaped the tendril-darkened brooks.

As the leathern cestus binds
  Tense the boxer's knotted hands,
So the strong wine round him winds,
  Binds his thews to iron bands.

Changeless are the gods—and bred
  All their wrath divine in him.
Bull-like fell his furious head,
  Swelled vast cords on breast and limb.

140

THE HELOT

As loud flaming stones are hurled
  From foul craters, thus the gods
Cast their just wrath on the world
  From the mire of Helot clods.

Still the furious Helot stood,
  Staring thro' the shafted space;
Dry-lipped for the Spartan blood,
  He of scourged Achea's race.

Sprang the Helot.   Roared the vine,
  Rent from grey, long-wedded stones,
From pale shaft and dusky pine;
  Beat the fury of his groans,

Thunders inarticulate,
  Wordless curses, deep and wild;
Reached the long-poised sword of Fate
  To the Spartan thro' his child.

On his knotted hands upflung,
  O'er his lowered front, all white,
Fair young Hermos quiv'ring hung.
  As the discus flashes bright

In the player's hand, the boy,
  Naked, blossom-pallid, lay.
Roused to lust of bloody joy,
  Throbbed the slave's embruted clay.

Loud he laughed.   The father sprang
  From the Spartan's iron mail.
Late!—the bubbling death-cry rang
  On the hot pulse of the gale.

ISABELLA VALANCY CRAWFORD

As the shining discus flies,
  From the thrower's strong hand whirled,
Hermos cleft the air, his cries
  Lance-like to the Spartan hurled.

As the discus smites the ground,
  Smote his golden head the stone
Of a tall shaft; burst a sound,
  And but one—his dying groan.

Lo, the tyrant's iron might!
  Lo, the Helot's yokes and chains!
Slave-slain in the throbbing light
  Lay the sole child of his veins.

Laughed the Helot loud and full,
  Gazing at his tyrant's face;
Lowered his front like captive bull,
  Bellowing from the fields of Thrace.

Rose the pale shaft redly flushed,
  Red with Bacchic light and blood;
On its stone the Helot rushed—
  Stone the tyrant Spartan stood.

Lo, the magic of the wine
  From far Marsh of Amyclae!
Biered upon the ruddy vine,
  Spartan dust and Helot clay!

Spouse of Bacchus, reeled the day,
  Red-tracked on the throbbing sods;
Dead—but free—the Helot lay.
  Just and changeless stand the gods!

142

INTO ANOTHER LAND

"HE AROSE AND WENT INTO ANOTHER LAND."

HE grasped an angel's hand and rose
　From the grand ruins of his clay,
And in the white day's silvery close
　Through the great city took his way.

His guide—O strange, familiar face
　And bright'ning smile he seemed to know,
And clinging hand and tender grace!
　O vision from the Long Ago!

From purple dark to purple dark
　The red lights of the city rolled;
Below the moon, a living spark,
　One bright star beat its wings of gold.

The clang of iron bells outburst,
　Shrill shrieks of engines swelled the tide;
Another day, both blest and curst
　With toil, had risen, lived and died.

The wave of labour rose and rolled
　From arch and alley, lane and street;
The harsh clocks thro' the city tolled,
　Roared the swift flood of hast'ning feet.

Swift opal quivered up the west,
　And cast its fires to hast'ning stars;
The clear moon beat her silver breast,
　Dove-like, against low saffron bars.

143

Like swords which smote a chill, pure flame
  From the clear breastplate of the night,
The long, swift north-blades went and came
  And set the mystic Pole alight.

And eve lay as the corpse of one
  Who had not lived till life was old:
Silver the bier she rested on,
  So pure, so beautiful, so cold.

O'er country snows, within the town,
  By circling lake, by dark pine tree,
Chill winds moaned, monk-like, up and down:
  " O Miserere, Domine!"

And loud or low in every soul
  Of all the hurrying throngs they met,
They heard the same chant upward roll,
  To each one's holiest anguish set.

His angel spake: " O hark and hear
  The living wail forever thus,
While we, the dead, sing high and clear
  A bold Te Deum Laudamus!"

He answered not, but on his soul
  A trembling wonder cloud-like lay:
Why seek they not some star-surfed goal?
  Why tread this old familiar way?

Then to his silent thought she said:
  " By this familiar way we go;
High Wisdom sends the happy dead
  To find their first of Heaven below.

144

INTO ANOTHER LAND

"O hearken, Love!" They paused a space
　　Where want made grim the squalid way;
Soft whispers stole about the place:
　　"God bless the man who died to-day,

"Friend of the poor." Her sweet eyes smiled.
　　"By this," she said, "they crown you king;
Of golden blessings undefiled
　　Are wrought the sceptre, crown, and ring."

Again they paused. In long-stretched ward,
　　Tranced from their pain, racked creatures lay;
From parched lips stole the whisper, "Lord,
　　Bless our dead friend who died to-day,

"Friend of the helpless!" Rapt he gazed.
　　What music struck the trembling air!
What glories round him beat and blazed!
　　May Heaven be here or Heaven be there?

He knew not, caring not to know:
　　He only knew—most grandly blest—
That on the wheeling earth below
　　The first of Heaven lay in his breast.

And as he scaled the star-based hill
　　Which toward the upper glories lay,
That sweet sound followed stronger still:
　　"God bless the man who died to-day!"

HIS CLAY.

HE died; he was buried, the last of his race,
And they laid him away in his burial-place.

And he said in his will, " When I have done
With the mask of clay that I have on,

" Bury it simply—I'm done with it,
At best is only a poor misfit.

" It cramped my brains and chained my soul,
And it clogged my feet as I sought my goal.

" When my soul and I were inclined to shout
O'er some noble thought we had chiselled out;

" When we'd polished the marble until it stood
So fair that we truly said: ' 'Tis good!'

" My soul would tremble, my spirit quail,
For it fell to the flesh to uplift the veil.

" It took our thought in its hands of clay,
And lo! how the beauty had passed away.

" When Love came in to abide with me,
I said, ' Welcome, Son of Eternity!'

" I built him an altar strong and white,
Such as might stand in God's own sight;

146

HIS CLAY

" I chanted his glorious litany—
　Pure Love is the Son of Eternity;

" But ever my altar shook alway
　'Neath the brute hands of the tyrant clay.

" Its voice, with its accents harsh and drear,
　Mocked at my soul and wailed in its ear:

" ' Why tend the altar and bend the knee?
　Love lives and dies in the dust with me.'

" So the flesh that I wore chanced ever to be
　Less of my friend than my enemy.

" Is there a moment this death-strong earth
　Thrills, and remembers her time of birth?

" Is there a time when she knows her clay
　As a star in the coil of the astral way?

" Who may tell?　But the soul in its clod
　Knows in swift moments its kinship to God—

" Quick lights in its chambers that flicker alway
　Before the hot breath of the tyrant clay.

" So the flesh that I wore chanced ever to be
　Less of my friend than my enemy.

" So bury it deeply—strong foe, weak friend—
　And bury it cheaply,—and there its end!"

ISABELLA VALANCY CRAWFORD

THE KING'S GARMENTS.

"I know no more powerful incentive to morality, at this stage of
human progress, than a profound conviction that by an inevitable
law our well-doing in this stage of existence decides our well-being
in that which is to come."—*Robert Dale Owen.*

"The divine moral government, which religion teaches us, im-
plies that the consequence of vice shall be misery in some future
state by the righteous judgment of God."—*Bishop Butler's "Analogy
of Religion."*

"SPEAK!" cried the King, "O seer, arise and speak,
　　For I am sick of revelry to-night;
Strange discords seem above the harps to break,
　　The wine itself hath lost its ruby light,
The dancers' feet are lead, the lutes but sigh;
"Arise, O seer, arise and prophesy!"

The ancient seer, with mild, majestic grace,
　　In the swift silence of the banquet halls
Rose white-robed, silver-bearded, in his place,
　　Gazed on the monarch, nobles, guests and thralls,
And clearly came his low and keen reply:
"O King, what wilt thou that I prophesy?

"For I am ready, but—thou give the theme."
　　Rolled round the hall the monarch's careless eyes.
"Well, since thou wilt not else, dream, seer—ay,
　　　　dream
　　What garments wait on kings in Paradise—
If crowns await them, and the purple dye—
Kings, sacred here—now, old man, prophesy!"

The watchful harpers touched the sweetest strings
　　Their tall harps owned; such soothing, dream-like
　　　　notes

148

THE KING'S GARMENTS

As murmur in the cups of deep, dusk springs
  In dreamy woods. The strain seductive floats
In trancing sounds, which, as they melting die
In ear and soul, breathe softly, " Prophesy !"

Loud cried the seer,—such passion thrilled his frame,
  Half sprang the monarch from his rich divan,
And paled his nobles as the bold words came:
  " I know no king to-night—thou art a man;
A man! and thou wert born and thou shalt die;
Of thy soul's garments must I prophesy.

" Doth Tyrian purple wait thy naked soul?
  O crownèd fool, beyond the Stygian gloom
That rolls its bitter billows 'tween thy goal
  In Paradise and thee I see a loom
And One who weaves thereat! I hear Him cry:
' Spare not, spare not, but loudly prophesy!'

" Yet, who shall name the terrors of His brow,
  The awful might of His resistless hand,
His unstained garments, whiter than the snow
  That crowns high mountains in a hilly land?
How shall a man dare raise his voice on high,
And of this flawless Weaver prophesy?

" To speak of that terrific loom who dare?
  Clearer than crystal, without mote or flaw,
It stands eternal in celestial air.
  And He who weaves thereat, His name is Law;
Star-like His fiery shuttles shoot and fly,
Weaving thy robes of which I prophesy.

" Whence come the warp, the woof? Behold, O King!
  From every deed of thine I see arise

Long filaments, dusk as the raven's wing
  That blots the melting azure of the skies;
Thy battles, murders, wine-red blasphemy
Yield warp and woof of which I prophesy.

" With hand that swerves not, just and most divine,
  Law weaves from these the garments of thy soul,
Black, black as hell; and thine, O tyrant, thine
  To wear them while remorseful ages roll,
Happy if in their mournful folds thou spy
One thread of gold! Thus, King, I prophesy.

" For Law immutable hath one decree,
  ' No deed of good, no deed of ill can die;
All must ascend unto my loom and be
  Woven for man in lasting tapestry,
Each soul his own.' Now, tyrant, dare to die
And claim thy robes of which I prophesy!"

SEPTEMBER IN TORONTO.

FROM shorn fields the victor comes,
  Rolls his triumph thro' the streets;
On his chariot's glowing sides
  Sound of shout and laughter beats.

Groan the burnished wheels that bear
  All the riches of the spoil:
Bearded sheaves and ruddy grapes,
  Treasure of the conquered soil.

Low the mighty kine, and rush
  Fleece to fleece the hurtling flocks;

SEPTEMBER IN TORONTO

Thunder the deep-breasted bulls
   To the shouting equinox.

High is borne the teeming hive,
   Wreathed with brown leaves of the vine;
Burn clear vases to sealed lips,
   Seething with the fierce new wine.

Ivory-sleek and shod with gold,
   Pulsing nostrils veiled in smoke,
Haught his chariot horses tread—
   Such before a god might yoke.

From the broad rock of his breast
   Hangs no sun of burnished shield;
Flows the gold-wrought toga—gold
   Red as glare of harvest-field.

In his chariot's quivering wake
   Close the months of summer ride—
Flowery shields and sun-tipped spears,
   Crocus-locked and sapphire-eyed.

Keenly white as moons of May
   Wheeling through deep-tinted stars,
Bright, majestical and tall,
   Roll the Vestals' shining cars,

Art and Science; trumpets call,
   Answer shrill the sharp-tongued flutes,
Swing great censers subtly filled
   With the scent of mellowed fruits.

Lo! the glare of wolf-red eyes—
   Hark! the groans of fetters vast—

" Io Triumphe !" scales the skies—
  Captive Famine cringes past.

Fierce with joy the wild trumps blare,
    Clash smooth cymbals loud and red,
Shakes the earth, as shield by shield
    The triumphant legions tread.

Rolls the pomp of victory on,
    Quake the stones and pulse the sods,
Roar tall trees in hymnic shouts
    To the strong son of the gods.

Sweeps his triumph by broad ways:
    Red September seeks the gates,
Bursting by the clam'rous tide
    Where his House of Victory waits.

THE LEGEND OF THE MISTLETOE.

WHILE Albion's woods, close-knotted, darkly spread
    About the Isle and fringed her virgin breast;
    While from the mystic arches of the West
The prophet Sea upreared his awful head,

And gazed upon her groves; with hoary hands
    Shook her tall, lonely rocks, and loud did peal
    Long thunders at her shores; nor could unseal
The secret to her ears, nor on her strands

Write with soft touches and with sapphire style
    The hidden things; nor with faint silver pipe
    Breathe it to her deep woods when acorns ripe
Hung brown in soft, still hazes; nor the while

152

THE LEGEND OF THE MISTLETOE

The mistletoe peered from the huge-maned oak—
   The dark, loud lion of all trees—when high
   Spring like a dove sailed low athwart the sky;
Nor while fierce summer thro' the copses broke,

A warrior, with the juice of flowers stained;
   So with weird voices inarticulate,
   And wordless thunders rounded with far fate,
The speechless Ocean mourned and sore complained.

Burthened with knowledge of the Titan, laid
   By the dim arches of the mystic West,
   And mourning still—a prophet most unblest—
Loud were the long laments the old seer made.

And nacreous-breasted, lone Albion stood,
   And felt his urgent hands and with blank eyes
   Gazed on his throes, nor plucked from his great cries
The secret of the one beyond his flood,

Nor hands pre-sensed yet, clasping close and vast
   Across the loud, bright waste, nor heard thro' calms
   Locked whispers from stern pines and supple palms,
Nor saw strange sails against her lone breast cast.

What time fierce Winter, like a wolf all lean,
   With sharp, white fangs bit at weak woodland things,
   Pierced furry breasts, and broke small painted wings,
And from dim homes all interlocked and green

Drove little spirits—those who love glossed leaves
   And glimmer in tall grasses—those who ride
   Glossed bubbles on the woodland's sheltered tide,
And make blue hyacinths their household eaves—

153

Then, moved with ruth of these small houseless sprites,
  The white-robed Druids led the people on
  To where the mistletoe all whitely shone
On the dark sacred oaks—stars in dim nights;

And chanting high, with golden sickles cut
  The kindly bough, and o'er the sharp-tipped snow
  And sere, bleak fields brought back the mistletoe,
And hung the starry branch in hall and hut.

Then to its shelter hurried airy throngs
  Of elves unhoused, and dwelt with kindly men,
  Till burned the heart of spring, and hill and glen
Throbbed to sweet bloom, and brooks and birds to songs.

Thus, from the first, faint Christ-lights lit the earth,
  As mistletoe shone on the dusky oak;
  Sweet Pity, star-like, in dark ages broke
And lent its flame divine to Yuletide mirth.

Ye lordly homes that with the Yuletide glow,
  And small, bright homes that spangle free, broad
      shores,
  Hang the white branch of Yule o'er wide-flung doors,
With Pity's bough—the strong soul's mistletoe.

WAR.

SHAKE, shake the earth with giant tread,
  Thou red-maned Titan bold;
For every step a man lies dead,
  A cottage hearth is cold.
Take up the babes with mailèd hands,
  Transfix them with thy spears,
Spare not the chaste young virgin-bands,
  Tho' blood may be their tears.

WAR

Beat down the corn, tear up the vine,
  The waters turn to blood;
And if the wretch for bread doth whine,
  Give him his kin for food.
Ay, strew the dead to saddle-girth,
  They make so rich a mold,
Thou wilt enrich the wasted earth—
  They'll turn to yellow gold.

On with thy thunders! Shot and shell
  Send screaming, featly hurled—
Science has made them in her cell
  To *civilize* the world.
Not, not alone where Christian men
  Pant in the well-armed strife,
But seek the jungle-throttled glen—
  The savage has a life!

He has a soul—so priests will say—
  Go, save it with thy sword!
Thro' his rank forests force thy way,
  Thy war cry, " For the Lord!"
Rip up his mines, and from his strands
  Wash out the gold with blood—
Religion raises blessing hands,
  " War's evil worketh good!"

When striding o'er the conquered land
  Silence thy rolling drum,
And, led by white-robed choiring band,
  With loud " *Te Deum* " come.
Seek the grim chancel, on its wall
  Thy blood-stiff banner hang;
They lie who say thy blood is gall,
  Thy tooth the serpent's fang.

See, the white Christ is lifted high,
  Thy conquering sword to bless!
Smiles the pure Monarch of the sky—
  Thy king can do no less.
Drink deep with him the festal wine,
  Drink with him drop for drop;
If like the sun his throne doth shine,
  Of it *thou* art the prop.

If spectres wait upon the bowl,
  Thou needst not be afraid;
Grin hell-hounds for thy bold, black soul,
  His purple be thy shade.
Go, feast with Commerce, be her spouse!
  She loves thee, thou art hers;
For thee she decks her board and house,
  Then how may others curse

If she, mild-seeming matron, leans
  Upon thine iron neck,
And leaves with thee her household scenes
  To follow at thy beck?
Bastard in brotherhood of kings,
  Their blood runs in thy veins;
For them the crowns; the sword that swings
  For thee, to hew their chains.

For thee the rending of the prey;
  They, jackals to the lion,
Tread after in the gory way
  Trod by the mightier scion.
O slave, that slayest other slaves,
  O'er vassals crowned a king,
O War, build high thy throne with graves,
  High as the vulture's wing!

THE SWORD.

AT the forging of the Sword
    The mountain roots were stirred
    Like the heart-beats of a bird;
    Like flax the tall trees waved,
So fiercely struck the Forgers of the Sword.

At the forging of the Sword
    So loud the hammers fell,
    The thrice-sealed gates of Hell
    Burst wide their glowing jaws,
Deep roaring, at the forging of the Sword.

At the forging of the Sword
    Kind mother Earth was rent
    Like an Arab's dusky tent,
    And, monster-like, she fed
On her children, at the forging of the Sword.

At the forging of the Sword,
    So loud the blows they gave,
    Up sprang the panting wave,
    And blind and furious slew,
Shrill-shouting to the Forgers of the Sword.

At the forging of the Sword
    The startled air swift whirled
    The red flames round the world,
    From the anvil where was smitten
The steel the Forgers wrought into the Sword.

At the forging of the Sword
    The maid and matron fled

And hid them with the dead;
Fierce prophets sang their doom,
More deadly than the wounding of the Sword.

At the forging of the Sword
Swift leaped the quiet hearts
In the meadows and the marts;
The tides of men were drawn
By the gleaming sickle-planet of the Sword.

Thus wert thou forged, O lissome Sword!
On such dusk anvil wert thou wrought,
In such red flames thy metal fused,
From such deep hells that metal brought.
O Sword, dread lord, thou speakst no word,
But dumbly rulest, king and lord!

Less than the gods by some small span,
Slim Sword, how great thy lieges be!
Glint but in *one* wild camp-fire's light,
Thy god-like vassals rush to thee.
O Sword, dread lord, thou speakst no word,
But dumbly rulest, king and lord!

Sharp god, how vast thy altars be!
Green valleys, sacrificial cups,
Flow with the purple lees of blood;
Its smoke is round the mountain tops.
O Sword, dread lord, thou speakst no word,
But dumbly rulest, king and lord!

O amorous god, fierce lover thou!
Bright sultan of a million brides,

PEACE

Thou knowst no rival to *thy* kiss,
  Thy loves are *thine* whate'er betides.
O Sword, dread lord, thou speakst no word,
But dumbly rulest, king and lord!

Unflesh thee, Sword! No more, no more,
  Thy steel no more shall sting and shine!
Pass thro' the fusing fires again,
  And learn to prune the laughing vine.
Fall Sword, dread lord—with one accord
The plough and hook we'll own as lord!

PEACE.

PEACE stands within the city wall;
Most like a god she towers tall,
And bugle-like she cries to all.

In place of sounds of nether hell,
In place of serpent hiss of shell,
Sounds sweet her powerful " All's well!"

Is she a willow by a stream?
The spirit of a dreamer's dream?
The pale moon's meek and phantom beam?

The mere desire of panting soul?
Water, not wine, within the bowl?
Rides she, a ghost, upon the roll

Of spectral seas? Nay, see her rise,
Strong flesh against the flushing skies,
Large calm within her watchful eyes.

ISABELLA VALANCY CRAWFORD

The olive darkling o'er her face,
Like one of Caryæ's sculptured race,
Her arms uphold the nation's place.

Like ivory beams, her strong white feet
Span over all the busy street;
Beneath their arch the merchants meet.

Her eyes are terrible and pure
As the stern, steadfast cynosure;
Before them bow and bend the poor.

Their thrilling pæans rise to her;
She mothers all the healthy stir
That beats the air with bruit and birr.

Below her feet War's banners furl,
The bounteous palms about her curl,
Above her head her strong doves whirl.

Her vesture, with giant lilies bound,
Falls like a slant of snow, and round
It whitens all the quiet ground.

Its cloven fringes are of gold;
By her vast calm made brave and bold,
Babes by their summer lightnings hold.

A helmet binds her lofty crest;
Strong scales of steel flash on her vest,
A strong shield on her ample breast.

IN EXCHANGE FOR HIS SOUL

Armed, armed she stands, from head to heel;
Afar strange navies meet and reel;
Far sounds the furious clash of steel.

Around her sounds the reaper's song,
Below her moves the busy throng;
So stands she—terrible and strong.

Ardent and awfully, afar
Blazes the blood-red wand'ring star
That rolls before the feet of war;

But wheels not nigh her sentried gate,
Her sinewed battlements that wait
Panting to guard her lofty state.

Her song is mild, but thro' it still
The blast of bugles, stern and shrill,
The calms about her pierce and thrill.

Armed, armed her head, her foot, her breast,
A spear defends her white dove's nest;
As Peace is strong so is she blest.

IN EXCHANGE FOR HIS SOUL.

LONG time one whispered in his ear:
  " Give me thy strong, pure soul; behold
'Tis mine to give what men hold dear—
  The treasure of red gold.

" I bribe thee not with crown and throne—
　　Pale spectres they of kingly power—
I give thee gold. Red gold alone
　　Can crown a king each hour."

　He frowned. Perchance he felt a throe,
　　Gold-hunger gnawing at his heart—
A passing pang, for, stern and low,
　　He bade the fiend depart.

　Again there came the voice and said:
　　" Gold for that soul of thine were shame;
Thine be that thing for which have bled
　　Both gods and men—high Fame.

" And in long ages yet to sweep
　　Their gloom and glory on the day,
When mouldering kings, forgot, shall sleep
　　In ashes, dust and clay,

" Thy name shall, star-like, pulse and burn
　　On heights most god-like and divine;
Immortal bays thy funeral urn
　　Shall lastingly entwine."

　He sighed. Perchance he felt the thrill,
　　The answering pulse to Fame's high call;
But answer made his steadfast will:
　　" I will not be thy thrall!"

　Again there came the voice and cried:
　　" Dost thou my kingly bribes disdain?
Yet shalt thou barter soul and pride
　　For things ignobly vain!

THE EARTH WAXETH OLD

" Two shameless eyes—two false, sweet eyes—
　　A sinful brow of sinless white
　Shall hurl thy soul from high clear skies
　　To *me* and Stygian night.

" Beneath the spell of gilded hair
　　Thy palms, like sickly weeds, shall die!
　God-strong resolves a sensuous air
　　Shall mock and crucify.

" Go to! My thrall at last thou art!
　　Ere bud to rounded blossom change
　Thou wilt, for wanton lips and heart
　　Most false, thy soul exchange!"

THE EARTH WAXETH OLD.

WHEN yellow-locked and crystal-eyed
　　I dreamed green woods among,
Where tall trees waved from side to side,
And in their green breasts deep and wide
I saw the building bluejay hide,
　　O then the earth was young!

The winds were fresh and brave and bold,
　　The red sun round and strong;
No prophet voice, chill, loud and cold,
Across my woodland dreamings rolled:
" The green earth waxeth sere and old
　　That once was fair and young."

I saw in scarred and knotty bole
　　The freshening of the sap;

When timid spring gave first small dole
Of sunbeams thro' bare boughs that stole,
I saw the brightening blossoms roll
   From summer's high-piled lap.

And where an ancient oak tree lay
   The forest stream across,
I mused above the sweet, shrill spray,
I watched the speckled trout at play,
I saw the shadows dance and sway
   On ripple and on moss.

I pulled the chestnut branches low,
   As o'er the stream they hung,
To see their bursting buds of snow;
I heard the sweet spring waters flow—
My heart and I, we did not know
   But that the earth was young.

I joyed in solemn woods to see,
   Where sudden sunbeams clung,
On open space of mossy lea
The violet and anemone
Wave their frail heads and beckon me—
   Sure then the earth was young!

I heard the fresh wild breezes birr
   New budded boughs among,
I saw the deeper tinting stir
In the green tassels of the fir,
I heard the pheasant rise and whirr
   Above her callow young.

I saw the tall fresh ferns down prest
   By scudding doe and fawn,

THE EARTH WAXETH OLD

I saw the grey dove's swelling breast
Above the margin of her nest,
When north and south and east and west
  Rolled all the red of dawn.

At eventide at length I lay,
  On grassy pillow flung;
I saw the parting bark of day—
With crimson sails and shrouds all gay
With golden fires—drift away
  The billowy clouds among.

I saw the stately planets sail
  On that blue ocean wide;
I saw, blown by some mystic gale—
Like silver ship in elfin tale
That bore some damsel rare and pale—
  The moon's slim crescent glide.

And every throb of spring that shook
  The rustling boughs among,
That filled the silver vein of brook,
That lit with bloom the mossy nook,
Cried to my boyish bosom: " Look!
  How fresh the earth and young!"

The winds were fresh, the days as clear
  As crystals set in gold.
No shape with prophet-mantle drear
Thro' those old woods came drifting near
To whisper in my wondering ear:
  " The green earth waxeth old."

ISABELLA VALANCY CRAWFORD

THE KING IS DEAD! LONG LIVE THE KING!

A HERALD stood upon the wold,
A round moon high above him rolled;
He blew a clear blast, shrill and bold,

Up to the star-touched hills, and low
To moor and valley deep in snow.
The long, fine, silver notes did blow

Where taper-jewelled cities lay,
Like mantles spread upon the way
The feet of queens might hap to stray.

On palace wall the loud blast beat,
Pierced the small vein of narrow street,
O'erblew the lute and dancers' feet.

The herald turned him east and west;
His silver beard rolled down his breast,
White samite glowed his spangled vest.

Again that shrill, clear blast took wing;
The round earth with its voice did ring:
" The King is dead!   Long live the King!"

To north, to south, he turned his head;
His trumpet spake: " The King is dead!
Long live the King!" again it said.

Said one of twain who heard the cry:
" The dear old year can never die;
He saw us wedded, thou and I.

166

THE KING IS DEAD! LONG LIVE THE KING!

" His days were flushed with flame of spring
    What time he blessed our nuptial ring;
    We heard his youngest robins sing.

" And if it chance that we should see
    From that fair day a century,
    My wife, together, it will be

" That when thy foot, dear heart, draws near,
    With thee shall come that happy year.
    To let them lay him on his bier,

" And let the shrill, sweet trumpet cry:
    ' The King is dead!'   He cannot die
    While love abides within our sky."

    By brooklet slim as silver sword,
    Ice-stifled thunders of the ford,
    Again the trumpet rang its word.

    Round the white moon its voice did cling;
    It smote the cold stars with its wing:
    " The King is dead!   Long live the King!"

    Said one who gazed upon the sky:
    " Oh, wherefore mock me with that cry?
    The bygone year can never die.

" His days were gilded tissues, spun
    By laughing earth and yellow sun;
    His roses like red planets shone.

" His breath was wine, his beard was gold,
    His leafy mantle richly rolled
    O'er forest, meadow, lea and wold.

" He came in state by town and lea;
　His blue eyes swelled on mine and me—
　I had my babe upon my knee.

" Her sweet, small head his lips caressed;
　He took my one babe from my breast—
　She in his flowery arms was pressed.

" Ah, God, dear God! was ever grief
　In mother heart more poorly brief
　Than time itself?　His bud and leaf

" A fresh, fair anguish still must be,
　Until some day again I see
　The babe he took upon my knee.

" To let them lay him on his bier!
　He lives; while grief can shed a tear
　He cannot die—the bygone year."

　　The earth was spangled with the eyes
　　Of children, as with stars and skies,
　　　Who watched the New Year in.
　　Lark-clear they sang from hut and hall:
　　" The new King is the baby small,
　　　Without a spot or sin.

" Our little King!　Our little King!
　The baby sweet with trumpets bring,
　　In snowy cloak and cope;
　But who shall hold him up that we
　His dimples and his smiles may see?
　　The Fairy Princess, Hope.

THE LILY BED

"O dear, bright stars, fly down, fly down,
  And make our baby such a crown
    As men shall joy to see!
  And who shall rock his cradle bed?
  First place his crown upon his head?
    Faith, Hope, and Charity."

THE LILY BED.

His cedar paddle, scented, red,
He thrust down through the lily bed;

Cloaked in a golden pause he lay,
Locked in the arms of the placid bay.

Trembled alone his bark canoe
As shocks of bursting lilies flew

Thro' the still crystal of the tide,
And smote the frail boat's birchen side;

Or, when beside the sedges thin
Rose the sharp silver of a fin;

Or when, a wizard swift and cold,
A dragon-fly beat out in gold

And jewels all the widening rings
Of waters singing to his wings;

Or, like a winged and burning soul,
Dropped from the gloom an oriole
169

On the cool wave, as to the balm
Of the Great Spirit's open palm

The freed soul flies.   And silence clung
To the still hours, as tendrils hung,

In darkness carven, from the trees,
Sedge-buried to their burly knees.

Stillness sat in his lodge of leaves;
Clung golden shadows to its eaves,

And on its cone-spiced floor, like maize,
Red-ripe, fell sheaves of knotted rays.

The wood, a proud and crested brave;
Bead-bright, a maiden, stood the wave.

And he had spoke his soul of love
With voice of eagle and of dove.

Of loud, strong pines his tongue was made;
His lips, soft blossoms in the shade,

That kissed her silver lips—her's cool
As lilies on his inmost pool—

Till now he stood, in triumph's rest,
His image painted in her breast.

One isle 'tween blue and blue did melt,—
A bead of wampum from the belt

THE LILY BED

Of Manitou—a purple rise
On the far shore heaved to the skies.

His cedar paddle, scented, red,
He drew up from the lily bed;

All lily-locked, all lily-locked,
His light bark in the blossoms rocked.

Their cool lips round the sharp prow sang,
Their soft clasp to the frail sides sprang,

With breast and lip they wove a bar.
Stole from her lodge the Evening Star;

With golden hand she grasped the mane
Of a red cloud on her azure plain.

It by the peaked, red sunset flew;
Cool winds from its bright nostrils blew.

They swayed the high, dark trees, and low
Swept the locked lilies to and fro.

With cedar paddle, scented, red,
He pushed out from the lily bed.

THE GHOSTS OF THE TREES.

THE silver fangs of the mighty axe
  Bit to the blood of our giant boles;
It smote our breasts and smote our backs.
  Thundered the front-cleared leaves.
        As sped in fire
  The whirl and flame of scarlet leaves,
        With strong desire
  Leaped to the air our captive souls.
While down our corpses thundered,
The Air at our strong souls gazed and wondered,
  And cried to us, " Ye
Are full of all mystery to me.
  I saw but your plumes of leaves,
    Your strong, brown greaves,
Your sinewy roots and lusty branches;
And, fond and anxious,
  I laid my ear and my restless breast
  By each pride-high crest;
        And softly stole
And listened by limb and listened by bole,
Nor ever the stir of a soul
        Heard I in ye.
    Great is the mystery !"

The strong brown Eagle plunged from his peak;
From the hollow iron of his beak
The wood pigeon fell, its breast of blue
Cold with sharp death all thro' and thro'.
      To our ghosts he cried,
    " With talons of steel
      I hold the storm;

172

THE GHOSTS OF THE TREES

Where the high peaks reel
   My young lie warm;
In the wind-rocked spaces of air I bide,
  My wings too wide,
Too angry-strong, for the emerald gyves
Of woodland cell where the meek dove thrives.
   And when at the bar
Of morn I smote with my breast its star,
     And under
My wings grew purple the jealous thunder,
  With the flame of the skies
Hot in my breast and red in my eyes,
  From peak to peak of sunrise piled,
That set space glowing
With flames from air-based craters blowing,
  I downward swept, beguiled
By the close-set forest, gilded and spread,
A sea for the lordly tread
  Of a god's war-ship.
I broke its leafy surf with my breast;
    My iron lip
I dipped in the cool of each whispering crest.
  From your leafy steeps
  I saw in the deeps
Red coral, the flame-necked oriole;
But never the stir of a soul
    Heard I in ye.
  Great is the mystery!"

   From its ferny coasts
The River gazed at our strong, free ghosts,
  And with rocky fingers shed
  Apart the silver curls of its head;
Laid its murmuring hands

173

On the reedy bands;
     And at gaze
Stood in the half-moon of brown, still bays.
Like glossed eyes of stags
Its round pools gazed from the rusty flags
  At our ghostly crests,
At the bark-shields strong on our phantom breasts;
     And its tide
Took lip and tongue and cried:

    " I have pushed apart
      The mountain's heart,
I have trod the valley down;
      With strong hands curled,
      Have caught and hurled
To the earth the high hill's crown.

    " My brow I thrust
      Through sultry dust
That the lean wolf howled upon;
      I drove my tides
      Between the sides
Of the bellowing canyon.

    " From crystal shoulders
      I hurled my boulders
On the bridge's iron span;
      When I reared my head
      From its old-time bed,
Shook the pale cities of man.

    " I have run a course
      With the swift, wild horse;
       174

THE GHOSTS OF THE TREES

I have thundered pace for pace
  With the rushing herds;
  I have caught the beards
Of the swift stars in the race.

" Neither moon nor sun
  Could me outrun;
Deep caged in my silver bars,
  I hurried with me
  To the shouting sea
Their light and the light of the stars.

" The reeling earth,
  In furious mirth,
With sledges of ice I smote;
  I whirled my sword
  Where the pale berg roared,
I took the ship by the throat.

" With stagnant breath
  I called chill Death,
My guest, to the hot bayou;
  I built men's graves
  With strong-thewed waves.
That thing that my strength might do

" I did right well.
  Men cried, ' From Hell
The might of thy hand is given !'
  By loose rocks stoned,
  The stout quays groaned;
Sleek sands by my spear were riven.

" O'er shining slides
  On my glossèd tides
The brown cribs, close woven, rolled;
  The stout logs sprung
  Their height among
My loud whirls of white and gold.

" The great raft prest
  My calm, broad breast—
A dream thro' my shady trance;
  The light canoe
  A spirit flew—
The pulse of my blue expanse.

" Winged swift, the ships
  My foaming lips
Made rich with dewy kisses,
  All night and morn,
  Thro' fields of corn;
And where the mill-wheel hisses,

" And shivers and sobs
  With labouring throbs,
With its whirls my strong palms played.
  I parted my flags
  For thirsty stags;
On the necks of arches laid,

" To the dry-vined town
  My tide rolled down:
Dry lips and throats a-quiver
  Rent sky and sod
  With shouts, ' From God
The strength of the mighty river !'

" I, listening, heard
    The soft-songed bird,
The beetle about your boles,
    The calling breeze
    In your crests, O trees,—
Never the voices of souls!"

We, freed souls of the trees, looked down
On the River's shining eyes of brown;
    And upward smiled
At the tender Air and its warrior child,
    The iron Eagle strong and wild.

    No will of ours,
The captive souls of our barky towers;
    His the deed
Who laid in the secret earth the seed,
And with strong hand
Knitted each woody fetter and band.

GISLI, THE CHIEFTAIN.

Part I.

To THE Goddess Lada prayed
    Gisli, holding high his spear
Bound with buds of spring, and laughed
    All his heart to Lada's ear.

Damp his yellow beard with mead;
    Loud the harps clanged thro' the day;
With bruised breasts triumphant rode
    Gisli's galleys in the bay.

Bards sang in the banquet hall,
   Set in loud verse Gisli's fame;
On their lips the war gods laid
   Fire to chant their warrior's name.

To the Love Queen Gisli prayed,
   Buds upon his tall spear's tip,
Laughter in his broad blue eyes,
   Laughter on his bearded lip.

To the Spring Queen Gisli prayed.
   She, with mystic distaff slim,
Spun her hours of love and leaves;
   Made the stony headlands dim—

Dim and green with tender grass;
   Blew on ice-fields with red mouth;
Blew on lovers' hearts and lured
   White swans from the blue-arched south.

To the Love Queen Gisli prayed.
   Groaned far icebergs, tall and blue,
As to Lada's distaff slim
   All their ice-locked fires flew.

To the Love Queen Gisli prayed.
   She, with red hands, caught and spun
Yellow flames from crater lips,
   Long flames from the waking sun.

To the Love Queen Gisli prayed.
   She with loom and beam and spell
All the subtle fires of earth
   Wove, and wove them strong and well.

GISLI, THE CHIEFTAIN

To the Spring Queen Gisli prayed.
  Low the sun the pale sky trod;
Mute her ruddy hand she raised,
  Beckoned back the parting god.

To the Love Queen Gisli prayed.
  Warp and weft of flame she wove,
Lada, Goddess of the Spring,
  Lada, Goddess strong of Love.

Sire of the strong chieftain's prayer,
  Victory, with his pulse of flame;
Mead, its mother,—loud he laughed,
  Calling on great Lada's name:

" Goddess Lada, Queen of Love,
  Here I stand and quaff to thee,
Deck for thee with buds my spear;
  Give a comely wife to me!

" Blow not to my arms a flake
  Of crisp snow in maiden guise,
Mists of pallid hair and tips
  Of long ice-spears in her eyes.

" When my death-sail skims the foam,
  Strain my oars on Death's black sea,
When my foot the Glass Hill seeks,
  Such a maid may do for me.

" Now, O Lada, mate the flesh;
  Mate the fire and flame of life;
Tho' the soul go still unwed,
  Give the flesh its fitting wife!
179

" As the galley runs between
 Skies with billows closely spun,
Feeling but the wave that leaps
 Closest to it in the sun,

" Throbs but to the present kiss
 Of the wild lips of the sea,
Thus a man joys in his life—
 Nought of the Beyond knows he.

" Goddess, here I cast bright buds,
 Spicy pine boughs at thy feet;
Give the flesh its fitting mate—
 Life is strong and life is sweet!"

To the Love Queen Gisli prayed.
 Warp and weft of flame she wove,
Lada, Goddess of the Spring,
 Lada, Goddess strong of love.

PART II.

From harpings and sagas and mirth of the town
Great Gisli, the chieftain, strode merrily down,

His ruddy beard stretched in the loom of the wind,
His shade like a dusky god striding behind.

Gylfag, his true hound, to his heel glided near,
Sharp-fanged, lank and red as a blood-rusted spear.

As crests of the green bergs flame white in the sky,
The town on its sharp hill shone brightly and high.

GISLI, THE CHIEFTAIN

In fiords roared the ice shields; below the dumb stroke
Of the Sun's red hammer rose blue mist like smoke.

It clung to the black pines and clung to the bay—
The galleys of Gisli grew ghosts of the day.

It followed the sharp wings of swans as they rose;
It fell to the wide jaws of swift riven floes;

It tamed the wild shriek of the eagle; grew dull
The cries, in its foldings, of osprey and gull.

" Arouse thee, bold wind," shouted Gisli, " and drive
Floe and berg out to sea, as bees from a hive!

" Chase this woman-lipped haze at top of thy speed;
The soul with it cloys, as the tongue cloys with mead!

" Come, buckle thy sharp spear again to thy breast;
Thy galley hurl forth from the seas of the West!

" With the long, hissing oars beat loud the North Sea;
The sharp gaze of day give the eagles and me!

" No cunning mists shrouding the sea and the sky,
Or the brows of the great gods, bold wind, love I!

" As Gylfag, my hound, lays his fangs in the flank
Of a grey wolf, shadowy, leather-thewed, lank,

" Bold wind, chase the blue mist, thy prow in its hair!
Sun, speed thy keen shafts thro' the breast of the air!"

PART III.

The shouting of Gisli, the chieftain,
Rocked the blue hazes, and, cloven
In twain by sharp prow of the west wind,
To north and to south fled the thick mist.

As in burnished walls of Valhalla,
In cleft of the mist stood the chieftain,
And up to the blue shield of Heaven
Flung the loud shaft of his laughter.

Smote the mist with shrill spear the swift wind;
Grey shapes fled like ghosts on the Hell Way;
Bayed after their long locks hoarse Gylfag;
Stared at them, triumphant, the eagles.

To mate and to eaglets the eagle
Shrieked, " Gone is my foe of the deep mist,
Rent by the vast hands of the kind gods
Who know the knife-pangs of our hunger!"

Shrill whistled the wind as his dun wings
Strove with it feather by feather;
Loud grated the rock as his talons
Spurned slowly its breast; and his red eyes

Like fires seemed to flame in the swift wind—
At his sides the darts of his hunger;
At his ears the shrieks of his eaglets;
In his breast the love of the quarry.

Unfurled to the northward and southward
His wings broke the air, and to eastward
His breast gave its iron; and godward
Pierced the shrill voice of his hunger.

GISLI, THE CHIEFTAIN

Bared were his great sides as he laboured
Up the steep blue of the broad sky,
His gaze on the fields of his freedom;
To the gods spake the prayers of his gyres.

Bared were his vast sides as he glided,
Black in the sharp blue of the north sky,
Black over the white of the tall cliffs,
Black over the arrow of Gisli.

THE SONG OF THE ARROW.

What know I,
As I bite the blue veins of the throbbing sky,
To the quarry's breast,
Hot from the sides of the sleek, smooth nest?

What know I
Of the will of the tense bow from which I fly?
What the need or jest
That feathers my flight to its bloody rest?

What know I
Of the will of the bow that speeds me on high?
What doth the shrill bow
Of the hand on its singing soul-string know?

Flame-swift speed I,
And the dove and the eagle shriek out and die.
Whence comes my sharp zest
For the heart of the quarry? The gods know best.

Deep pierced the red gaze of the eagle
The breast of a cygnet below him.

Beneath his dun wing from the eastward
Shrill chanted the long shaft of Gisli;

Beneath his dun wing from the westward
A shaft shook that laughed in its biting—
Met in the fierce breast of the eagle
The arrows of Gisli and Brynhild.

PART IV.

A ghost along the Hell Way sped:
The Hell shoes shod his misty tread;
A phantom hound beside him sped.

Beneath the spandrels of the Way
Worlds rolled to night—from night to day;
In Space's ocean suns were spray.

Grouped worlds, eternal eagles, flew;
Swift comets fell like noiseless dew;
Young earths slow budded in the blue.

The waves of space, inscrutable,
With awful pulses rose and fell,
Silent and godly—terrible.

Electric souls of strong suns laid
Strong hands along the awful shade
That God about His God-work made.

Ever from all ripe worlds did break
Men's voices, as when children speak,
Eager and querulous and weak;

184

GISLI, THE CHIEFTAIN

And pierced to the All-worker thro'
His will that veiled Him from the view:
" What hast Thou done?   What dost Thou do?"

And ever from His heart did flow,
Majestical, the answer low—
The benison—" Ye shall not know !"

The wan ghost on the Hell Way sped,
Nor yet Valhalla's lights were shed
Upon the white brow of the Dead.

Nor sang within his ears the roll
Of trumpets calling to his soul;
Nor shone wide portals of the goal.

His spear grew heavy on his breast;
Dropped, like a star, his golden crest;
Far, far the vast Halls of the Blest !

His heart grown faint, his feet grown weak,
He scaled the knit mists of a peak
That ever parted grey and bleak,

And, as by unseen talons nipped,
To the deep abysses slowly slipped.
Then, swift as thick smoke strongly ripped

By whirling winds from ashy ring
Of dank weeds blackly smouldering,
The peak sprang upward, quivering;

And, perdurable, set its face
Against the pulsing breast of space.
But for a moment; to its base

Refluent rolled the crest, new sprung,
In clouds with ghastly lightnings stung;
Faint thunders to their black feet clung.

His faithful hound ran at his heel;
His thighs and breast were bright with steel;
He saw the awful Hell Way reel.

But far along its bleak peaks rang
A distant trump—its airy clang
Like light through deathly shadows sprang.

He knew the blast—the voice of love
(Cleft lay the throbbing peak above)
Sailed light, winged like a silver dove.

On strove the toiling ghost, his soul
Stirred like strong mead in wassail bowl
That quivers to the shout of " Skoal!"

Strode from the mist, close-curved and cold
As is a writhing dragon's fold,
A warrior with shield of gold.

A sharp blade glittered at his hip;
Flamed like a star his lance's tip;
His bugle sang at bearded lip.

Beneath his golden sandals flew
Stars from the mist, as grass flings dew,
Or red fruit falls from the dark yew.

As under sheltering wreaths of snow
The dark blue north flowers richly blow,
Beneath long locks of silver glow

GISLI, THE CHIEFTAIN

Clear eyes that, burning on a host,
Would win a field at sunset lost,
Ere stars from Odin's hand were tost.

He stretched his hand, he bowed his head;
The wan ghost to his bosom sped—
Dead kissed the bearded lips of Dead.

" What dost thou here, my youngest born?
Thou, scarce yet fronted with life's storm,
Why art thou from the dark earth torn?

" When high Valhalla pulsed and rang
With harps that shook as grey bards sang,
'Mid the loud joy I heard the clang

" Of Death's dark doors; to me alone
Smote in thine awful dying groan—
My soul recalled its blood and bone.

" Viewless the cord which draws from far,
To the round sun, some mighty star;
Viewless the strong knit soul cords are.

" I felt thy dying gasp—thy soul
Toward mine a kindred wave in roll;
I left the harps, I left the bowl,

" I sought the Hell Way—I, the blest—
That thou, new death-born son, should rest
Upon the strong rock of my breast.

" What dost thou here, young, fair and bold?
Sleek with youth's gloss thy locks of gold;
Thy years by flowers might yet be told.

" What dost thou at the ghostly goal,
While yet thy years were to thy soul
As mead yet shallow in the bowl?"

His arm about the pale ghost cast,
The warrior blew a clear, loud blast;
Like frightened wolves the mists fled past.

Grew firm the Way; worlds flamed to light
The awful peak that thrust its height
With swift throbs upward; like a flight

Of arrows from a host close set,
Long meteors pierced its breast of jet.
Again the trump his strong lips met,

And, at its blast, blew all the day
In broad winds on the awful Way;
Sun smote at sun across the gray.

As reindeer smite the high-piled snow
To find the green moss far below,
They struck the mists, thro' which did glow

Bright vales; and on a sea afar
Lay, at a sunlit harbour bar,
A galley gold-sailed like a star.

Spake the pale ghost as onward sped,
Heart pressed to heart, the valiant dead
(Soft the green paths beneath their tread):

" I loved—this is my tale—and died.
The fierce chief hungered for my bride:
The spear of Gisli pierced my side.

188

GISLI, THE CHIEFTAIN

" And she—her love filled all my need;
  Her vows were sweet and strong as mead;
  Look, father! doth my heart still bleed?

" I built her round with shaft and spear;
  I kept her mine for one brief year—
  She laughed above my blood-stained bier!

" Upon a far and ice-peaked coast
  My galleys by long winds were tost:
  There Gisli feasted with his host

" Of warriors triumphant.   He
  Strode out from harps and revelry,
  And sped his shaft above the sea.

" Look, father! doth my heart bleed yet?
  His arrow Brynhild's arrow met—
  My galleys anchored in their net.

" Again their arrows meet—swift lies
  That pierced me from their smiling eyes.
  How fiercely hard a man's heart dies!

" She false—he false!   There came a day
  Pierced by the fierce chief's spear I lay—
  My ghost rose shrieking from its clay.

" I saw on Brynhild's golden vest
  The shining locks of Gisli rest—
  I sought the Hell Way to the Blest.

" Father, put forth thy hand and tear
  Their twin shafts from my heart, all bare
  To thee—they rankle death-like there."

Said the voice of Evil to the ear of Good,
  " Clasp thou my strong right hand,
Nor shall our clasp be known or understood
  By any in the land.

" I, the dark giant, rule strong on the earth;
  Yet thou, bright one, and I
Sprang from the one great mystery—at one birth
  We looked upon the sky.

" I labour at my bleak, stern toil, accursed
  Of all mankind; nor stay
To rest, to murmur ' I hunger!' or ' I thirst!'
  Nor for my joy delay.

" My strength pleads strong with thee; doth any beat
  With hammer and with stone,
Past tools, to use them to his deep defeat,
  To turn them on his throne,

" Then I, of God the mystery—toil with me,
  Brother; but in the sight
Of men who know not, I stern son shall be
  Of Darkness—thou of Light!"

Book III.

MALCOLM'S KATIE: A LOVE STORY.

PART I.

MAX placed a ring on little Katie's hand,
A silver ring that he had beaten out
From that same sacred coin—first well prized wage
For boyish labour, kept thro' many years.
"See, Kate," he said, "I had no skill to shape
Two hearts fast bound together, so I graved
Just 'K' and 'M,' for Katie and for Max."

"But look! you've run the lines in such a way
That 'M' is part of 'K,' and 'K' of 'M,'"
Said Katie, smiling. "Did you mean it thus?
I like it better than the double hearts."

"Well, well," he said, "but womankind is wise!
Yet tell me, dear, will such a prophecy
Not hurt you sometimes when I am away?
Will you not seek, keen-eyed, for some small break
In those deep lines to part the 'K' and 'M'
For you? Nay, Kate, look down amid the globes
Of those large lilies that our light canoe
Divides, and see within the polished pool
That small rose face of yours, so dear, so fair,—
A seed of love to cleave into a rock
And bourgeon thence until the granite splits
Before its subtle strength. I being gone—
Poor soldier of the axe—to bloodless fields
(Inglorious battles, whether lost or won),
That sixteen-summered heart of yours may say:
'I but was budding, and I did not know
My core was crimson and my perfume sweet;

I had not seen the sun, and blind I swayed
To a strong wind, and thought because I swayed
'Twas to the wooer of the perfect rose—
That strong, wild wind has swept beyond my ken,
The breeze I love sighs thro' my ruddy leaves.' "

" O words !" said Katie, blushing, " only words !
You build them up that I may push them down.
If hearts are flowers, I know that flowers can root,
Bud, blossom, die—all in the same loved soil.
They do so in my garden. I have made
Your heart my garden. If I am a bud
And only feel unfoldment feebly stir
Within my leaves, wait patiently ; some June
I'll blush a full-blown rose, and queen it, dear,
In your loved garden. Tho' I be a bud,
My roots strike deep, and torn from that dear soil
Would shriek like mandrakes—those witch things I
        read
Of in your quaint old books.   Are you content ?"

" Yes, crescent-wise, but not to round, full moon.
Look at yon hill that rounds so gently up
From the wide lake ; a lover king it looks,
In cloth of gold, gone from his bride and queen,
And yet delayed because her silver locks
Catch in his gilded fringe. His shoulders sweep
Into blue distance, and his gracious crest,
Not held too high, is plumed with maple groves—
One of your father's farms : a mighty man,
Self-hewn from rock, remaining rock through all."

" He loves me, Max," said Katie.

MALCOLM'S KATIE

       " Yes, I know—
A rock is cup to many a crystal spring.
Well, he is rich; those misty, peak-roofed barns—
Leviathans rising from red seas of grain—
Are full of ingots shaped like grains of wheat.
His flocks have golden fleeces, and his herds
Have monarchs worshipful as was the calf
Aaron called from the furnace; and his ploughs,
Like Genii chained, snort o'er his mighty fields.
He has a voice in Council and in Church—"

" He worked for all," said Katie, somewhat pained.

" Ay, so, dear love, he did. I heard him tell
How the first field upon his farm was ploughed.
He and his brother Reuben, stalwart lads,
Yoked themselves, side by side, to the new plough;
Their weaker father, in the grey of life—
But rather the wan age of poverty
Than many winters—in large, gnarlèd hands
The plunging handles held; with mighty strains
They drew the ripping beak through knotted sod,
Thro' tortuous lanes of blackened, smoking stumps,
And past great flaming brush-heaps, sending out
Fierce summers, beating on their swollen brows.
O such a battle! had we heard of serfs
Driven to like hot conflict with the soil,
Armies had marched and navies swiftly sailed
To burst their gyves. But here's the little point—
The polished-diamond pivot on which spins
The wheel of difference—they OWNED the soil,
And fought for love—dear love of wealth and power—
And honest ease and fair esteem of men.
One's blood heats at it!"

                    " Yet you said such fields
Were all inglorious," Katie, wondering, said.

" Inglorious? Yes! They make no promises
Of Star or Garter, or the thundering guns
That tell the earth her warriors are dead.
Inglorious? Ay, the battle done and won
Means not a throne propped up with bleaching bones,
A country saved with smoking seas of blood,
A flag torn from the foe with wounds and death,
Or Commerce, with her housewife foot upon
Colossal bridge of slaughtered savages,
The Cross laid on her brawny shoulder, and
In one sly, mighty hand her reeking sword,
And in the other all the woven cheats
From her dishonest looms.   Nay, none of these.
It means—four walls, perhaps a lowly roof;
Kine in a peaceful posture; modest fields;
A man and woman standing hand in hand
In hale old age, who, looking o'er the land,
Say, ' Thank the Lord, it all is mine and thine!'
It means, to such thewed warriors of the Axe
As your own father—well, it means, sweet Kate,
Outspreading circles of increasing gold,
A name of weight, one little daughter heir
Who must not wed the owner of an axe,
Who owns naught else but some dim, dusky woods
In a far land, two arms indifferent strong,—"

" And Katie's heart," said Katie, with a smile;—
For yet she stood on that smooth violet plain
Where nothing shades the sun; nor quite believed
Those blue peaks closing in were aught but mist
Which the gay sun could scatter with a glance.
For Max, he late had touched their stones, but yet

He saw them seamed with gold and precious ores,
Rich with hill flowers and musical with rills,—
" Or that same bud that will be Katie's heart
Against the time your deep, dim woods are cleared,
And I have wrought my father to relent."

" How will you move him, sweet? Why, he will rage
And fume and anger, striding o'er his fields,
Until the last bought king of herds lets down
His lordly front and, rumbling thunder from
His polished chest, returns his chiding tones.
How will you move him, Katie, tell me how?"

" I'll kiss him and keep still; that way is sure,"
Said Katie, smiling; " I have often tried."

" God speed the kiss," said Max, and Katie sighed,
With prayerful palms close sealed, " God speed the
    axe!"

O light canoe, where dost thou glide?
Below thee gleams no silvered tide,
But concave heaven's chiefest pride.

Above thee burns Eve's rosy bar;
Below thee throbs her darling star;
Deep 'neath thy keel her round worlds are.

Above, below—O sweet surprise
To gladden happy lover's eyes!
No earth, no wave—all jewelled skies.

PART II.

The South Wind laid his moccasins aside,
Broke his gay calumet of flowers, and cast
His useless wampum, beaded with cool dews,
Far from him northward; his long, ruddy spear
Flung sunward, whence it came, and his soft locks
Of warm, fine haze grew silvery as the birch.
His wigwam of green leaves began to shake;
The crackling rice-beds scolded harsh like squaws;
The small ponds pouted up their silver lips;
The great lakes eyed the mountains, whispered " Ugh!
Are ye so tall, O chiefs? Not taller than
Our plumes can reach," and rose a little way,
As panthers stretch to try their velvet limbs
And then retreat to purr and bide their time.

At morn the sharp breath of the night arose
From the wide prairies, in deep-struggling seas,
In rolling breakers, bursting to the sky;
In tumbling surfs, all yellowed faintly thro'
With the low sun; in mad, conflicting crests,
Voiced with low thunder from the hairy throats
Of the mist-buried herds. And for a man
To stand amid the cloudy roll and moil,
The phantom waters breaking overhead,
Shades of vexed billows bursting on his breast,
Torn caves of mist walled with a sudden gold—
Resealed as swift as seen—broad, shaggy fronts,
Fire-eyed, and tossing on impatient horns
The wave impalpable—was but to think
A dream of phantoms held him as he stood.
The late, last thunders of the summer crashed
Where shrieked great eagles, lords of naked cliffs.

MALCOLM'S KATIE

The pulseless forest, locked and interlocked
So closely bough with bough and leaf with leaf,
So serfed by its own wealth, that while from high
The moons of summer kissed its green-glossed locks,
And round its knees the merry West Wind danced,
And round its ring, compacted emerald,
The South Wind crept on moccasins of flame,
And the red fingers of th' impatient Sun
Plucked at its outmost fringes, its dim veins
Beat with no life, its deep and dusky heart
In a deep trance of shadow felt no throb
To such soft wooing answer.   Thro' its dream
Brown rivers of deep waters sunless stole;
Small creeks sprang from its mosses, and, amazed,
Like children in a wigwam curtained close
Above the great, dead heart of some red chief,
Slipped on soft feet, swift stealing through the gloom,
Eager for light and for the frolic winds.

In this shrill moon the scouts of Winter ran
From the ice-belted north, and whistling shafts
Struck maple and struck sumach, and a blaze
Ran swift from leaf to leaf, from bough to bough,
Till round the forest flashed a belt of flame,
And inward licked its tongues of red and gold
To the deep-crannied inmost heart of all.
Roused the still heart—but all too late, too late!
Too late the branches, welded fast with leaves,
Tossed, loosened, to the winds; too late the Sun
Poured his last vigour to the deep, dark cells
Of the dim wood.   The keen two-bladed Moon
Of Falling Leaves rolled up on crested mists,
And where the lush, rank boughs had foiled the Sun
In his red prime, her pale, sharp fingers crept
After the wind and felt about the moss,

199

And seemed to pluck from shrinking twig and stem
The burning leaves, while groaned the shuddering
    wood.

Who journeyed where the prairies made a pause
Saw burnished ramparts flaming in the sun
With beacon fires, tall on their rustling walls.
And when the vast horned herds at sunset drew
Their sullen masses into one black cloud,
Rolling thundrous o'er the quick pulsating plain,
They seemed to sweep between two fierce, red suns
Which, hunter-wise, shot at their glaring balls
Keen shafts with scarlet feathers and gold barbs.

By round, small lakes with thinner forests fringed—
More jocund woods that sung about the feet
And crept along the shoulders of great cliffs—
The warrior stags, with does and tripping fawns,
Like shadows black upon the throbbing mist
Of evening's rose, flashed thro' the singing woods,
Nor tim'rous sniffed the spicy cone-breathed air;
For never had the patriarch of the herd
Seen, limned against the farthest rim of light
Of the low-dipping sky, the plume or bow
Of the red hunter; nor, when stooped to drink,
Had from the rustling rice-bed heard the shaft
Of the still hunter hidden in its spears—
His bark canoe close knotted in its bronze,
His form as stirless as the brooding air,
His dusky eyes two fixed, unwinking fires,
His bow-string tightened, till it subtly sang
To the long throbs and leaping pulse that rolled
And beat within his knotted, naked breast.

There came a morn the Moon of Falling Leaves

MALCOLM'S KATIE

With her twin silver blades had only hung
Above the low set cedars of the swamp
For one brief quarter, when the Sun arose
Lusty with light and full of summer heat,
And, pointing with his arrows at the blue
Closed wigwam curtains of the sleeping Moon,
Laughed with the noise of arching cataracts,
And with the dove-like cooing of the woods,
And with the shrill cry of the diving loon,
And with the wash of saltless rounded seas,
And mocked the white Moon of the Falling Leaves:

" Esa! esa! shame upon you, Pale Face!
Shame upon you, Moon of Evil Witches!
Have you killed the happy, laughing Summer?
Have you slain the mother of the flowers
With your icy spells of might and magic?
Have you laid her dead within my arms?
Wrapped her, mocking, in a rainbow blanket?
Drowned her in the frost-mist of your anger?
She is gone a little way before me;
Gone an arrow's flight beyond my vision.
She will turn again and come to meet me
With the ghosts of all the stricken flowers,
In a blue mist round her shining tresses,
In a blue smoke in her naked forests.
She will linger, kissing all the branches;
She will linger, touching all the places,
Bare and naked, with her golden fingers,
Saying, ' Sleep and dream of me, my children;
Dream of me, the mystic Indian Summer,—
I who, slain by the cold Moon of Terror,
Can return across the path of Spirits,
Bearing still my heart of love and fire,
Looking with my eyes of warmth and splendour,

201

Whisp'ring lowly thro' your sleep of sunshine.
I, the laughing Summer, am not turnèd
Into dry dust, whirling on the prairies,
Into red clay, crushed beneath the snowdrifts.
I am still the mother of sweet flowers
Growing but an arrow's flight beyond you
In the Happy Hunting-Ground—the quiver
Of great Manitou, where all the arrows
He has shot from His great bow of Power,
With its clear, bright singing cord of Wisdom,
Are re-gathered, plumed again and brightened,
And shot out, re-barbed with Love and Wisdom;
Always shot, and evermore returning.
Sleep, my children, smiling in your heart-seeds
At the spirit words of Indian Summer.'
Thus, O Moon of Falling Leaves, I mock you!
Have you slain my gold-eyed squaw, the Summer?"

The mighty Morn strode laughing up the land,
And Max, the lab'rer and the lover, stood
Within the forest's edge beside a tree—
The mossy king of all the woody tribes—
Whose clatt'ring branches rattled, shuddering,
As the bright axe cleaved moon-like thro' the air,
Waking strange thunders, rousing echoes linked,
From the full lion-throated roar to sighs
Stealing on dove-wings thro' the distant aisles.
Swift fell the axe, swift followed roar on roar,
Till the bare woodland bellowed in its rage
As the first-slain slow toppled to his fall.
" O King of Desolation, art thou dead?"
Cried Max, and laughing, heart and lips, leaped on
The vast prone trunk. " And have I slain a king?
Above his ashes will I build my house;
No slave beneath its pillars, but—a king!"

MALCOLM'S KATIE

Max wrought alone but for a half-breed lad
With tough, lithe sinews, and deep Indian eyes
Lit with a Gallic sparkle. Max the lover found
The lab'rer's arms grow mightier day by day,
More iron-welded, as he slew the trees;
And with the constant yearning of his heart
Toward little Kate, part of a world away,
His young soul grew and shewed a virile front,
Full-muscled and large-statured like his flesh.

Soon the great heaps of brush were builded high,
And, like a victor, Max made pause to clear
His battle-field high strewn with tangled dead.
Then roared the crackling mountains, and their fires
Met in high heaven, clasping flame with flame;
The thin winds swept a cosmos of red sparks
Across the bleak midnight sky; and the sun
Walked pale behind the resinous black smoke.

And Max cared little for the blotted sun,
And nothing for the startled, outshone stars;
For love, once set within a lover's breast,
Has its own sun, its own peculiar sky,
All one great daffodil, on which do lie
The sun, the moon, the stars, all seen at once
And never setting, but all shining straight
Into the faces of the trinity—
The one beloved, the lover, and sweet love.

It was not all his own, the axe-stirred waste.
In these new days men spread about the earth
With wings at heel, and now the settler hears,
While yet his axe rings on the primal woods,
The shrieks of engines rushing o'er the wastes;
Nor parts his kind to hew his fortunes out.

And as one drop glides down the unknown rock
And the bright-threaded stream leaps after it
With welded billions, so the settler finds
His solitary footsteps beaten out
With the quick rush of panting human waves
Upheaved by throbs of angry poverty,
And driven by keen blasts of hunger from
Their native strands, so stern, so dark, so drear!
O then to see the troubled, groaning waves
Throb down to peace in kindly valley beds,
Their turbid bosoms clearing in the calm
Of sun-eyed Plenty, till the stars and moon,
The blessed sun himself, have leave to shine
And laugh in their dark hearts!

                    So shanties grew
Other than his amid the blackened stumps;
And children ran with little twigs and leaves
And flung them, shouting, on the forest pyres
Where burned the forest kings; and in the glow
Paused men and women when the day was done.
There the lean weaver ground anew his axe,
Nor backward looked upon the vanished loom,
But forward to the ploughing of his fields,
And to the rose of plenty in the cheeks
Of wife and children; nor heeded much the pangs
Of the roused muscles tuning to new work.
The pallid clerk looked on his blistered palms
And sighed and smiled, but girded up his loins
And found new vigour as he felt new hope.
The lab'rer with trained muscles, grim and grave,
Looked at the ground, and wondered in his soul
What joyous anguish stirred his darkened heart
At the mere look of the familiar soil,
And found his answer in the words, *" Mine own!"*

204

Then came smooth-coated men with eager eyes
And talked of steamers on the cliff-bound lakes,
And iron tracks across the prairie lands,
And mills to crush the quartz of wealthy hills,
And mills to saw the great wide-armèd trees,
And mills to grind the singing stream of grain.
And with such busy clamour mingled still
The throbbing music of the bold, bright Axe—
The steel tongue of the present; and the wail
Of falling forests—voices of the past.

Max, social-souled, and with his practised thews,
Was happy, boy-like, thinking much of Kate,
And speaking of her to the women-folk,
Who, mostly happy in new honeymoons
Of hope themselves, were ready still to hear
The thrice-told tale of Katie's sunny eyes
And Katie's yellow hair and household ways;
And heard so often, " There shall stand our home
On yonder slope, with vines about the door,"
That the good wives were almost made to see
The snowy walls, deep porches, and the gleam
Of Katie's garments flitting through the rooms;
And the black slope all bristling with burnt stumps
Was known amongst them all as " Max's house."

O Love builds on the azure sea,
    And Love builds on the golden sand,
And Love builds on the rose-winged cloud,
    And sometimes Love builds on the land!

O if Love build on sparkling sea,
    And if Love build on golden strand,
And if Love build on rosy cloud,
    To Love these are the solid land!

205

O Love will build his lily walls,
  And Love his pearly roof will rear
On cloud, or land, or mist, or sea—
  Love's solid land is everywhere!

PART III.

The great farmhouse of Malcolm Graem stood,
Square-shouldered and peak-roofed, upon a hill,
With many windows looking everywhere,
So that no distant meadow might lie hid,
Nor corn-field hide its gold, nor lowing herd
Browse in far pastures, out of Malcolm's ken.
He loved to sit, grim, grey, and somewhat stern,
And thro' the smoke-clouds from his short clay pipe
Look out upon his riches, while his thoughts
Swung back and forth between the bleak, stern past
And the near future; for his life had come
To that close balance when, a pendulum,
The memory swings between the " then " and " now."
His seldom speech ran thus two different ways:
" When I was but a laddie, thus I did ";
Or, " Katie, in the fall I'll see to build
Such fences or such sheds about the place;
And next year, please the Lord, another barn."
Katie's gay garden foamed about the walls,
Assailed the prim-cut modern sills, and rushed
Up the stone walls to break on the peaked roof.
And Katie's lawn was like a poet's sward,
Velvet and sheer and diamonded with dew;
For such as win their wealth most aptly take
Smooth urban ways and blend them with their own.
And Katie's dainty raiment was as fine
As the smooth, silken petals of the rose,

MALCOLM'S KATIE

And her light feet, her nimble mind and voice,
In city schools had learned the city's ways,
And, grafts upon the healthy, lovely vine,
They shone, eternal blossoms 'mid the fruit;
For Katie had her sceptre in her hand
And wielded it right queenly there and here,
In dairy, store-room, kitchen—every spot
Where woman's ways were needed on the place.

And Malcolm took her through his mighty fields
And taught her lore about the change of crops,
And how to see a handsome furrow ploughed,
And how to choose the cattle for the mart,
And how to know a fair day's work when done,
And where to plant young orchards; for he said,
" God sent a lassie, but I need a son—
" Bethankit for His mercies all the same."
And Katie, when he said it, thought of Max,
Who had been gone two winters and two springs,
And sighed and thought, " Would he not be your
    son?"
But all in silence, for she had too much
Of the firm will of Malcolm in her soul
To think of shaking that deep-rooted rock;
But hoped the crystal current of his love
For his one child, increasing day by day,
Might fret with silver lip until it wore
Such channels thro' the rock that some slight stroke
Of circumstance might crumble down the stone.

The wooer too, Max prophesied, had come;
Reputed wealthy; with the azure eyes
And Saxon-gilded locks, the fair, clear face
And stalwart form that most of women love;
And with the jewels of some virtues set

207

On his broad brow; with fires within his soul
He had the wizard skill to fetter down
To that mere pink, poetic, nameless glow
That need not fright a flake of snow away,
But, if unloosed, could melt an adverse rock,
Marrowed with iron, frowning in his way.

And Malcolm balanced him by day and night,
And with his grey-eyed shrewdness partly saw
He was not one for Kate, but let him come
And in chance moments thought, " Well, let it be;
They make a bonnie pair; he knows the ways
Of men and things; can hold the gear I give,
And, if the lassie wills it, let it be;"
And then, upstarting from his midnight sleep,
With hair erect and sweat upon his brow
Such as no labour e'er had beaded there,
Would cry aloud, wide staring thro' the dark,
" Nay, nay! She shall not wed him! Rest in peace!"
Then, fully waking, grimly laugh and say,
" Why did I speak and answer when none spake?"
But still lie staring, wakeful, through the shades,
List'ning to the silence, and beating still
The ball of Alfred's merits to and fro,
Saying, between the silent arguments,
" But would the mother like it, could she know?
I would there were a way to ring a lad
Like silver coin, and so find out the true.
But Kate shall say him ' Nay ' or say him ' Yea '
At her own will."

                And Katie said him " Nay "
In all the maiden, speechless, gentle ways
A woman has. But Alfred only laughed
To his own soul, and said in his walled mind,

MALCOLM'S KATIE

" O Kate, were I a lover I might feel
Despair flap o'er my hopes with raven wings,
Because thy love is given to other love.
And did I love, unless I gained thy love
I would disdain the golden hair, sweet lips,
True violet eyes and gentle air-blown form,
Nor crave the beauteous lamp without the flame,
Which in itself would light a charnel house.
Unloved and loving, I would find the cure
Of Love's despair in nursing Love's disdain—
Disdain of lesser treasure than the whole.
One cares not much to place against the wheel
A diamond lacking flame, nor loves to pluck
A rose with all its perfume cast abroad
To the bosom of the gale.   Not I, in truth!
If all man's days are three-score years and ten,
He needs must waste them not, but nimbly seize
The bright, consummate blossom that his will
Calls for most loudly.   Gone, long gone the days
When Love within my soul forever stretched
Fierce hands of flame, and here and there I found
A blossom fitted for him, all up-filled
With love as with clear dew:—they had their hour
And burned to ashes with him as he drooped
In his own ruby fires.   No phœnix he
To rise again, because of Katie's eyes,
On dewy wings from ashes such as his!
But now another passion bids me forth
To crown him with the fairest I can find,
And makes me lover, not of Katie's face,
But of her father's riches.   O high fool,
Who feels the faintest pulsing of a wish
And fails to feed it into lordly life,
So that, when stumbling back to Mother Earth,
His freezing lip may curl in cold disdain

Of those poor, blighted fools who starward stare
For that fruition, nipped and scanted here!
And while the clay o'ermasters all his blood,
And he can feel the dust knit with his flesh,
He yet can say to them, ' Be ye content;
I tasted perfect fruitage thro' my life,
Lighted all lamps of passion till the oil
Failed from their wicks; and now, O now I know
There is no Immortality could give
Such boon as this—to simply cease to be!
There lies your Heaven, O ye dreaming slaves,
If ye would only live to make it so,
Nor paint upon the blue skies lying shades
Of—*what is not*. Wise, wise and strong the man
Who poisons that fond haunter of the mind,
Craving for a hereafter with deep draughts
Of wild delights so fiery, fierce, and strong,
That when their dregs are deeply, deeply drained,
What once was blindly craved of purblind Chance—
Life, life eternal, throbbing thro' all space—
Is strongly loathed; and, with his face in dust,
Man loves his only heaven—six feet of earth.
So, Katie, tho' your blue eyes say me ' Nay,'
My pangs of love for gold must needs be fed,
And shall be, Katie, if I know my mind."

Events were winds close nestling in the sails
Of Alfred's bark, all blowing him direct
To his wished harbour. On a certain day
All set about with roses and with fire—
One of three days of heat which frequent slip,
Like triple rubies, in between the sweet,
Mild, emerald days of summer—Katie went,
Drawn by a yearning for the ice-pale blooms,
Natant and shining, firing all the bay

MALCOLM'S KATIE

With angel fires built up of snow and gold.
She found the bay close packed with groaning logs
Prisoned between great arms of close-hinged wood,
All cut from Malcolm's forests in the west
And floated thither to his noisy mills,
And all stamped with the potent " M " and " G "
Which much he loved to see upon his goods—
The silent courtiers owning him their king.
Out clear beyond, the rustling rice-beds sang,
And the cool lilies starred the shadowed wave.
"This is a day for lily-love," said Kate,
While she made bare the lilies of her feet
And sang a lily-song that Max had made
That spoke of lilies—always meaning Kate:

" While, Lady of the silvered lakes—
Chaste goddess of the sweet, still shrine
   The jocund river fitful makes
   By sudden, deep gloomed brakes—
Close sheltered by close warp and woof of vine,
Spilling a shadow gloomy-rich as wine
Into the silver throne where thou dost sit,
Thy silken leaves all dusky round thee knit!

" Mild Soul of the unsalted wave,
   White bosom holding golden fire,
  Deep as some ocean-hidden cave
   Are fixed the roots of thy desire,
Thro' limpid currents stealing up,
And rounding to the pearly cup.
   Thou dost desire,
With all thy trembling heart of sinless fire,
   But to be filled
   With dew distilled
From clear, fond skies that in their gloom

Hold, floating high, thy sister moon.
Pale chalice of a sweet perfume,
Whiter-breasted than a dove,
To thee the dew is—love!"

Kate bared her little feet and poised herself
On the first log close grating on the shore;
And with bright eyes of laughter and wild hair—
A flying wind of gold—from log to log
Sped, laughing as they wallowed in her track
Like brown-scaled monsters, rolling as her foot
Spurned deftly each in turn with rose-white sole.
A little island, out in middle wave,
With its green shoulder held the great drive braced
Between it and the mainland,—here it was
The silver lilies drew her with white smiles—
And as she touched the last great log of all
It reeled, upstarting, like a column braced
A second on the wave, and when it plunged
Rolling upon the froth and sudden foam,
Katie had vanished, and with angry grind
The vast logs rolled together; nor a lock
Of drifting, yellow hair, an upflung hand,
Told where the rich man's chiefest treasure sank
Under his wooden wealth.

                       But Alfred, prone
With pipe and book upon the shady marge
Of the cool isle, saw all, and seeing hurled
Himself, and hardly knew it, on the logs.
By happy chance a shallow lapped the isle
On this green bank; and when his iron arms
Dashed the barked monsters, as frail stems of rice,
A little space apart, the soft, slow tide

212

But reached his chest, and in a flash he saw
Kate's yellow hair, and by it drew her up,
And lifting her aloft, cried out, " O Kate!"
And once again cried, " Katie! is she dead?"
For like the lilies broken by the rough
And sudden riot of the armoured logs,
Kate lay upon his hands; and now the logs
Closed in upon him, nipping his great chest,
Nor could he move to push them off again
For Katie in his arms.   " And now," he said,
" If none should come, and any wind arise
To weld these woody monsters 'gainst the isle,
I shall be cracked like any broken twig;
And as it is, I know not if I die,
For I am hurt—ay, sorely, sorely hurt!"
Then looked on Katie's lily face, and said,
" Dead, dead or living?   Why, an even chance.
O lovely bubble on a troubled sea,
I would not thou shouldst lose thyself again
In the black ocean whence thy life emerged,
But skyward steal on gales as soft as love,
And hang in some bright rainbow overhead,
If only such bright rainbow spanned the earth."
Then shouted loudly, till the silent air
Roused like a frightened bird, and on its wings
Caught up his cry and bore it to the farm.
There Malcolm, leaping from his noontide sleep,
Upstarted as at midnight, crying out,
" She shall not wed him!   Rest you, wife, in peace!"

They found him, Alfred, haggard-eyed and faint,
But holding Katie ever toward the sun,
Unhurt, and waking in the fervent heat.
And now it came that Alfred, being sick
Of his sharp hurts and tended by them both

213

With what was like to love—being born of thanks—
Had choice of hours most politic to woo,
And used his deed, as one might use the sun
To ripe unmellowed fruit; and from the core
Of Katie's gratitude hoped yet to nurse
A flower all to his liking—Katie's love.

But Katie's mind was like the plain, broad shield
Of a table diamond, nor had a score of sides;
And in its shield, so precious and so plain,
Was cut thro' all its clear depths Max's name.
And so she said him " Nay " at last, in words
Of such true-sounding silver that he knew
He might not win her at the present hour,
But smiled and thought, " I go, and come again;
Then shall we see.   Our three-score years and ten
Are mines of treasure, if we hew them deep,
Nor stop too long in choosing out our tools."

PART IV.

From his far wigwam sprang the strong North Wind
And rushed with war-cry down the steep ravines,
And wrestled with the giants of the woods;
And with his ice-club beat the swelling crests
Of the deep watercourses into death;
And with his chill foot froze the whirling leaves
Of dun and gold and fire in icy banks;
And smote the tall reeds to the hardened earth,
And sent his whistling arrows o'er the plains,
Scattering the lingering herds; and sudden paused,
When he had frozen all the running streams,
And hunted with his war-cry all the things

That breathed about the woods, or roamed the bleak,
Bare prairies swelling to the mournful sky.

" White squaw !" he shouted, troubled in his soul,
" I slew the dead, unplumed before; wrestled
With naked chiefs scalped of their leafy plumes;
I bound sick rivers in cold thongs of death,
And shot my arrows over swooning plains,
Bright with the paint of death, and lean and bare.
And all the braves of my loud tribe will mock
And point at me when our great chief, the Sun,
Relights his council fire in the Moon
Of Budding Leaves: ' Ugh, ugh! he is a brave!
He fights with squaws and takes the scalps of babes !'
And the least wind will blow his calumet,
Filled with the breath of smallest flowers, across
The war-paint on my face, and pointing with
His small, bright pipe, that never moved a spear
Of bearded rice, cry, ' Ugh! he slays the dead !'
O my white squaw, come from thy wigwam grey,
Spread thy white blanket on the twice-slain dead,
And hide them ere the waking of the Sun !"

High grew the snow beneath the low-hung sky,
And all was silent in the wilderness;
In trance of stillness Nature heard her God
Rebuilding her spent fires, and veiled her face
While the Great Worker brooded o'er His work.

" Bite deep and wide, O Axe, the tree !
What doth thy bold voice promise me ?"

" I promise thee all joyous things
That furnish forth the lives of kings;

215

" For every silver ringing blow
  Cities and palaces shall grow."

" Bite deep and wide, O Axe, the tree!
  Tell wider prophecies to me."

" When rust hath gnawed me deep and red
  A nation strong shall lift his head.

" His crown the very heavens shall smite,
  Æons shall build him in his might."

" Bite deep and wide, O Axe, the tree!
  Bright Seer, help on thy prophecy!"

Max smote the snow-weighed tree and lightly laughed.
" See, friend," he cried to one that looked and smiled,
" My axe and I, we do immortal tasks;
We build up nations—this my axe and I."

" Oh!" said the other with a cold, short smile,
  " Nations are not immortal.   Is there now
One nation throned upon the sphere of earth
That walked with the first gods and with them saw
The budding world unfold its slow-leaved flower?
Nay, it is hardly theirs to leave behind
Ruins so eloquent that the hoary sage
Can lay his hand upon their stones and say:
' These once were thrones!'

                    " The lean, lank lion peals
His midnight thunders over lone, red plains,
Long-ridged and crested on their dusty waves
With fires from moons red-hearted as the sun,

And deep re-thunders all the earth to him;
For, far beneath the flame-flecked, shifting sands,
Below the roots of palms, and under stones
Of younger ruins, thrones, towers and cities
Honeycomb the earth.   The high, solemn walls
Of hoary ruins—their foundings all unknown
But to the round-eyed worlds that walk
In the blank paths of Space and blanker Chance—
At whose stones young mountains wonder, and the
      seas'
New-silvering, deep-set valleys pause and gaze—
Are reared upon old shrines whose very gods
Were dreams to the shrine-builders of a time
They caught in far-off flashes—as the child
Half thinks he can remember how one came
And took him in her hand and showed him that,
He thinks, she called the sun.

                    " Proud ships rear high
On ancient billows that have torn the roots
Of cliffs, and bitten at the golden lips
Of firm, sleek beaches, till they conquered all
And sowed the reeling earth with salted waves;
Wrecks plunge, prow foremost, down still, solemn
      slopes,
And bring their dead crews to as dead a quay—
Some city built, before that ocean grew,
By silver drops from many a floating cloud,
By icebergs bellowing in their throes of death,
By lesser seas tossed from their rocking cups,
And leaping each to each; by dewdrops flung
From painted sprays, whose weird leaves and flowers
Are moulded for new dwellers on the earth,
Printed in hearts of mountains and of mines.

217

" Nations immortal?   Where the well-trimmed lamps
Of long-past ages?   When Time seemed to pause
On smooth, dust-blotted graves that, like the tombs
Of monarchs, held dead bones and sparkling gems,
She saw no glimmer on the hideous ring
Of the black clouds; no stream of sharp, clear light
From those great torches passed into the black
Of deep oblivion.   She seemed to watch, but she
Forgot her long-dead nations.   When she stirred
Her vast limbs in the dawn that forced its fire
Up the black East, and saw the imperious red
Burst over virgin dews and budding flowers,
She still forgot her mouldered thrones and kings,
Her sages and their torches and their gods,
And said, ' This is my birth—my primal day!'
She dreamed new gods, and reared them other shrines,
Planted young nations, smote a feeble flame
From sunless flint, re-lit the torch of mind.
Again she hung her cities on the hills,
Built her rich towers, crowned her kings again;
And with the sunlight on her awful wings
Swept round the flowery cestus of the earth,
And said, ' I build for Immortality!'
Her vast hand reared her towers, her shrines, her
        thrones;
The ceaseless sweep of her tremendous wings
Still beat them down and swept their dust abroad.
Her iron finger wrote on mountain sides
Her deeds and prowess, and her own soft plume
Wore down the hills.   Again drew darkly on
A night of deep forgetfulness; once more
Time seemed to pause upon forgotten graves;
Once more a young dawn stole into her eyes;
Again her broad wings stirred, and fresh, clear airs
Blew the great clouds apart; again she said,

' This is my birth—my deeds and handiwork
Shall be immortal!' Thus and so dream on
Fooled nations, and thus dream their dullard sons.
Naught is immortal save immortal—Death!"

Max paused and smiled: " O preach such gospel,
      friend,
To all but lovers who most truly love;
For *them*, their gold-wrought scripture glibly reads,
All else is mortal but immortal—Love!"

" Fools! fools!" his friend said, " most immortal fools!
But pardon, pardon, for perchance you love?"

" Yes," said Max, proudly smiling, " thus do I
Possess the world and feel eternity."

Dark laughter blackened in the other's eyes:
" Eternity! why did such Iris arch
Enter our worm-bored planet? Never lived
One woman true enough such tryst to keep."

" I'd swear by Kate," said Max; " and then I had
A mother, and my father swore by her."

" By Kate? Ah, that were lusty oath, indeed!
Some other man will look into her eyes
And swear me roundly, ' By true Catherine!'
As Troilus swore by Cressèd—so they say."

" You never knew my Kate," said Max, and poised
His axe again on high; " but let it pass.
You are too subtle for me; argument
Have I none to oppose yours with but this:

Get you a Kate, and let her sunny eyes
Dispel the doubting darkness in your soul."

" And have not I a Kate?   Pause, friend, and see.
She gave me this faint shadow of herself
The day I slipped the watch-star of our loves—
A ring—upon her hand; she loves me, too.
Yet tho' her eyes be suns, no gods are they
To give me worlds, or make me feel a tide
Of strong eternity set toward my soul;
And tho' she loves me, yet am I content
To know she loves me by the hour, the year,
Perchance the second—as all women love."

The bright axe faltered in the air and ripped
Down the rough bark and bit the drifted snow,
For Max's arm fell, withered in its strength,
'Long by his side.   " Your Kate," he said, " your
    Kate?"

" Yes, mine—while holds her mind that way, my Kate;
I saved her life, and had her love for thanks.
Her father is Malcolm Graem—Max, my friend,
You pale!   What sickness seizes on your soul?"

Max laughed, and swung his bright axe high again:
" Stand back a pace; a too far-reaching blow
Might level your false head with yon prone trunk!
Stand back and listen while I say, ' You lie!'
That is my Katie's face upon your breast,
But 'tis my Katie's love lives in my breast!
Stand back, I say! my axe is heavy, and
Might chance to cleave a liar's brittle skull!
Your Kate! your Kate! your Kate!—hark, how the
    woods

220

Mock at your lie with all their woody tongues!
O silence, ye false echoes! Not his Kate
But mine—I'm certain! I will have your life!"
All the blue heaven was dead in Max's eyes;
Doubt-wounded lay Kate's image in his heart,
And could not rise to pluck the sharp spear out.

" Well, strike, mad fool," said Alfred, somewhat pale;
" I have no weapon but these naked hands!"

" Ay, but," said Max, " you smote my naked heart!
O shall I slay him? Satan, answer me;
I cannot call on God for answer here!
O Kate—!"

A voice from God came thro' the silent woods
And answered him; for suddenly a wind
Caught the great tree-tops, coned with high-piled
      snow,
And smote them to and fro, while all the air
Was sudden filled with busy drifts; and high
White pillars whirled amid the naked trunks,
And harsh, loud groans, and smiting, sapless boughs
Made hellish clamour in the quiet place.
With a shrill shriek of tearing fibres, rocked
The half-hewn tree above his fated head,
And, tott'ring, asked the sudden blast, " Which way?"
And, answering, its windy arms down crashed
Thro' other lacing boughs with one loud roar
Of woody thunder. All its pointed boughs
Pierced the deep snow; its round and mighty corpse,
Bark-flayed and shudd'ring, quivered into death.
And Max, as some frail, withered reed, the sharp
And piercing branches caught at him, as hands

221

In a death-throe, and beat him to the earth;
And the dead tree upon its slayer lay.

" Yet hear we much of gods! If such there be,
They play at games of chance with thunderbolts,"
Said Alfred, " else on me this doom had come.
This seals my faith in deep and dark unfaith.
Now, Katie, are you mine, for Max is dead—
Or will be soon, imprisoned by those boughs,
Wounded and torn, soothed by the deadly palms
Of the white, traitorous frost; and buried then
Under the snows that fill those vast, grey clouds,
Low sweeping on the fretted forest roof.
And Katie shall believe you false—not dead.
False, false!—And I? O she shall find me true—
True as a fabled devil to the soul
He longs for with the heat of all Hell's fires.
These myths serve well for simile, I see,
And yet—down, Pity! knock not at my breast,
Nor grope about for that dull stone, my heart.
I'll stone thee with it, Pity! Get thee hence!
Pity, I'll strangle thee with naked hands;
For thou dost bear upon thy downy breast
Remorse, shaped like a serpent, and her fangs
Might dart at me and pierce my marrow thro'!
Hence, beggar, hence—and keep with fools, I say!
He bleeds and groans! Well, Max, thy God or mine,
Blind Chance, here played the butcher—'twas not I.
Down, hands! ye shall not lift his fallen head!
What cords tug at ye? What? Ye'd pluck him up
And staunch his wounds? There rises in my breast
A strange, strong giant, throwing wide his arms
And bursting all the granite of my heart.
How like to quivering flesh a stone may feel!
Why, it has pangs! I'll none of them! I know

Life is too short for anguish and for hearts!
So I wrestle with thee, giant, and my will
Turns the thumb, and thou shalt take the knife!
Well done! I'll turn thee on the arena dust
And look on thee—What? thou wert Pity's self,
Stolen in my breast; and I have slaughtered thee!
But hist! where hast thou hidden thy fell snake,
Fire-fanged Remorse? Not in my breast, I know,
For all again is chill and empty there,
And hard and cold—the granite knitted up!

" So lie there, Max—poor fond and simple Max!
'Tis well thou diest! Earth's children should not call
Such as thee father—let them ever be
Fathered by rogues and villains fit to cope
With the black dragon Chance and the black knaves
Who swarm in loathsome masses in the dust!
True Max, lie there, and slumber into death!"

Part V.

Said the high hill, in the morning, " Look on me!
Behold, sweet earth, sweet sister sky, behold
The red flames on my peaks, and how my pines
Are cressets of pure gold, my quarried scars
Of black crevasse and shadow-filled canyon
Are traced in silver mist. Now on my breast
Hang the soft purple fringes of the night;
Close to my shoulder droops the weary moon,
Dove-pale, into the crimson surf the sun
Drives up before his prow; and blackly stands
On my slim, loftiest peak an eagle with
His angry eyes set sunward, while his cry

Falls fiercely back from all my ruddy heights,
And his bald eaglets, in their bare, broad nest,
Shrill pipe their angry echoes: ' Sun, arise,
And show me that pale dove beside her nest,
Which I shall strike with piercing beak and tear
With iron talons for my hungry young!'

" And that mild dove, secure for yet a space,
    Half wakened, turns her ringed and glossy neck
To watch dawn's ruby pulsing on my breast,
    And see the first bright golden motes slip down
The gnarlèd trunks about her leaf-deep nest,
    Nor sees nor fears the eagle on the peak."

" Ay, lassie, sing! I'll smoke my pipe the while;
    And let it be a simple, bonnie song,
Such as an old, plain man can gather in
    His dulling ear, and feel it slipping thro'
The cold, dark, stony places of his heart."

" Yes, sing, sweet Kate," said Alfred in her ear;
    " I often heard you singing in my dreams
When I was far away the winter past."
So Katie on the moonlit window leaned,
And in the airy silver of her voice
Sang of the tender blue Forget-me-not:

        Could every blossom find a voice
            And sing a strain to me,
        I know where I would place my choice,
            Which my delight should be.
        I would not choose the lily tall,
            The rose from musky grot,

But I would still my minstrel call
  The blue Forget-me-not.

And I on mossy bank would lie,
  Of brooklet, rippling clear;
And she of the sweet azure eye,
  Close at my listening ear,
Should sing into my soul a strain
  Might never be forgot—
So rich with joy, so rich with pain,
  The blue Forget-me-not.

Ah, every blossom hath a tale,
  With silent grace to tell,
From rose that reddens to the gale
  To modest heather-bell;
But O the flower in every heart
  That finds a sacred spot
To bloom, with azure leaves apart,
  Is the Forget-me-not.

Love plucks it from the mosses green
  When parting hours are nigh,
And places it Love's palms between
  With many an ardent sigh;
And bluely up from grassy graves
  In some loved churchyard spot,
It glances tenderly and waves—
  The dear Forget-me-not.

And with the faint, last cadence stole a glance
At Malcolm's softened face—a bird-soft touch
Let flutter on the rugged, silver snarls
Of his thick locks—and laid her tender lips
A second on the iron of his hand.

" And did you ever meet," he sudden asked
  Of Alfred, sitting pallid in the shade,
  " Out by yon unco place, a lad,—a lad
  Named Maxwell Gordon; tall and straight and strong;
  About my size, I take it, when a lad?"

And Katie at the sound of Max's name,
  First spoken for such space by Malcolm's lips,
  Trembled and started, and let down her brow,
  Hiding its sudden rose on Malcolm's arm.

" Max Gordon?   Yes.   Was he a friend of yours?"

" No friend of mine, but of the lassie's here.
  How comes he on?   I wager he's a drone,
  And never will put honey in the hive."

" No drone," said Alfred, laughing; " when I left,
  He and his axe were quarreling with the woods
  And making forests reel.   Love steels a lover's arm."

O blush that stole from Katie's swelling heart,
  And with its hot rose brought the happy dew
  Into her hidden eyes!

                    " Ay, ay! is that the way?"
  Said Malcolm, smiling. " Who may be his love?"

" In that he is a somewhat simple soul;
  Why, I suppose he loves—" he paused, and Kate
  Looked up with two forget-me-nots for eyes,
  With eager jewels in their centres set
  Of happy, happy tears, and Alfred's heart
  Became a closer marble than before—

226

" Why, I suppose he loves—his lawful wife."

" His wife! his wife!" said Malcolm, in amaze,
  And laid his heavy hand on Katie's head;
   " Did you two play me false, my little lass?
  Speak and I'll pardon. Katie, lassie, what?"

" He has a wife," said Alfred, " lithe and bronzed,
  An Indian woman, comelier than her kind,
  And on her knee a child with yellow locks,
  And lake-like eyes of mystic Indian brown."

" And so you knew him; he is doing well?"
" False, false!" cried Katie, lifting up her head;
" Oh, you know not the Max my father means!"
" He came from yonder farm-house on the slope."
" Some other Max—we speak not of the same."
" He has a red mark on his temple set."
" It matters not—'tis not the Max we know."
" He wears a turquoise ring slung round his neck."
" And many wear them; they are common stones."
" His mother's ring—her name was Helen Wynde."
" And there be many Helens who have sons."
" O Katie, credit me—it is the man!"
" O not the man! Why, you have never told
  Us of the true soul that the true Max has;
  The Max we know has such a soul, I know."

" How know you that, my foolish little lass?"
  Her father said, a storm of anger bound
  Within his heart like Samson with green withes;
  " Belike it is the false young cur we know."

" No, no," said Katie, simply, and low-voiced,
  " If he be traitor I must needs be false,

For long ago love melted our two hearts,
And time has moulded those two hearts in one,
And he is true since I am faithful still."
She rose and parted, trembling as she went,
Feeling the following steel of Alfred's eyes,
And with the icy hand of scorned mistrust
Searching about the pulses of her heart,
Feeling for Max's image in her breast.

" Tonight she conquers Doubt; tomorrow's noon
His following soldiers sap the golden wall,
And I shall enter and possess the fort,"
Said Alfred, in his mind.   " O Katie, child,
Wilt thou be Nemesis with yellow hair
To rend my breast? for I do feel a pulse
Stir when I look into thy pure-barbed eyes.
Oh, am I breeding that false thing, a heart,
Making my breast all tender for the fangs
Of sharp Remorse to plunge their hot fire in?
I am a certain dullard.   Let me feel
But one faint goad, fine as a needle's point,
And it shall be the spur in my soul's side
To urge the maddening thing across the jags
And cliffs of life into the soft embrace
Of that cold mistress, who is constant, too,
And never flings her lovers from her arms,—
Not Death, for she is still a fruitful wife,
Her spouse the Dead ; and their cold marriage yields
A million children, born of mouldering flesh.
So Death and Flesh live on; immortal they !
I mean the blank-eyed queen whose wassail bowl
Is brimmed from Lethe, and whose porch is red
With poppies, as it waits the panting soul.
She, she alone is great !   No sceptred slave
Bowing to blind, creative giants, she !

No forces seize her in their strong, mad hands,
Nor say, ' Do this—be that !'   Were there a God,
His only mocker, she, great Nothingness ;
And to her, close of kin, yet lover, too,
Flies this large nothing that we call the soul."

Doth true Love lonely grow?
                                   Ah, no ! ah, no !
Ah, were it only so,
That it alone might show
   Its ruddy rose upon its sapful tree,
      Then, then in dewy morn
      Joy might his brow adorn
   With Love's young rose as fair and glad as he.

But with Love's rose doth blow,
                                   Ah, woe ! ah, woe !
Truth, with its leaves of snow,
And Pain and Pity grow
   With Love's sweet roses on its sapful tree !
      Love's rose buds not alone,
      But still, but still doth own
   A thousand blossoms cypress-hued to see !

Part VI.

Who curseth Sorrow knows her not at all.
Dark matrix she, from which the human soul
Has its last birth ; whence it, with misty thews
Close knitted in her blackness, issues out
Strong for immortal toil up such great heights
As crown o'er crown rise through Eternity.
Without the loud, deep clamour of her wail,

229

The iron of her hands, the biting brine
Of her black tears, the soul, but lightly built
Of indeterminate spirit, like a mist
Would lapse to chaos in soft, gilded dreams,
As mists fade in the gazing of the sun.
Sorrow, dark mother of the soul, arise!
Be crowned with spheres where thy blest children
    dwell,
Who, but for thee, were not. No lesser seat
Be thine, thou Helper of the Universe,
Than planet on planet piled—thou instrument
Close clasped within the great Creative Hand!

The Land had put his ruddy gauntlet on,
Of harvest gold, to dash in Famine's face;
And like a vintage wain deep dyed with juice
The great moon faltered up the ripe, blue sky,
Drawn by silver stars—like oxen white
And horned with rays of light. Down the rich land
Malcolm's small valleys, filled with grain lip high,
Lay round a lonely hill that faced the moon
And caught the wine kiss of its ruddy light.
A cusped, dark wood caught in its black embrace
The valleys and the hill, and from its wilds,
Spiced with dark cedars, cried the whippoorwill.
A crane, belated, sailed across the moon.
On the bright, small, close linked lakes green islets
    lay—
Dusk knots of tangled vines, or maple boughs,
Or tufted cedars, bossed upon the waves.
The gay, enamelled children of the swamp
Rolled a low bass to treble, tinkling notes
Of little streamlets leaping from the woods.
Close to old Malcolm's mills two wooden jaws

MALCOLM'S KATIE

Bit up the water on a sloping floor;
And here, in season, rushed the great logs down
To seek the river winding on its way.
In a green sheen, smooth as a naiad's locks,
The water rolled between the shuddering jaws,
Then on the river level roared and reeled
In ivory-armèd conflict with itself.

"Look down," said Alfred, "Katie, look and see
How that but pictures my mad heart to you.
It tears itself in fighting that mad love
You swear is hopeless. Hopeless—is it so?"
"Ah, yes," said Katie, "ask me not again!"
"But Katie, Max is false; no word has come,
Nor any sign from him for many months,
And—he is happy with his Indian wife."

She lifted eyes fair as the fresh, grey dawn
With all its dews and promises of sun.
"O Alfred, saver of my little life,
Look in my eyes and read them honestly!"
He laughed till all the isles and forests laughed.
"O simple child! what may the forest flames
See in the woodland ponds but their own fires?
And have you, Katie, neither fears nor doubts?"
She with the flower-soft pinkness of her palm
Covered her sudden tears, then quickly said,
"Fears—never doubts, for true love never doubts."

Then Alfred paused a space, as one who holds
A white doe by the throat and searches for
The blade to slay her. "This your answer still?
You doubt not—doubt not this far love of yours,
Tho' sworn a false young recreant, Kate, by me?"
"He is as true as I am," Katie said,

" And did I seek for stronger simile
I could not find such in the universe."
" And were he dead? what, Katie, were he dead—
A handful of brown dust, a flame blown out—
What then? would love be strongly true to—
    naught?"
" Still true to love my love would be," she said,
And, faintly smiling, pointed to the stars.

" O fool!" said Alfred, stirred as craters rock
To their own throes, while over his pale lips
Rolled flaming stone—his molten heart. " Then, fool,
Be true to what thou wilt, for he is dead,
And there have grown this gilded summer past
Grasses and buds from his unburied flesh!
I saw him dead. I heard his last, loud cry,
' O Kate!' ring thro' the woods; in truth I did!"
She half-raised up a piteous, pleading hand,
Then fell along the mosses at his feet.

" Now will I show I love you, Kate," he said,
" And give you gift of love; you shall not wake
To feel the arrow feather-deep within
Your constant heart. For me, I never meant
To crawl an hour beyond what time I felt
The strange fanged monster that they call Remorse
Fold round my wakened heart. The hour has come;
And as Love grew the welded folds of steel
Slipped round in horrid zones. In Love's flaming
    eyes
Stared its fell eyeballs, and with hydra head
It sank hot fangs in breast and brow and thigh.
Come, Kate! O Anguish is a simple knave
Whom hucksters could outwit with small trade lies,
When thus so easily his smarting thralls

May flee his knout!   Come, come, my little Kate;
The black porch with its fringe of poppies waits,—
A propylæum hospitably wide,—
No lictors with their fasces at its jaws,
Its floor as kindly to my fire-veined feet
As to thy silver-lilied, sinless ones!
O you shall slumber soundly, tho' the white,
Wild waters pluck the crocus of your hair,
And scaly spies stare with round, lightless eyes
At your small face laid on my stony breast!
Come, Kate; I must not have you wake, dear heart,
To hear you cry, perchance, on your dead Max!"

He turned her still face close upon his breast,
And with his lips upon her soft-ringed hair
Leaped from the bank, low shelving o'er the knot
Of frantic waters at the long slide's foot.
And as the severed waters crashed and smote
Together once again, within the wave-
Stunned chamber of his ear there pealed a cry,
"O Kate!   Stay, madman, traitor, stay!   O Kate!"

Max, gaunt as prairie wolves in famine time
With long-drawn sickness, reeled upon the bank,
Katie, new rescued, waking in his arms.
On the white riot of the waters gleamed
The face of Alfred, calm, with close sealed eyes,
And blood red on his temple where it smote
The mossy timbers of the groaning slide.

" O God!" cried Max, as Katie's opening eyes
   Looked up to his, slow budding to a smile
   Of wonder and of bliss, " my Kate, my Kate!"
She saw within his eyes a larger soul
Than that light spirit that before she knew,

And read the meaning of his glance and words.
" Do as you will, my Max; I would not keep
You back with one light falling finger-tip!"
And cast herself from his large arms upon
The mosses at his feet, and hid her face
That she might not behold what he would do;
Or lest the terror in her shining eyes
Might bind him to her, and prevent his soul
Work out its greatness; and her long, wet hair
Drew massed about her ears, to shut the sound
Of the vexed waters from her anguished brain.

Max looked upon her, turning as he looked.
A moment came a voice in Katie's soul:
" Arise, be not dismayed, arise and look;
If he shall perish, 'twill be as a god,
For he will die to save his enemy."
But answered her torn heart: " I cannot look—
I cannot look and see him sob and die
In those pale, angry arms. O let me rest
Blind, blind and deaf until the swift-paced end.
My Max! O God! was that his Katie's name?"
Like a pale dove, hawk-hunted, Katie ran,
Her fear's beak in her shoulder; and below,
Where the coiled waters straightened to a stream,
Found Max all bruised and bleeding on the bank,
But smiling with man's triumph in his eyes
When he has on fierce Danger's lion neck
Placed his right hand and plucked the prey away.
And at his feet lay Alfred, still and white,
A willow's shadow trembling on his face.
" There lies the false, fair devil, O my Kate,
Who would have parted us, but could not, Kate!"
" But could not, Max," said Katie. " Is he dead?"
But, swift perusing Max's strange, dear face,

Close clasped against his breast, forgot him straight
And every other evil thing upon
The broad green earth.

Part VII.

Again rang out the music of the axe,
And on the slope, as in his happy dreams,
The home of Max with wealth of drooping vines
On the rude walls, and in the trellised porch
Sat Katie, smiling o'er the rich, fresh fields.
And by her side sat Malcolm, hale and strong,
Upon his knee a little smiling child
Named—Alfred, as the seal of pardon set
Upon the heart of one who sinned and woke
To sorrow for his sins; and whom they loved
With gracious joyousness, nor kept the dusk
Of his past deeds between their hearts and his.
Malcolm had followed with his flocks and herds
When Max and Katie, hand in hand, went out
From his old home; and now, with slow, grave smile,
He said to Max, who twisted Katie's hair
About his naked arm, bare from his toil:
" It minds me of old times, this house of yours;
It stirs my heart to hearken to the axe,
And hear the windy crash of falling trees.
Ay, these fresh forests make an old man young."

" Oh, yes !" said Max, with laughter in his eyes;
" And I do truly think that Eden bloomed
Deep in the heart of tall, green maple groves,
With sudden scents of pine from mountain sides,
And prairies with their breasts against the skies.
And Eve was only little Katie's height."

" Hoot, lad ! you speak as every Adam speaks
  About his bonnie Eve ; but what says Kate ? "

" Oh, Adam had not Max's soul," she said ;
  " And these wild woods and plains are fairer far
  Than Eden's self. O bounteous mothers they,
  Beckoning pale starvelings with their fresh, green
      hands,
  And with their ashes mellowing the earth,
  That she may yield her increase willingly !
  I would not change these wild and rocking woods,
  Dotted by little homes of unbarked trees,
  Where dwell the fleers from the waves of want,
  For the smooth sward of selfish Eden bowers,
  Nor—Max for Adam, if I knew my mind ! "

CANADA TO ENGLAND.

GONE are the days, old Warrior of the Seas,
When thine armed head, bent low to catch my voice,
Caught but the plaintive sighings of my woods,
And the wild roar of rock-dividing streams,
And the loud bellow of my cataracts,
Bridged with the seven splendours of the bow.
When Nature was a Samson yet unshorn,
Filling the land with solitary might,
Or as the Angel of the Apocalypse,
One foot upon the primeval bowered land,
One foot upon the white mane of the sea,
My voice but faintly swelled the ebb and flow
Of the wild tides and storms that beat upon
Thy rocky girdle,—loud shrieking from the Ind
Ambrosial-breathing furies; from the north
Thundering with Arctic bellows, groans of seas

CANADA TO ENGLAND

Rising from tombs of ice disrupted by
The magic kisses of the wide-eyed sun.

The times have won a change.   Nature no more
Lords it alone and binds the lonely land
A serf to tongueless solitudes; but Nature's self
Is led, glad captive, in light fetters rich
As music-sounding silver can adorn;
And man has forged them, and our silent God
Behind His flaming worlds smiles on the deed.
" Man hath dominion "—words of primal might;
" Man hath dominion "—thus the words of God.

If destiny is writ on night's dusk scroll,
Then youngest stars are dropping from the hand
Of the Creator, sowing on the sky
My name in seeds of light.   Ages will watch
Those seeds expand to suns, such as the tree
Bears on its boughs, which grows in Paradise.

How sounds my voice, my warrior kinsman, now?
Sounds it not like to thine in lusty youth—
A world-possessing shout of busy men,
Veined with the clang of trumpets and the noise
Of those who make them ready for the strife,
And in the making ready bruise its head?
Sounds it not like to thine—the whispering vine,
The robe of summer rustling thro' the fields,
The lowing of the cattle in the meads,
The sound of Commerce, and the music-set,
Flame-brightened step of Art in stately halls,—
All the infinity of notes which chord
The diapason of a Nation's voice?

My infants' tongues lisp word for word with thine;
We worship, wed, and die, and God is named
That way ye name Him,—strong bond between
Two mighty lands when as one mingled cry,
As of one voice, Jehovah turns to hear.
The bonds between us are no subtle links
Of subtle minds binding in close embrace,
Half-struggling for release, two alien lands,
But God's own seal of kindred, which to burst
Were but to dash His benediction from
Our brows. " Who loveth not his kin,
Whose face and voice are his, how shall he love
God whom he hath not seen ?"

TORONTO.

SHE moves to meet the centuries, her feet
All shod with emerald, and her light robe
Fringed with leaves singing in the jazel air.
Her tire is rich, not with stout battlements,
Prophets of strife, but wealthy with tall spires
All shining Godward, rare with learning's domes,
And burning with young stars that promise suns
To clasp her older brows. On her young breast
Lie linked the fair, clear pearls of many homes,—
Mighty and lovely chain, from its white strength
Hangs on her heart the awful jewel, Hope.

She moves to meet the centuries, nor lies
All languid waiting, with the murmuring kiss
Of the large waters on white, nerveless feet,
And dim, tranced gaze upon the harbour bar,
And dusk, still boughs knit over her prone head,

TORONTO

And rose-soft hands that idly pluck the turf,
And rose lips singing idly thro' her dream.

She hears the marching centuries which Time
Leads up the dark peaks of Eternity:
The pulses of past warriors bound in her;
The pulses of dead sages beat in her;
The pulses of dead merchants stir in her;
The roses of her young feet turn to flame,
Yet ankle-deep in tender buds of spring;
Till, with the perfumes of close forests thick
Upon her tender flesh, she to her lips
Lifts the bold answering trump, and, winding shrill
With voices of her people and her waves
Notes of quick joy, half queen, half child, she bounds
To meet the coming Time, and climbs the steps
Of the tall throne he builds upon her strand.

Toronto, joy and peace! When comes the day
Close domes of marble rich with gold leap up
From porphyry pillars to the eye-clear sky,
And when the wealthy fringes of thy robe
Sweep outward league on league, and to thee come
The years all bowed with treasures for thy house,
On lusty shoulders, still remember thee
Of thy first cradle on the lilies' lap
In the dim woods; and tho' thy diadem
Make a new sunrise, still, amid its flame,
Twine for the nursing lilies' sake the glow
Of God-like lilies round about thy brows—
Honour and Peace and sweet-breathed Charity!

SAID THE WEST WIND.

I LOVE old earth! Why should I lift my wings,
My misty wings, so high above her breast
That flowers would shake no perfumes from their
    hearts,
And waters breathe no whispers to the shores?
I love deep places builded high with woods,
Deep, dusk, fern-closed, and starred with nodding
    blooms,
Close watched by hills, green, garlanded and tall.

On hazy wings, all shot with mellow gold,
I float, I float thro' shadows clear as glass;
With perfumed feet I wander o'er the seas,
And touch white sails with gentle finger-tips;
I blow the faithless butterfly against
The rose-red thorn, and thus avenge the rose;
I whisper low amid the solemn boughs,
And stir a leaf where not my loudest sigh
Could move the emerald branches from their calm,—
Leaves, leaves, I love ye much, for ye and I
Do make sweet music over all the earth!

I dream by glassy ponds, and, lingering, kiss
The gold crowns of their lilies one by one,
As mothers kiss their babes who be asleep
On the clear gilding of their infant heads,
Lest if they kissed the dimple on the chin,
The rose flecks on the cheek or dewy lips,
The calm of sleep might feel the touch of love,
And so be lost. I steal before the rain,
The longed-for guest of summer; as his fringe
Of mist drifts slowly from the mountain peaks,

ESTHER

The flowers dance to my fairy pipe and fling
Rich odours on my wings, and voices cry,
"The dear West Wind is damp, and rich with scent;
We shall have fruits and yellow sheaves for this."

At night I play amid the silver mists,
And chase them on soft feet until they climb
And dance their gilded plumes against the stars;
At dawn the last round primrose star I hide
By wafting o'er her some small fleck of cloud,
And ere it passes comes the broad, bold Sun
And blots her from the azure of the sky,
As later, toward his noon, he blots a drop
Of pollen-gilded dew from violet cup
Set bluely in the mosses of the wood.

ESTHER.

UNHEARD of others, voices called all night:—
The babble of young voices, the strong cries
Of men and women mourned amid the palms,
And gathered in mine ear, as winds that blow
About the earth and, gathering in some cave,
Give ghostly utterance of ghostly things—
"Esther, the Queen, arise and move the King
To sheathe the sword that lies upon the throats
Of thine own people!"

       When the sun sprang up
His tresses were as blood that stained the courts
And beat upon the walls, and sent its tide
To bathe my naked feet when I thrust back
The golden tissue of the door to catch

16   241

Some sweetness of the morn upon my brow;
And lo! my God, a sweetness filled my soul
That came not from the morning but from Thee!

The winds that stirred the foldings of my robe
Were children's fingers—ghostly, clinging clasps
That said, " O Esther, plead before the King!"
Ah me! how often when a little maid,
Playing amid the fountains and the flowers
Of mine own people, have such dimpled hands
Caught at my flying robe in mimic fright,
And great round eyes buried themselves therein;
But then the voices laughed, " O Esther, stay
That wicked brother, for he chases us,
And pelts with blushing roses."   Now I hear,
" O Esther, stay the King, he slaughters us!"

Alas! my courage is so weak a blade
It trembles at a breath.   God, temper it to strength!
I perish if I go uncalled before the King.
Yea! let him smite me down a sacrifice
For Israel! Perchance that, dying thus, my blood
May creep about his heart and soften it
To those for whom I die. O God, when Thou
Didst veil Thy handmaid's soul in this fair flesh
'Twas for some strait sore as the present need!

What is it that glimmers ready by my couch?
The symbol of my state, the crown the King
Hath set upon my brows. On, crown, and deck
My triumph or my death! O robes of state,
Ye jewelled splendours, how ye mock this flesh
That quivers with monitions of that hour
When this night's moon shall peer above the palms
And find no life in Esther but that cold, cold life,

242

BETWEEN THE WIND AND RAIN

Blazing from diamond crown and golden robe,
Mocks of her life's brief sun and briefer state.

But still will Esther go. Jehovah calls!
And if I die—Hark! as I go by court
And golden pillar, sweet, shrill voices cry,
Unheard of others, " Esther, stay the King!"
O yea, my lambs of Israel! how your hands
Cling to my robes and pluck me to the King!
God, lift his sceptre up before my face!
But if I die—I die!

BETWEEN THE WIND AND RAIN.

" THE storm is in the air," she said, and held
Her soft palm to the breeze; and, looking up,
Swift sunbeams brushed the crystal of her eyes,
As swallows leave the skies to skim the brown,
Bright, woodland lakes. " The rain is in the air.
O Prophet Wind, what hast thou told the rose
That suddenly she loosens her red heart
And sends long perfumed sighs about the place?
O Prophet Wind, what hast thou told the swift
That from the airy eave she, shadow-grey,
Smites the blue pond and speeds her glancing wing
Close to the daffodils? What hast thou told small
    bells
And tender buds that—all unlike the rose—
They draw green leaves close, close about their breasts
And shrink to sudden slumber? The sycamores
In every leaf are eloquent with thee,
The poplars busy all their silver tongues
With answering thee, and the round chestnut stirs
Vastly but softly at thy prophecies.

The vines grow dusky with a deeper green
And with their tendrils snatch thy passing harp
And keep it by brief seconds in their leaves.

" O Prophet Wind, thou tellest of the rain,
  While, jacinth-blue, the broad sky folds calm palms,
  Unwitting of all storm, high o'er the land!
  The little grasses and the ruddy heath
  Know of the coming rain; but toward the sun
  The eagle lifts his eyes, and with his wings
  Beats on a sunlight that is never marred
  By cloud or mist, shrieks his fierce joy to air
  Ne'er stirred by stormy pulse."

" The eagle mine," I said, " oh, I would ride
  His wings like Ganymede, nor ever care
  To drop upon the stormy earth again,
  But circle star-ward, narrowing my gyres
  To some great planet of eternal peace."

" Nay," said my wise, young love, " the eagle falls
  Back to his cliff, swift as a thunder-bolt;
  For there his mate and naked eaglets dwell,
  And there he rends the dove, and joys in all
  The fierce delights of his tempestuous home;
  And tho' the stormy earth throbs thro' her poles,
  And rocks with tempests on her circling path,
  And bleak, black clouds snatch at her purple hills,
  While mate and eaglets shriek upon the rock,
  The eagle leaves the hylas to its calm,
  Beats the wild storm apart that rings the earth,
  And seeks his eyrie on the wind-dashed cliff.
  O Prophet Wind, close, close the storm and rain!"

244

BETWEEN THE WIND AND RAIN

Long swayed the grasses like a rolling wave
Above an undertow; the mastiff cried;
Low swept the poplars, groaning in their hearts;
And iron-footed stood the gnarlèd oaks,
And braced their woody thews against the storm.
Lashed from the pond, the ivory cygnets sought
The carven steps that plunged into the pool;
The peacocks screamed and dragged forgotten plumes;
On the sheer turf all shadows subtly died
In one large shadow sweeping o'er the land;
Bright windows in the ivy blushed no more;
The ripe, red walls grew pale, the tall vane dim.
Like a swift offering to an angry god,
O'erweighted vines shook plum and apricot
From trembling trellis, and the rose trees poured
A red libation of sweet, ripened leaves
On the trim walks; to the high dove-cote set
A stream of silver wings and violet breasts,
The hawk-like storm down swooping on their track.

" Go," said my love, " the storm would whirl me off
As thistle-down. I'll shelter there, but you—
You love no storms!"

                        " Where'er thou art," I said,
" Is all the calm I know. Wert thou enthroned
In maelstrom or on pivot of the winds,
Thou holdest in thy hand my palm of peace;
And, like the eagle, I would break the belts
Of shouting tempests to return to thee,
Were I above the storm on mighty wings.
Yet no she-eagle thou! a small, white girl
I clasp and lift and carry from the rain
Across the windy lawn."

ISABELLA VALANCY CRAWFORD

With this I wove
Her floating lace about her floating hair
And crushed her snowy raiment to my breast,
And while she thought of frowns, but smiled instead,
And wrote her heart in crimson on her cheeks,
I bounded with her up the breezy slopes,
The storm about us with such airy din,
As of a thousand bugles, that my heart
Took courage in the clamour, and I laid
My lips upon the flower of her pink ear,
And said, " I love thee; give me love again!"
And here she paled,—love has its dread,—and then
She clasped its joy and reddened in its light,
Till all the daffodils I trod were pale
Beside the small flower red upon my breast.

And ere the dial on the slope was passed,
Between the last loud bugle of the Wind
And the first silver coinage of the rain
Upon my flying hair, there came her kiss
Gentle and pure upon my face—and thus
Were we betrothed between the wind and rain.

CÆSAR'S WIFE.

NAY! swear no more, thou woman whom I called
Star, Empress, Wife! Were Dian's self to lean
From her white altar and with goddess lip
Swear thee as pure as her pale breast divine,
I could not deem thee purer than I know
Thou art indeed.

Once, when my triumphs rolled
Along old Rome and blood of roses washed

CAESAR'S WIFE

The battle-stains from off my chariot-wheels,
And triumph's thunders round my legions roared,
And kings in kingly bondage golden bound
Shook at my charger's foot, past the hot din
Of Victory—whose heart of golden pride is wound
Most subtly through with fire of subtlest pain—
My soul on prouder pinion rose above
The Roman shouting, to an air more clear
Than that Jove darks with hurtling thunderbolts,
Or stains with Jovian revels—that separate sphere,
Unshared of gods or man, where thy white feet
Caught their sole staining from my ruddy heart,
Blazing beneath them ; where, when Rome looked up,
'Twas with the eyes close shaded with the hand,
As at some glory terrible and pure,—
For no man being pure, a terror dwells
Holy and awful in a sinless thing—
And Cæsar's wife, the Empress-Matron, sat
Above a doubt—as high above a stain.

Nay! how know I what hell first belched abroad
Tall flames and slanderous vomitings of smoke,
Blown by infernal breathings, till they scaled
Thy throne of whiteness, and the very slaves
Who crouched in Roman kennels wagged the tongue
Against the wife of Cæsar : " Ha! we need not now
An opal-shaded stone wherewith to view
A stainless glory."   In that day my neck
Was bound and yoked with my twin-Cæsar's yoke—
Man's master, Sorrow.

   I know thee pure—
But Cæsar's wife must throne herself so high
Upon the hills that touch their snowy crests
So close on Heaven that no slanderous Hell

Can dash its lava up their swelling sides.
I love thee, woman, know thee pure, but thou
No more art wife of Cæsar. Get thee hence!
My heart is hardened as a lonely crag,
Grey granite lifted to a greyer sky,
And where against its solitary crown
Eternal thunders bellow.

THE WISHING STAR.

DAY floated down the sky—a perfect day—
Leaving a footprint of pale primrose gold
Along the west that, when her lover, Night,
Fled with his starry lances in pursuit
Across the sky, the way she went might shew.

From the faint-tinged ridges of the sea the Moon
Sprang up like Aphrodite from the wave,
Which, as she climbed the jewelled sky, still held
Her golden tresses to its swelling breast,
Where wide dispread their quivering glories lay,
Or as the shield of Night, full-disked, and red
As flowers that look forever toward the Sun.

A terrace with a fountain and an oak
Looked out upon the sea.   The fountain danced
Beside the huge old tree as some slim nymph,
Robed in light silver, might her frolics shew
Before some hoary king, while high above
He shook his wild, long locks upon the breeze,
And sighed deep sighs of " All is vanity!"
Behind, a wall of Norman William's time
Rose mellow, hung with ivy, here and there

THE WISHING STAR

Torn wide apart to let a casement peer
Upon the terrace.

On a carved sill I leant—
A *fleur-de-lis* bound with an English rose—
And looked above me into two such eyes
As would have dazzled from that ancient page
That new-old cry that hearts so often write
In their own ashes, "All is vanity!"
"Knowst thou," she said, with tender eyes far fixed
On the wide arch that domes our little earth,
"That when a star hurls on with shining wings
On some swift message from his throne of light,
The ready heart may wish, and the ripe fruit,
Fulfilment, drop into the eager palm?"
"Then let us watch for such a star," quoth I.
"Nay, love," she said, "'tis but an idle tale!"
But some swift feeling smote upon her brow
A rosy shadow.

I turned and watched the sky.
Calmly the cohorts of the night swept on,
Led by the wide-winged vesper; and, 'gainst the moon,
Where low her globe trembled upon the edge
Of the wide amethyst that clearly paved
The dreamy sapphire of the night, there lay
The jetty spars of some tall ship that looked
The Night's device upon his ripe-red shield.
And suddenly down towards the moon there ran,
From some high space deep veiled in solemn blue,
A little star, a point of trembling gold,
Gone swift as seen.

"My wishing star," quoth I;
"Shall tell my wish? Didst note that little star?

Its brightness died not; it but disappeared
To whirl undimmed thro' space. I wished our love
Might blot the ' All is vanity ' from life,
Burning brightly as that star and winging on
Thro' unseen space of veiled Eternity,
Brightened by Immortality—not lost."
" Awful and sweet the wish!" she said, and so
We rested in the silence of content.

EGYPT, I DIE!

EGYPT, I die! Thy hand, thy lip, thy kiss
Press thy wild pulses into mine; ay, this
I borrow from thee that will plume my shade
Strong as a god to Hades—not every man
Breathes out his ghost like strong Falerian poured
On the cold marble set before the gods!
I die! ay, Queen, as dies thy mighty Nile,
Which vaster swells the large, calm, waiting sea!

I die! I die! I die! O gods, to feel
The shard burst back and let my unarmed head
Rise to the clouds, my giant arms swing out
O'er hills and vales and deserts, and my feet,
Colossus-wise, tread down two separate worlds!

Egypt, this death? Was I before a man?
Did I thrust spear in battle? Was it I
That wedded Fulvia? Methinks I dreamed,
With moments half aroused in which I loved
Thee, Egypt,—ay, that was the fiery cloud
Which wrapped the ardent sun that now I feel
Strike on these eyes. When thou again shalt look
Up to the stars—why, Antony's crest is there;

VASHTI, THE QUEEN.

When the wild lightning leaps before the roar
Of purple-fronted thunder, Antony's glance
Seeks for his Queen before he shouts her name.

I die—I live! Man is a god enchained,
Blinded by motes, deafened, my Queen, by sounds
No louder than the murmuring of a gnat.
Egypt and I will course amid the stars
With veins enlarged for those more crystal fires
Rolling through space to pour their clear flames through
This pulsing flesh. Unlace my helmet. Know,
The bite of a sword, the little loathsome nip
Of an asp, can free a god! I never guessed,
Save in chance moments which but came and went
Swift as the dip of gilded oar upon
Deep-bosomed Cydnus, how this passing pang
Might mean a godhood!

        Nay, my love, my Queen,
Kiss not again this little mask of clay
Which shrouded Antony even from himself,
But follow, Egypt, follow! Our great ghosts
Shall tower together while all time is told
On beads of dying worlds. I die—I live!

VASHTI, THE QUEEN.

Vashti, the Queen, appear? Nay, slaves, begone
Before mine anger blaze fierce as the sun
On the red plains that stretch beyond the shades
Of palm-defended Shushan! I, Vashti, stand
Unveiled before the revellers, see them poise
The flashing goblet in mid-air, and cry
Aloud upon my beauty? No eye abashed,

251

No knee smite on the ground to do my state
Fit honour, for behold the King, great lord,
Leans from his throne and guides the vacant eyes
With " Lo, the Queen!"—and Vashti stands unveiled.

And so, my lord, who lives in sacred state
Beside the gold-vestured sun, in Vashti breathes
Dishonoured, bereft of that most kingly thing
That honoured his great state, the sacredness
Of the Queen's beauty! Vashti, the Queen,
So fallen, fallen! Lo, now I see the hall,—
The vision hurts mine eye,—Ahasuerus set
Upon his throne; the purple curtains sway
Between great pillars; and the princes, crowned
Each as his state; the golden goblets brimmed
With royal wine that blushes as the wind
Whispers its shameful tale of " Vashti comes!"

Nay, now, thou Sun, defend me; smite aside
The sheltering palms of Shushan; fold thine arms
Of fire about me; burn my royal beauty
To loathsomeness with thy quick kisses;
Drink the proud blood that leaps about my heart;
Yea, slay me ere I go before the King
In other sort than as the Wife and Queen!

That day when Vashti leaves her sacred state,
As holy to her lord and life, the King,
And decks her beauty servant to the eyes
Of those who gorge as on a fair-limbed toy,
Then let her be accursèd of all queens
Who thro' all time shall share a throne; and of
All wives who would be sacred in their husbands' eyes,
As they do centre, to such wives, the world!

THE VESPER STAR.

THE VESPER STAR.

UNFOLD thy pinions, drooping to the sun,
Just plunged behind the round-browed mountain, deep
Crowned with the snows of hawthorn, avalanched
All down its sloping shoulder with the bloom
Of orchards, blushing to the ardent South,
And to the evening oriflamme of rose
That arches the blue concave of the sky.

O rosy Star, thy trembling glory part
From the great sunset splendour that its tides
Sends rushing in swift billows to the east,
And on their manes of fire outswell thy sails
Of light-spun gold; and as the glory dies,
Throbbing thro' changeful rose to silver mist,
Laden with souls of flowers wooed abroad
From painted petals by the ardent Night,
Possess the heavens for one short splendid hour—
Sole jewel on the Egypt brow of Night,
Who steals, dark giant, to caress the Earth,
And gathers from the glassy mere and sea
The silver foldings of his misty robe,
And hangs upon the air with brooding wings
Of shadow, shadow, stretching everywhere.

AN INTERREGNUM.

LOUD trumpets blow among the naked pines,
Fine spun as sere-cloth rent from royal dead.
Seen ghostly thro' high-lifted vagrant drifts,
Shrill blaring, but no longer loud to moons

Like a brown maid of Egypt stands the Earth,
Her empty valley palms stretched to the Sun
For largesse of his gold.   Her mountain tops
Still beacon winter with white flame of snow,
Fading along his track; her rivers shake
Wild manes, and paw their banks as though to flee
Their riven fetters.

                      Lawless is the time,
Full of loud kingless voices that way gone:
The Polar Cæsar striding to the north,
Nor yet the sapphire-gated south unfolds
For Spring's sweet progress; the winds, unkinged,
Reach gusty hands of riot round the brows
Of lordly mountains waiting for a lord,
And pluck the ragged beards of lonely pines—
Watchers on heights for that sweet, hidden king,
Bud-crowned and dreaming yet on other shores—
And mock their patient waiting.   But by night
The round Moon falters up a softer sky,
Drawn by silver cords of gentler stars
Than darted chill flames on the wintry earth.

Within his azure battlements the Sun
Regilds his face with joyance, for he sees,
From those high towers, Spring, earth's fairest lord,
Soft-cradled on the wings of rising swans,
With violet eyes slow budding into smiles,
And small, bright hands with blossom largesse full,
Crowned with an orchard coronal of white,
And with a sceptre of a ruddy reed
Burnt at its top to amethystine bloom.

A BATTLE

Come, Lord, thy kingdom stretches barren hands!
Come, King, and chain thy rebels to thy throne
With tendrils of the vine and jewelled links
Of ruddy buds pulsating into flower!

A BATTLE.

SLOWLY the Moon her banderoles of light
Unfurls upon the sky; her fingers drip
Pale, silvery tides; her armoured warriors
Leave Day's bright tents of azure and of gold,
Wherein they hid them, and in silence flock
Upon the solemn battlefield of Night
To try great issues with the blind old king,
The Titan Darkness, who great Pharoah fought
With groping hands, and conquered for a span.

The starry hosts with silver lances prick
The scarlet fringes of the tents of Day,
And turn their crystal shields upon their breasts,
And point their radiant lances, and so wait
The stirring of the giant in his caves.

The solitary hills send long, sad sighs
As the blind Titan grasps their locks of pine
And trembling larch to drag him toward the sky,
That his wild-seeking hands may clutch the Moon
From her war-chariot, scythed and wheeled with light,
Crush bright-mailed stars, and so, a sightless king,
Reign in black desolation!   Low-set vales
Weep under the black hollow of his foot,
While sobs the sea beneath his lashing hair
Of rolling mists, which, strong as iron cords,
Twine round tall masts and drag them to the reefs.

Swifter rolls up Astarte's light-scythed car;
Dense rise the jewelled lances, groves of light;
Red flouts Mars' banner in the voiceless war
(The mightiest combat is the tongueless one) ;
The silvery dartings of the lances prick
His fingers from the mountains, catch his locks
And toss them in black fragments to the winds,
Pierce the vast hollow of his misty foot,
Level their diamond tips against his breast,
And force him down to lair within his pit
And thro' its chinks thrust down his groping hands
To quicken Hell with horror—for the strength
That is not of the Heavens is of Hell.

CURTIUS.

How spake the Oracle, my Curtius, how?
Methought, while on the shadowed terraces
I walked and looked toward Rome, an echo came
Of legion wails, blent into one deep cry.
" O Jove!" I thought, " the Oracles have said,
And, saying, touched some swiftly answering chord
General to every soul."   And then my heart
(I being here alone) beat strangely loud,
Responsive to the cry, and my still soul
Informed me thus: " Not such a harmony
Could spring from aught within the souls of men,
But that which is most common to all souls.
Lo! that is sorrow!"

      Nay, Curtius, I could smile
To tell thee, as I listened to the cry,
How on the silver flax which blew about
The ivory distaff in my languid hand

CURTIUS

I found large tears; such big and rounded drops
As gather thro' dark nights on cypress boughs.
And I was sudden angered, for I thought:
"Why should a general wail come home to me
With such vibration in my trembling heart
That such great tears should rise and overflow?"
Then shook them on the marble where I paced,
Where instantly they vanished in the sun,
As diamonds fade in flames. 'Twas foolish, Curtius!

And then methought how strange and lone it seemed,
For till thou camest I seemed to be alone
On the vined terrace, prisoned in the gold
Of that still noontide hour. No widows stole
Up the snow-glimmering marble of the steps
To take my alms and bless the gods and me;
No orphans touched the fringes of my robe
With innocent babe fingers, nor dropped the gold
I laid in their soft palms, to laugh, and stroke
The jewels on my neck, or touch the rose
Thou sayest, Curtius, lives upon my cheek.
Perchance all lingered in the Roman streets
To catch first tidings from the Oracles.
The very peacocks drowsed in distant shades,
Nor sought my hand for honeyed cake; and high
A hawk sailed blackly in the clear blue sky
And kept my doves from cooing at my feet.

My lute lay there, bound with the small white buds
Which, laughing, this bright morn thou brought and
        wreathed
Around it as I sang; but with that wail
Dying across the vines and purple slopes,
And breaking on its strings, I did not care
To waken music—nor in truth could force

17   257

My voice or fingers to it. So I strayed
Where hangs thy best loved armour on the wall,
And pleased myself by filling it with thee.
'Tis yet the goodliest armour in proud Rome,
Say all the armourers; all Rome and I
Know *thee* the lordliest bearer of a sword.
Yet, Curtius, stay, there is a rivet lost
From out the helmet, and a ruby gone
From the short sword-hilt—trifles both which can
Be righted by tomorrow's noon. Tomorrow's noon!—
Was there a change, my Curtius, in my voice
When spake I these three words, " tomorrow's noon "?
Oh, I am full of dreams—methought there was.

Why, love, how darkly gaze thine eyes in mine!
If loved I dismal thoughts I well could deem
Thou sawest not the blue of my fond eyes,
But looked between the lips of that dread pit,—
O Jove! to name it seems to curse the air
With chills of death! We'll speak not of it, Curtius.

When I had dimmed thy shield with kissing it
I went between the olives to the stalls.
White Audax neighed out to me as I came,
As I had been Hippona to his eyes,
New dazzling from the one small mystic cloud
That, like a silver chariot, floated low
In the ripe blue of noon, and seemed to pause,
Stayed by the hilly round of yon aged tree.
He stretched the ivory arch of his vast neck,
Smiting sharp thunders from the marble floor
With hoofs impatient of a peaceful earth;
Shook the long silver of his burnished mane
Until the sunbeams smote it into light
Such as a comet trails across the sky.

CURTIUS

I love him, Curtius! Such magnanimous fires
Leap from his eyes! And I do truly think
That with thee seated on him, thy strong knees
Against his sides, the bridle in his jaws
In thy loved hand, to pleasure thee he'd spring
Sheer from the verge of Earth into the breast
Of Death and Chaos. Of Death and Chaos!—
What omens seem to strike my soul to-day!

What is there in this blossom-hour should knit
An omen in with every simple word?
Should make yon willows with their hanging locks
Dusk sybils, muttering sorrows to the air?
The roses, clamb'ring round yon marble Pan,
Wave like red banners floating o'er the dead?
The dead—there 'tis again! My Curtius, come,
And thou shalt tell me of the Oracles
And what sent hither that long cry of woe.
Yet wait, yet wait, I care not much to hear.

While on thy charger's throbbing neck I leaned,
Romeward there passed across the violet slopes
Five sacrificial bulls, with silver hides,
And horns as cusped and white as Dian's bow,
And lordly breasts which laid the honeyed thyme
Into long swarths, whence smoke of yellow bees
Rose up in puffs, dispersing as it rose.
For the great temple they. And as they passed
With quiet gait I heard their drivers say
The bulls were for the Altars, when should come
Word from the Oracles as to the Pit.
O Curtius, Curtius, in my soul I see
How black and fearful is its glutton throat!
I will not look!
O Soul, be blind and see not!

259

                              Then the men
Waved their long goads, still juicy from the vine
And plumed with bronzy leaves, and each to each
Showed the sleek beauty of the rounded sides,
The mighty curving of the lordly breasts,
The level lines of backs, the small, fine heads,
And laughed and said, " The gods will have it thus,
The choicest of the earth for sacrifice,
Let it be man or maid, or lowing bull!"
Where lay the witchcraft in their clownish words
To shake my heart?   I know not; but it thrilled
As Daphne's leaves thrill to a wind so soft
One might not feel it on the open palm.
I cannot choose but laugh, for what have I
To do with altars and with sacrifice?

MY IRISH LOVE.

BESIDE the saffron of a curtain lit
With broidered flowers, below a golden fringe
That on her silver shoulder made a glow
Like the sun kissing lilies in the dawn,
She sat, my Irish love, slim, light and tall.
Between his mighty paws her stag-hound held
(Love-jealous he) the foam of her pale robes,
Rare laces of her land, and his red eyes
Half loved me, grown familiar at her side;
Half pierced me—doubting my soul's right to stand
His lady's wooer in the courts of Love.
Above her, knitted-silver, fell a web
Of light from waxen tapers slipping down,
First to the wide-winged star of emeralds set
On the black crown with its blue burnished points
Of raven light; thence, fonder, to the cheek,

MY IRISH LOVE

O'er which flew drifts of rose leaves, wild and rich,
With lilied pauses in the wine-red flight:
For when I whispered, like a wind in June
My whisper tossed the roses to and fro
In her dear face, and when I paused they lay
Still in her heart.

                  Then lower fell the light—
A silver chisel cutting the round arm
Clear from the gloom—and dropped like dew
On the crisp lily, diamond-clasped, that lay
In happy kinship on her pure, proud breast;
And thence it sprang, like Cupid, nimble-winged,
To the quaint love-ring on her finger bound,
And set it blazing like a watch-fire lit
To guard a treasure. Then up sprang the flame
Mad for her eyes; but those grey worlds were deep
In seas of native light, and when I spoke
They wandered shining to the shining moon,
That gazed at us between the parted folds
Of yellow, rich with gold and daffodils,
Dropping her silver cloak on Innisfail.
O worlds, those eyes! There Laughter lightly tossed
His gleaming cymbals; large and most divine,
Pity stood in their crystal doors with hands
All generous outspread; in her pure depths
Moved Modesty, chaste goddess, snow-white of brow
And shining vestal limbs; rose-fronted stood,
Blushing yet strong, young Courage, knightly in
His virgin arms; and simple, russet Truth
Played like a child amongst her tender thoughts—
Thoughts white as daisies snowed upon the lawn.

Unheeded, Dante on the cushion lay,
His golden clasps yet locked. No poet tells

The tale of Love with such a wizard tongue
That lovers slight dear Love himself to list!
Our wedding eve, and I had brought to her
The jewels of my house new set for her,
As I did set the immemorial pearl
Of our old honour in the virgin gold
Of her high soul. With grave and well pleased eyes,
And critic lips, and kissing finger-tips,
She praised the white tiara and its train
Of lesser splendours, nor blushed nor smiled:
They were but fitting pages to her state,
And had no tongues to speak between our souls.

But I would have her smile ripe for me then—
Swift treasure of a moment—so I laid
Between her palms a little simple thing,
A golden heart graved with my name alone,
And round it, twining close, small shamrocks linked
Of gold, mere gold:—no jewels made it rich
Until twin diamonds shattered from her eyes
And made the red gold rare. "True Knight," she
    said,
"Your English heart with Irish shamrocks bound!"
"A golden prophet of eternal truth,"
I said, and kissed the roses of her palms,
And then the shy, bright roses of her lips;
And all the jealous jewels shone forgot
In necklace and tiara as I clasped
The gold heart and its shamrocks round her neck.
My fair, pure soul! My noble Irish love!

Book IV.

OLD SPOOKSES' PASS.

WE'D camped thet night on Yaller Bull Flat,—
   Thar wus Possum Billy, an' Tom, an' me.
Right smart at throwin' a lariat
   Wus them two fellers, as ever I see ;
An' fur ridin' a broncho, or argyin' squar
   With the devil rolled up in the hide uv a mule,
Them two fellers thet camped with me thar
   Would hev made an' or'nary feller a fool.

Fur argyfyin' in any way
   Thet hed tew be argyed with sinew an' bone
I never see'd fellers could argy like them ;
   But jest right here I will hev tew own
Thet whar brains cum in in the game uv life
   They held the poorest keerds in the lot ;
An' when hands wus shown, sum other chap
   Raked in the hull uv the blamed old pot.

We wus short uv hands, the herd wus large,
   An' watch an' watch we divided the night ;
We could hear the coyotes howl an' whine,
   But the durned critters kept out uv sight
Uv the camp-fire blazin' ; an' now an' then
   Thar cum a rustle an' sort uv rush—
A rattle a-sneakin' away frum the blaze
   Thru the rattlin', cracklin' grey sage bush.

We'd chanced thet night on a pootyish lot
   With a tol'ble show uv tall, sweet grass,—
We wus takin' Speredo's drove across
   The Rockies, by way uv " Old Spookses' Pass "—

An' a mite uv a crick went crinklin' down,
  Like a " pocket " bust in the rocks overhead,
Consid'able shrunk by the summer drought
  Tew a silver streak in its gravelly bed.

'Twus a fairish spot fur tew camp a' night;
  An' chipper I felt, tho' sort uv skeered
Thet them two cowboys, with only me,
  Couldn't boss three thousand head uv a herd.
I took the fust uv the watch myself;
  An' es the red sun down the mountains sprang,
I rolled a fresh quid, an' got on the back
  Uv my peart leetle chunk uv a tough mustang.

An' Possum Billy wus sleepin' sound
  Es only a cowboy knows how tew sleep;
An' Tommy's snores would hev made a old
  Buffalo bull feel kind o' cheap.
Wal, pard, I reckon thar's no sech time
  Fur dwindlin' a chap in his own conceit
Es when them mountains an' awful stars
  Jest hark tew the tramp uv his mustang's feet.

It 'pears tew me thet them solemn hills
  Beckon them stars so big an' calm,
An' whisper, " Make tracks this way, my friends,
  We've ringed in here a specimen man;
He's here alone, so we'll take a look
  Thru his ganzy an' vest, an' his blood an' bone,
An' post ourselves es tew whether his heart
  Is *flesh,* or a rotten, made-up stone."

An' it's often seemed, on a midnight watch,
  When the mountains blackened the dry, brown sod,

266

OLD SPOOKSES' PASS

Thet a chap, if he shet his eyes, might grip
  The great, kind hand uv his Father God.
I rode round the herd at a sort uv walk;
  The shadders cum stealin' thick an' black;
I'd jest got tew leave tew thet thar chunk
  Uv a mustang tew keep in the proper track.

Ever see'd a herd ringed in at night?
  Wal, it's sort uv cur'us,—the watchin' sky,
The howl uv coyotes, a great black mass
  With here an' thar the gleam uv a eye
An' the white uv a horn, an' now an' then
  An old bull liftin' his shaggy head
With a beller like a broke-up thunder growl,
  An' the summer lightnin', quick an' red,

Twistin' an' turnin' amid the stars,
  Silent as snakes at play in the grass,
An' plungin' thair fangs in the bare old skulls
  Uv the mountains frownin' above the Pass;
An' all so still, thet the leetle crick,
  Twinklin' an' crinklin' frum stone tew stone,
Grows louder an' louder an' fills the air
  With a cur'us sort uv a singin' tone.
It ain't no matter wharever ye be,—
  I'll 'low it's a cur'us sort uv case—
Whar thar's runnin' water, it's sure tew speak
  Uv folks tew home an' the old home place;

An' yer bound tew listen an' hear it talk,
  Es yer mustang crunches the dry, bald sod,
Fur I reckon the hills an' stars an' crick
  Are all uv 'em preachers sent by God.
An' them mountains talk tew a chap this way:
  " Climb, if ye can, ye degenerate cuss !"

An' the stars smile down on a man, an' say,
   " Cum higher, poor critter, cum up tew us!"

An' I reckon, pard, thar is One above
   The highest old star thet a chap can see,
An' He sez, in a solid, etarnal way,
   " Ye never can stop till ye get tew *Me!*"
Good fur Him, tew! fur I calculate
   He ain't the One tew dodge an' tew shirk,
Or waste a mite uv the things He's made,
   Or knock off till He's finished His great day's work.

We've got tew labour an' strain an' snort
   Along thet road thet He's planned an' made;
Don't matter a mite He's cut His line
   Tew run over a 'tarnal tough up-grade.
An' if sum poor sinner ain't built tew hold
   Es big a head uv steam es the next,
An' keeps slippin' an' slidin' 'way down hill,
   Why, He don't make out thet He's awful vext;

Fur He knows He made Him in thet thar way,
   Sumwhar tew fit in His own great plan;
An' He ain't the Bein' tew pour His wrath
   On the head uv thet slimpsy an' slippery man;
An' He sez tew the feller, "Look here, My son,
   You're the worst hard case thet ever I see,
But be thet it takes ye a million yars,
   Ye never can stop till ye git tew *Me!*"

Them's my idees es I panned them out;
   Don't take no stock in them creeds thet say
Thar's a chap with horns thet's took control
   Uv the rollin' stock on thet up-grade way,

OLD SPOOKSES' PASS

Thet's free tew tote up es ugly a log
    Es grows in his big bush grim an' black,
An' slyly put it across the rails
    Tew hist a poor critter clar off the track;

An' when he's pooty well busted an' smashed,
    The devil cums smilin' an' bowin' round,
An' sez tew the Maker, " Guess ye don't care
    Tew trouble with stock thet ain't parfactly sound;
Lemme tote him away—best ye can do—
    Neglected, I guess, tew build him with care;
I'll hide him in hell—better thet folks
    Shouldn't see him laid up on the track fur repair!'

Don't take no stock in them creeds at all;
    Ain't one uv them cur'us sort uv moles
Thet think the Maker is bound tew let
    The devil git up a " corner " in souls.
Ye think I've put up a biggish stake?
    Wal, I'll bet fur all I'm wuth, d'ye see?
He ain't wuth shucks thet won't dar tew lay
    All his pile on his own idee.

Ye bet yer boots I'm es safe tew win
    Es the chap thet's able tew smilin' smack
The ace he's been hidin' up his sleeve
    Kerslap on top uv a feller's jack.
Es I wus sayin', the night wus dark,
    The lightnin' skippin' frum star tew star;
Thar wa'n't no clouds but a thread uv mist,
    No sound but the coyotes' yell afar,

An' the noise uv the crick as it called tew me,
    " Pard, don't ye mind the mossy, green spot

Whar a crick stood still fur a drowzin' spell
 Right in the midst uv the old home lot?
Whar, right at sundown on Sabba'day,
 Ye skinned yerself uv yer meetin' clothes,
An' dove like a duck whar the water clar
 Shone up like glass thru the lily-blows?

" Yer soul wus white es yer skin them days,
 Yer eyes es clar es the crick at rest;
The wust idee in yer head thet time
 Wus robbin' a bluebird's swingin' nest.
Now ain't ye changed? Declar fur it, pard,
 Thet crick would question, it 'pears tew me,
Ef ye looked in its waters agin tew night,
 ' Who may this old cuss uv a sinner be?' "

Thet wus the style thet thet thar crick
 In "Old Spookses' Pass" in the Rockies talked;
Drowzily list'nin' I rode round the herd,
 When all uv a sudden the mustang baulked,
An' shied with a snort. I never knowed
 Thet tough leetle critter tew show a scare
In storm or dark; but he jest scrouched down,
 With his nostrils snuffin' the damp, cool air,

An' his flanks a-quiver. Shook up? Wal, yas;
 Guessed we'd hev heaps uv tarnation fun;
I calculated quicker'n light
 Thet the herd would be off on a healthy run.
But thar wa'n't a stir tew horn or hoof;
 The herd, like a great black mist, lay spread,
While here an' thar a grazin' bull
 Loomed up like a mighty " thunder head."

OLD SPOOKSES' PASS

I riz in my saddle an' stared around.
  On the mustang's neck I felt the sweat;
Thar wus nuthin' tew see—sort uv felt the har
  Commencin' tew crawl on my scalp, ye bet!
Felt kind uv cur'us—own up I did;
  Felt sort uv dry in my mouth an' throat.
Sez I, " Ye ain't goin' tew scare, old hoss,
  At a prowlin' cuss uv a blamed coyote?"

But 'twa'n't no coyote nor prowlin' beast,
  Nor rattle a-wrigglin' thru the grass,
Nor a lurkin' redskin—twa'n't my way
  In a game like thet tew sing out, " I pass!"
But I knowed when I glimpsed the rollin' whites,
  The sparks frum the black uv the mustang's eye,
Thar wus *sumthin'* waltzin' up thet way
  Thet would send them critters off on the fly.

In the night-air's tremblin,' shakin' hands,
  Felt it beatin' kerslap onter me,
Like them waves thet chased thet President chap
  Thet went on the war-trail in old Judee.
The air wus bustin'—but silent es death;
  An' lookin' up, in a second I see'd
The sort uv sky thet allus looks down
  On the rush an' the roar uv a night stampede.

Tearin' along the indigo sky
  Wus a drove uv clouds, snarled an' black,
Scuddin' along to'ard the risin' moon,
  Like the sweep uv a durned hungry pack
Uv prairie wolves to'ard a bufferler,
  The heft uv the herd left out uv sight.
I drored my breath right hard, fur I knowed
  We wus in fur a 'tarnal run thet night.

Quiet? Ye bet! The mustang scrouched,
  His neck stretched out an' his nostrils wide;
The moonshine swept, a white river, down
  The black uv the mighty mountain's side,
Lappin' over an' over the stuns an' brush
  In whirls an' swirls uv leapin' light,
Makin' straight fur the herd, whar black an' still
  It stretched away tew the left an' right

On the level lot;—I tell ye, pard,
  I knowed when it touched the first black hide
Me an' the mustang would hev a show
  Fur a breezy bit uv an' evenin' ride.
One! it flowed over a homely pine
  Thet riz frum a cranny, lean an' lank,
A cleft uv the mountain;—reckonin' *two,*
  It slapped onter an old steer's heavin' flank,

Es sound he slept on the skirt uv the herd,
  Dreamin' his dreams uv the sweet blue grass
On the plains below; an' afore it touched
  The other wall uv " Old Spookses' Pass "
The herd wus up,—not one at a time,
  Thet ain't the style in a midnight run—
They wus up an' off like es all thair minds
  Wus rolled in the hide uv only one.

I've fit in a battle an' heerd the guns
  Blasphemin' God with thair devils' yell;
Heerd the stuns uv a fort like thunder crash
  In frunt uv the scream uv a red-hot shell;
But thet thar poundin' uv iron hoofs,
  The clatter uv horns, the peltin' sweep
Uv three thousand head uv a runnin' herd,
  Made all uv them noises kind uv cheap.

OLD SPOOKSES' PASS

The Pass jest opened its giant throat
  An' its lips uv granite, an' let a roar
Uv answerin' echoes; the mustang bucked,
  Then answered the bridle, an', pard, afore
The twink uv a fire-bug, lifted his legs
  Over stuns an' brush, like a lopin' deer—
A smart leetle critter! An' thar wus I
  'Longside uv the plungin' leadin' steer—

A low-set critter, not much account
  Fur heft or looks, but one uv them sort
Thet kin fetch a herd at his durned heels
  With a toss uv his horns or a mite uv a snort,
Fur a fight or a run; an' thar wus I,
  Pressin' clus tew the steel uv his heavin' flank,
An' cussin' an' shoutin'—while overhead
  The moon in the black clouds tremblin' sank

Like a bufferler overtook by the wolves
  An' pulled tew the ground by the scuddin' pack.
The herd rushed on with a din an' crash,
  Dim es a shadder vast an' black;
Couldn't tell ef a hide wus black or white,
  But frum the dim surges a-roarin' by
Bust long red flashes—the flamin' light
  Frum sum old steer's fur'us an' scareful eye.

Thet Pass in the Rockies fairly roared;
  An' sudden es winkin' came the bang
An' rattle uv thunder. Tew see the grit
  Uv thet peart leetle chunk uv a tough mustang
Not a buck nor a shy!—he gev a snort
  Thet shook the foam on his steamin' hide
An' leaped along. Wal, pard, ye bet
  I'd a healthy show fur a lively ride!

18   273

An' them cowboys slept in the leetle camp,
　　Calm es three kids in a truckle bed;
Declar' the crash wus enough tew put
　　Life in the dust uv the sleepin' dead.
The thunder kept droppin' its awful shells,
　　One at a minute, on mountain an' rock:
The Pass with its stone lips thundered back;
　　An' the rush an' roar an' whirlin' shock
Uv the runnin' herd wus fit tew bust
　　A tenderfoot's heart, hed he chanced along;
But I jest let out uv my lungs an' throat
　　A rippin' old verse uv a herdsman's song,

An' sidled the mustang closer up
　　'Longside uv the leader, an' hit him flat
On his steamin' flank with a lightsum stroke
　　Uv the end uv my limber lariat.
He never swerved, an' we thundered on,
　　Black in the blackness, red in the red
Uv the lightnin', blazin' with ev'ry clap
　　Thet bust frum the black guns overhead.

The mustang wus shod, an' the lightnin' bit
　　At his iron shoes each step he run,
Then plunged in the yearth. We rode in flame,
　　Fur the flashes rolled inter only one,
Same es the bellers made one big roar;
　　Yet thru the whirl uv din an' flame
I sung an' shouted, an' called the steer
　　I sidled agin by his own frunt name,

An' struck his side with my fist an' foot.
　　'Twus jest like hittin' a rushin' stone,
An' he thundered ahead—I couldn't boss
　　The critter a mossel, I'm free tew own.
274

OLD SPOOKSES' PASS

The sweat cum a-pourin' down my beard;
  Ef ye wonder wharfor, jest ye spread
Yerself fur a ride with a runnin' herd,
  A yawnin' gulch half a mile ahead,

Three hundred foot from its grinnin' lips
  Tew the roarin' stream on its stones below.
Once more I hurled the mustang up
  Agin the side uv the cuss called Joe;
'Twa'n't a mite uv use—he riz his heels
  Up in the air, like a scuddin' colt;
The herd massed closer, an' hurled down
  The roarin' Pass like a thunderbolt.

I couldn't rein off—seemed swept along
  In the rush an' roar an' thunderin' crash;
The lightnin' struck at the runnin' herd
  With a crack like the stroke uv a cowboy's lash.
Thar! I could see it—I tell ye, pard,
  Things seemed whittled down sort uv fine—
We wusn't five hundred feet frum the gulch,
  With its mean leetle fringe uv scrubby pine.

What could stop us? I grit my teeth;
  Think I prayed,—ain't sartin uv that,—
When, whizzin' an' singin', thar came the rush
  Right past my face uv a lariat!
"Bully fur you, old pard!" I roared,
  Es it whizzed roun' the leader's steamin' chest,
An' I wheeled the mustang fur all he wus wuth
  Kerslap on the side uv the old steer's breast.

He gev a snort, an' I see him swerve—
  I follered his shoulder clus an' tight;

Another swerve, an' the herd begun
  Tew swing around. Shouts I, " All right!
Ye've fetched 'em now !" The mustang gev
  A small, leetle whinny; I felt him flinch.
Sez I, " Ye ain't goin' tew weaken now,
  Old feller, an' me in this durned pinch?"

" No," sez he, with his small, prickin' ears,
  Plain es a human could speak; an' me,
I turned my head tew glimpse, ef I could,
  Who might the chap with the lariat be.
Wal, pard, I weakened—ye bet yer life!
  Thar wa'n't a human in sight around,
But right in frunt uv me cum the beat
  Uv a hoss's hoofs on the tremblin' ground—

Steddy an' heavy—a slingin' lope;
  A hefty critter with biggish bones
Might make jest sich—could hear the hoofs
  Es they struck on the rattlin', rollin' stones—
The jingle uv bit—an' clar an' shrill
  A whistle es ever left cowboy's lip;
An', cuttin' the air, the long, fine hiss
  Uv the whirlin' lash uv a cowboy's whip.

I crowded the mustang back ontil
  He riz on his haunches—an' I sed,
" In the Maker's name, who may ye be?"
  Sez a vice, " Old feller, jest ride ahead!"
" All right!" sez I, an' I shook the rein;
  " Ye've turned the herd in a hansum style;
Whoever ye be, I'll not back down!"
  An' I didn't, nuther—ye bet yer pile!

OLD SPOOKSES' PASS

Clus on the heels uv thet unseen hoss,
  I rode on the side uv the turnin' herd,
An' once in a while I answered back
  A shout or a whistle or cheerin' word
Frum lips no lightnin' wus strong tew show.
  'Twus sort uv scareful, thet midnight ride;
But we'd got our backs tew the gulch—fur that
  I'd hev follered a cur'user sort uv guide.

'Twus kind uv scareful tew watch the herd
  Es the plungin' leaders squirmed an' shrank,
Es I heerd the flick uv the unseen lash
  Hiss on the side uv a steamin' flank.
Guess the feller wus smart at the work!
  We worked them leaders round ontil
They overtook the tail uv the herd,
  An' the hull uv the crowd begun tew "mill."

Round spun the herd in a great black wheel,
  Slower an' slower—ye've seen beneath
A biggish torrent a whirlpool spin,
  Its waters black es the face uv Death?
'Peared sort uv like thet, the "millin'" herd.
  We kept by the leaders—*him* an' me—
Neck by neck, an' he sung a tune
  About a young gal named Betsey Lee.

Jine in the chorus? Wal, yas, I did.
  He sung like a reg'lar mockin'-bird,
An' us cowboys allus sing out tew calm
  The scare, ef we can, uv a runnin' herd.
Slower an' slower wheeled round the "mill";
  The maddest old steer uv a leader slowed;
Slower an' slower sounded the hoofs
  Uv the hoss thet *him* in frunt uv me rode.

Fainter an' fainter growed thet thar song
  Uv Betsey Lee an' her har uv gold;
Fainter an' fainter grew the sound
  Uv the unseen hoofs on the tore-up mould.
The leadin' steer, thet cuss uv a Joe,
  Stopped an' shook off the foam an' the sweat,
With a stamp an' a beller; the run wus done—
  Wus glad uv it tew, yer free tew bet!

The herd slowed up an' stood in a mass
  Uv blackness lit by the lightnin's eye;
An' the mustang cowered es *sumthin'* swept
  Clus tew his wet flank in passin' by.
" Good night tew ye, pard!" " Good night!" sez I,
  Strainin' my sight on the empty air;
The har riz rustlin' up on my head,
  Now thet I hed the time tew scare.

The mustang flinched till his saddle girth
  Scraped on the dust uv the tremblin' ground;—
Thar cum a laugh, the crack uv a whip,
  A whine like the cry uv a well-pleased hound,
The noise uv a hoss thet reared an' sprang
  At the touch uv a spur—then all wus still
But the sound uv the thunder dyin' down
  On the stony breast uv the nighest hill.

The herd went back tew its rest an' feed,
  Es quiet a crowd es ever wore hide;
An' them boys in camp never heerd a lisp
  Uv the thunder an' crash uv thet run an' ride.
An' I'll never furget while a wildcat claws
  Or a cow loves a nibble uv sweet blue grass,
The cur'us pardner thet rode with me
  In the night stampede in "Old Spookses' Pass."

278

OLD SPENSE.

You've seen his place, I reckon, friend?
　'Twus rather kind uv tryin'
The way he made the dollars fly,
　Sech gimcrack things a-buyin'—
　　He spent a big share uv a fortun
　　On pesky things thet went a-snortin'

An' hollerin' over all the fields,
　An' ploughin' ev'ry furrow;
We sort uv felt discouraged, fur
　Spense wusn't one tew borrow;
　　An' wuss—the old chap wouldn't lend
　　A cent's wuth tew his dearest friend.

Good lands! the neighbours see'd tew wunst
　Them snortin', screamin' notions
Wus jest enough tew drown the yearth
　In wrath, like roarin' oceans;
　　An' "guessed the Lord would giv old Spense
　　Blue fits fur fightin' Pruvidence."

Spense wus thet hardened when the yearth
　Wus like a baked pertater,
Insted uv prayin' hard fur rain,
　He fetched an irrigator.
　　"The wicked flourish like green bays!"
　　Sed folks fur comfort in them days.

I will allow his place wus grand,
　With not a stump upon it;

The loam wus jest es rich an' black
  Es schoolma'am's velvet bonnit;
    But tho' he flourished folks all knowed
    What spiritooal ear-marks he showed.

Spense hed a notion in his mind,
  Ef sum poor human grapples
With pesky worms thet eat his vines
  An' spile his summer apples,
    It don't seem enny kind uv sense
    Tew call thet " cheekin' Pruvidence !"

An' ef a chap on Sabbath sees
  A thunder cloud a-strayin'
Above his fresh cut clover, an'
  Gits down tew steddy prayin',
    An' tries tew shew the Lord's mistake
    Insted uv tacklin' tew his rake,

He ain't got enny kind uv show
  Tew talk uv chast'ning trials
When thet thar thunder cloud lets down
  Its sixty billion vials.
    No! when it looks tew rain on hay,
    First take yer rake an' then yer pray.

Old Spense wus one uv them thar chaps
  Thet in this life uv tussle
An' rough-an-tumble sort uv set
  A mighty store on muscle;
    Believed in hustlin' in the crop,
    An' prayin' on the last load top.

An' yet he hed his p'ints—his heart
  Wus builded sort uv spacious
280

OLD SPENSE

An' solid, ev'ry beam an' plank;
  An', Stranger, now, veracious,
    A wore-out hoss he never shot,
    But turned him in the clover lot.

I've see'd up tew the meetin'-house
  The winkin' an' the nudgin'
When preacher sed, " No doubt thet Dives,
  Bein' drefful mean an' grudgin'
    Tew church work, sealed his awful fate
    Whar thar ain't no foolin' with the gate."

I mind the preacher met old Spense,
  Beneath the maples laggin';
The day wus hot, an' he'd a pile
  Uv 'cetrees in his waggon—
    A sack of flour, a hansum hog,
    Sum butter, an' his tarrier dog.

Preacher, he halted up his hoss,
  Asked fur Miss Spense an' Deely,
Tew limber up his tongue a mite,
  An' sez right slick an' mealy:
    " Brother, I reelly want tew know
    Hev you got religion?   Samson, whoa !"

Old Spense, he bit a noble chaw,
  An' sort uv meditated;
Samson, he nibbled at the grass,
  An' preacher smiled an' waited;
    Ye'd see it writ upon his face:
    " I've got Spense in a tightsum place !"

The old man curled his whip-lash round
  An alto-viced muskitter;

Preacher, sort uv triumphant, stroked
  His or'nary old critter;
    Spense p'ints tew flour, an' hog, an' jar—
    Sez he, " I've got religion thar.

" Them's goin' down tew Spinks's place,
  Whar old man Spinks is stayin';
The bank he dealt at bust last month,
  An' folks is mostly sayin',
    Him bein' aged, an' poor, an' sick,
    They'll put him in the poorhouse slick.

" But no, they don't!   Not while I own
  The name uv Jedediah.
Yer movin'?   How's yer gran'ma Green,
  An' yer cousin, Ann Maria?
    Boss, air they?   Yas, sirree, I dar
    Tew say, I've got religion thar."

Preacher, he in his stirrups riz,
  His visage kind uv cheerin',
An' keerful looked along the road,
  Over sugar bush an' clearin';
    Thar wa'n't a deacon within sight;
    Sez he, " My brother, guess you're right!

" You keep yer waggon Zionward,
  With that religion on it;
I calculate we'll meet"—jest here
  A caliker sunbonnet,
    On a sister's head, cum round the jog,
    An' preacher disparsed like mornin' fog.

One day a kind uv judgment cum.
  The lightnin'-rod conductor

OLD SPENSE

Got broke; the fluid struck his aunt,
    An' in the root-house chucked her.
      It laid her up fur quite a while,
      An' the judgment made the neighbours smile.

Old Spense he swore a mighty swar;
    He didn't mince nor chew it,
Fur when he spoke, 'most usual,
    It hed a backbone tew it;
      He sed he'd find a healthy plan
      Tew squar things with the Agent man

Who'd sold him thet thar useless rod
    Tew put upon his roofin';
An' ef he found him round the place,
    He'd send the scamp a-hoofin'.
      " Ye sort uv understand my sense?"
      " Yes, pa," sed pooty Deely Spense.

" Yes, pa," sez she, es mild es milk,
    Tew thet thar strong oration;
An' when a woman acts like *that*,
    It's bin my obsarvation—'
      An' reckon thet ye'll find it sound—
      She means tew turn creation round,

An' fix the univarse the way
    She sort uv feels the notion.
So Deely let the old man rave,
    Nor kicked up no commotion;
      Tho' thet cute Agent man an' she
      Were knowed es steddy company.

He'd chance around when Spense wus out,
    A feller sort o' airy;

An' poke around free es the wind
   With Deely in the dairy.
      (Old Spense he'd got a patent churn
      Thet gev the church a drefful turn.)

I am a married man myself,
   More sot on steddy ploughin'
An' cuttin' rails than praisin' gals,
   Yet honestly allowin'
      A man must be main hard tew please
      Thet didn't freeze tew Deely's cheese.

I reckon tho' old Spense hed signed
   With Satan queer law papers,
He'd filled thet dairy up chock-full
   Uv them thar patent capers.
      Preacher once took fur sermon text—
      " Rebellious patent vats—what next?"

I've kind uv strayed frum thet thar scare
   Thet cum on Spense—tho' reelly,
I'll allus hold it wus a shine
   Uv thet thar pooty Deely.
      Thar's them es holds, thru thin an' thick,
      'Twus a friendly visit frum Old Nick.

Es time went on old Spense, he seemed
   More sot on patent capers;
So he went right off tew fetch a thing
   He'd read uv in the papers.
      'Twus a moony night in airly June.
      The whippoorwills wus all in tune,

The katydids wus callin' clar,
   The fire-bugs wus a-glowin',

OLD SPENSE

The smell uv clover filled the air.
  Thet day old Spense'd bin mowin'
    With a mower yellin' drefful screams,
    Like them skreeks we hear in nightmare dreams.

Miss Spense wus in the keepin'-room
  O'erlookin' last yar's cherries;
The help wus settin' on the bench
  A-hullin' airly berries;
    The hired man sot on the step
    An' chawed an' watched the crickets lep.

Not one uv them thar folks thet thought
  Uv Deely in the dairy:
The help thought on the hired man,
  An' he uv Martin's Mary;
    Miss Spense, she pondered thet she'd found
    Crushed sugar'd riz a cent a pound.

I guess hed you an' I bin thar,
  A-peepin' thru the shutter
Uv thet thar dairy, we'd 'a' swore
  Old Spense's cheese an' butter
    Wus gilded, frum the manner that
    Deely, she smiled on pan an' vat.

The Agent, he hed chanced around
  In evenin's peaceful shadder;
He'd glimpsed Spense an' his tarrier go
  Across the new-mown medder
    To'ard Crampville; so he shewed his sense
    By slidin' o'er the garden fence;

An' kind of unassumin' glode,
  Beneath the bendin' branches,

Tew the dairy door whar Deely watched,
  A-twitterin' an' anxious.
    It didn't suit Miss Deely's plan
    Her pa should ketch thet Agent man.

I kind uv mind, them days I went
  With Betsy Ann a-sparkin',
Time hed a drefful sneakin' way
  Uv passin' without markin'
    A single blaze upon a post,
    An' walkin' noiseless es a ghost.

I guess thet Adam found it thus
  Afore he hed to grapple
With thet conundrum Satan raised
  About the blamed old apple;
    He found time sort uv smart tew pass
    Afore Eve took tew apple-sass.

Thar ain't no changes cum about
  Sence them old days in Eden,
Except thet lovers take a spell
  Uv mighty hearty feedin';
    Now Adam makes his Eve rejice
    By orderin' up a lemon-ice.

He ain't got enny kind uv show
  Tew hear the merry pealin's
Uv them thar weddin' bells, unless
  He kind uv stirs her feelin's
    By treatin' her tew ginger-pop,
    An' pilin' peanuts in a-top.

Thet Agent man knowed how tew run
  The business real handy;

OLD SPENSE

An' him an' Deely sot an' laughed
  An' scrunched a pile o' candy;
    An' talk'd about the singin' skule—
    An' stars—an' Spense's kickin' mule—

An' other elevatin' facts
  In skyence an' in natur.
An' time, es I wus sayin', glode
  Past like a champion skater,
    When—thunder! round the orchard fence
    Cum thet thar tarrier dog an' Spense,

An' made straight fur the dairy door.
  Thar's times in most experence
We feel how trooly wise 'twould be
  Tew make a rapid clearance;
    Nor wait tew practise them thar rules
    We larn tew city dancin' skules.

The Agent es a gen'ral plan
  Wus polished es the handles
Uv my old plough, an' slick an' smooth
  Es Betsey's taller candles;
    But when he see'd old Spense—wal, now,
    He acted homely es a cow!

His manners wusn't in the grain,
  His wool wus sorter shoddy;
His courage wus a poorish sort,
  It hedn't got no body;
    An' when he see'd old Spense, he shook
    Es ef he'd see'd his gran'ma's spook.

Deely, she wrung her pooty hands—
  She felt her heart a-turnin'

Es poor es milk when all the cream
  Is taken off fur churnin';
    When all tew once her eyes fell pat
    Upon old Spense's patent vat.

The Agent took no sort uv stock
  Thet time in etiquettin';
It would hev made a punkin laugh
  Tew see his style uv gettin';
    In thet thar empty vat he slid,
    An' Deely shet the hefty lid.

Old Spense wus smilin' jest es clar
  Es stars in the big " Dipper ";
An' Deely made believe tew hum
  " Old Hundred " gay an' chipper,—
    But thinkin' what a tightsum squeeze
    The vat wus fur the Agent's knees.

Old Spense, he sed, " I guess, my gal,
  Ye've bin a sort uv dreamin';
I see ye hevn't set the pans,
  Nor turned the mornin's cream in.
    Now, ain't ye spry? Now, durn my hat
    Ef the milk's run inter thet thar vat!"

Thar's times one's feelin's swell like bread
  In summer-time a-risin',
An' Deely's heart swole in a way
  Wus mightily surprisin',
    When Spense gripped one uv them thar pans
    Uv yaller cream in his big han's.

The moon glode underneath a cloud,
  The breeze sighed loud an' airy;

OLD SPENSE

The pans, they faint-like glimmered on
　　The white walls uv the dairy.
　　　　Deely, she trembled like an ash,
　　　　An' leaned agin the old churn dash.

" Tarnation darksum," growled old Spense,
　　An', liftin' up the cover,
He turned the pan uv cream quite spry
　　On Deely's Agent lover.
　　　　Good sakes alive! a curdlin' skreek
　　　　Frum thet thar Agent man did break!

All drippin' white he rosed tew view,
　　His curly locks a-flowin'
With clotted cream, an' in the dusk
　　His eyes with terror glowin'.
　　　　He made one spring—'tis sartin, reely,
　　　　He never sed " Good night " tew Deely.

Old Spense, he riz up frum the ground,
　　An' with a kind uv wonder
He looked inter thet patent vat,
　　An' simply sed, " By thunder!"
　　　　Then looked at Deely hard, and sed,
　　　　" The milk will sop clar thru his head."

Folks looked right solemn when they heerd
　　The hull uv thet thar story,
An' sed, " It might be plainly seen
　　'Twus clar agin the glory
　　　　Uv Pruvidence tew use a vat
　　　　Thet Satan in hed boldly sat!"

They shook thair heads when Spense declared
　　'Twus Deely's beau in hidin';

They guessed they knowed a thing or two,
   An' wusn't so confidin':
     " 'Twus the Devourin' Lion cum
     Tew ask old Spense tew step down hum!"

Old Spense, he kinder spiled the thing
   Fur thet thar congregation
By holdin' on tew life in spite
   Uv Satan's invitation;
     An' hurts thair feelin's ev'ry Spring,
     Buyin' sum pesky patent thing.

The Agent man slid out next day
   Tew peddle round Young Hyson;
An' Deely fur a fortnight thought
   Uv drinkin' sum rat pison;
     Didn't put no papers in her har,
     An' dined out uv the pickle jar.

Then at Aunt Hesby's sewin'-bee
   She met a slick young feller,
With a city partin' tew his har
   An' a city umbereller.
     He see'd her hum thet night, an' he
     Is now her steddy company.

THE DEACON AND HIS DAUGHTER.

HE saved his soul an' saved his pork
   With old time presarvation;
He didn't hold with creosote
   Or new plans uv salvation:
He sed thet " works would show the man,
The smokehouse tell upon the ham."

THE DEACON AND HIS DAUGHTER

He didn't, when he sunk a well,
  Inspect the stuns and gravel
Tew prove thet Moses wus a dunce
  Unfit fur furrin travel:
He marvelled at them works uv God—
An' broke 'em up tew mend the road.

An' when the circus cum around,
  He hitched his sleek old horses,
An' in his rattlin' waggon took
  His dimpled household forces—
The boys tew wonder at the clown
An' think his lot life's highest crown.

He wondered at the zebras wild,
  Nor knew 'em painted donkeys;
An' when he gev the boys a dime
  Fur cakes tew feed the monkeys,
He never thought, in enny shape,
He hed descended frum an ape.

An' when he saw sum shaller-pate,
  With smallest brain possession,
He uttered no filosofy
  On Natur's retrogression
Tew ancient types, by Darwin's rule;
He simply sed, " Wal, durn a fool!"

He never hed an enemy
  But once a year, tew meetin',
When he and Deacon Maybee fought
  On questions uv free seatin',
Or which should be the one t' rebuke
Pastor fur kissin' sister Luke.

His farm wus well enough, but stones
  Kind uv stern, ruthless facts is;
An' he jest made out tew save a mite
  An' pay his righteous taxes,
An' mebbe tote sum flour an' pork
Tew poor old critters past their work.

But on the neatest thing he hed
  Around the place or dwellin'
I guess he never paid a red
  Uv taxes. No mushmelon
Wus rounder, pinker, sweeter than
The old man's daughter, Minta Ann.

I've been at Philadelfy's show
  An' other sim'lar fusses,
An' seen a mighty sight uv stone
  Minarveys and Venusses,
An' Sikeys clad in flowers an' wings,
But not much show uv factory things.

I've seen the hull entire crowd
  Uv Jove's female relations,
An' I feel tew make a solemn swar
  On them thar " Lamentations,"
Thet as a sort uv gen'ral plan
I'd ruther spark with Minta Ann.

You'd ought tew see her dimpled chin,
  With one red freckle on it,
Her brown eyes glancing underneath
  Her tilted shaker bonnet:
I vow, I often did desire
They'd set the plaguey thing a-fire.

292

THE DEACON AND HIS DAUGHTER

You'd ought tew hear thet thar gal sing
  On Sabbath, up tew meetin',
You'd kind uv feel high lifted up,
  Yer soul fur Heaven fleetin'.
An' then, came supper, down she'd tie
Ye tew this earth with punkin pie!

I tell ye, stranger, 'twus a sight
  Fur poetry and speeches
Tew see her sittin' on the stoop
  A-peelin' scarlet peaches
Inter the kettle at her feet,—
I tell ye, 'twus a show complete.

Drip-droppin' thru the rustlin' vine
  The sunbeams cum a-flittin',
An' sort uv danced upon the floor,
  Chased by the tabby kitten;
Losh! tew see the critter's big surprise
When them beams slipped inter Minta's eyes!

An' down her brow her pretty har
  Cum curlin', crinklin', creepin'
In leetle yaller mites uv rings,
  Inter them bright eyes peepin',
Es run the tendrils uv the vine
Tew whar the merry sunbeams shine.

But losh! her smile wus drefful shy
  An' kept her white lids under;
Jest as when darkens up the sky
  An' growls away the thunder,
Them skeery speckled trout will hide
Beneath them white pond-lilies' pride.

An' then her heart, 'twas made clar thru
   Uv Californy metal,
Chock full uv things es sugar sweet
   Es a presarvin' kettle.
The beaux went crazed fur menny a mile
When I got the kettle on the bile.

The good old deacon's gone tew whar
   Thar ain't no wild contentions
On Buildin' Funds' Committees an'
   No taxes nor exemptions;
Yet still I sorter feel he preaches,
An' Minta Ann presarves my peaches.

FARMER STEBBINS' OPINIONS.

No, PARSON, 'tain't bin in my style
   (Nor none uv my relations)
Tew dig about the gnarly roots
   Uv prophetic spekkleations,
Tew see what Malachai meant
   Or Solomon wus hintin',
Or round what jog o' futur's road
   Isaiah wus a-squintin'.

I've lost my rest a-keepin' out
   The hogs frum our cowcumbers,
But never lost a wink, ye bet,
   By 'rastlin' over Numbers.
I never took no comfort, when
   The year wus bald with losses,
A-spekkleatin' on them chaps
   Thet rode them varus hosses.

It never gev my soul a boost,
   When grief an' it wus matin',
Tew figger out thet thet thar Pope
   Wus reely twins with Satan.
I took no stock in countin' up
   How menny head uv cattle
Frum Egypt's ranches Moses drove;
   I never fit a battle
On p'ints thet frequently giv rise
   Tew pious spat an' grumble,
An' make the brethren clinch an' yell
   In spiritooal rough-an'-tumble.

I never bet on Paul agin
   The argyments uv Peter;
I never made the good old Book
   A kind uv moral teeter
Tew pass a choreless hour away,
   An' get the evenin' over;
I swallered it jest as it stood,
   Frum cover clar tew cover.

Hain't hed no time tew disputate,
   Except with axe an' arm,
With stump an' rampike an' with stuns,
   Upon my half-clared farm;
An' when sech argyments as them
   Fill six days out uv seven,
A man on Sabbath wants tew crawl
   By quiet ways tew Heaven.

Agin he gets the waggon out,
   An' hitches up the sorrels

An' rides ten miles tew meetin', he
    Ain't braced fur pious quarrels;
No, sir, he ain't! thet waggon rolls
    Frum corduroy to puddle,
An' thet thar farmer gets his brains
    Inter an easy muddle.

His back is stiff frum six days' toil—
    So God takes hold an' preaches
In boughs uv rustlin' maple an'
    In whisperin' leaves uv beeches.
Sez He tew thet thar farmin' chap
    (Likewise tew the old woman),
" I guess I'm built tew comprehend
    Thet you an' her be's human.

" So jest take hold on this here day,
    Recowperate yer muscle;
Let up a mite this day on toil,
    'Tain't made fur holy bustle.
Let them old sorrels jog along
    With mighty slack-like traces,
Half dreamin', es My sunbeams fleck
    Their venerable faces.

" I guess they did their share uv work
    Since Monday's dew wus hoary;
Don't try tew lick 'em tew a trot
    Upon the road tew Glory;
Jest let 'em laze a spell whar thick
    My lily-buds air blowin',
An' whar My trees cast shadders on
    My silver cricklet flowin'.

" An' while their red, rough tongues push back
 The stems uv reed an' lily,
Jest let 'em dream uv them thar days
 When they wus colt an' filly,
An' spekkleate, es fetlock deep
 They eye My cool crick flowin',
On whar I loosed it frum My hand,
 Whar be its crisp waves goin';
An' how in snow-white lily cup
 I built them yaller fires,
An' bronzed them reeds thet rustle up
 Agin the waggon tires;

" An' throw a forrard eye along
 Whar thet bush roadway passes,
A-spekkleating on the chance
 Uv nibbling roadside grasses.
Jest let them lines rest on their necks—
 Restrain yer moral twitters—
An' paste this note inside yer hat:
 I talk tew all My critters,

" Be they on four legs or on two,
 In broadcloth, scales or feathers,
No matter what may be the length
 Uv all their mental tethers,
In ways mayn't suit the minds uv them
 Thet thinks themselves their betters,—
I talk tew them in simple style
 In words uv jest three letters,
Spelled out in lily-blow an' reed,
 In soft winds on them blowin',
In juicy grass by wayside streams,
 In coolin' waters flowin'.

"An' so jest let them sorrels laze
   My ripplin' silver creek in;
They're listenin' in their own dumb way,
   An' I, Myself, am speakin'."

THE FARMER'S DAUGHTER CHERRY.

THE farmer quit what he was at,
   The bee-hive he was smoking;
He tilted back his old straw hat—
   Said he, " Young man, yer joking!
O lordy! (Lord, forgiv the swar!)
   Ain't ye a cheeky sinner?
Cum, if I giv ye my gal thar,
   Whar would *you* find her dinner?

" Now look at *me*; I settled down
   When I wus one an' twenty,
Me an' my axe an' Mrs. Brown,
   An' stony land a-plenty.
Look up thar! ain't thet humsted fine?
   An' look at them thar cattle;
I tell ye, since thet airly time
   I've fit a tidy battle.

" It kinder 'rastles down a man
   Tew fight the stuns an' mire,
But I sort uv clutched tew thet thar plan
   Uv David and Goliar.
Want wus the mean old Philistine
   Thet strutted round the clearin';
Uv pebbles I'd a hansum line,
   An' flung 'em nuthin' fearin',

298

" They hit him squar, right whar they ought,–
   Them times I *had* an arm—
I licked the giant an' I bought
   A hundred-acre farm.
My gal wus born about them days,—
   I wus mowin' in the medder,
When sumone cums along an' sez,
   ' The wife's gone thru the shadder.'

" Times thought it wus God's will she went—
   Times thought she worked tew slavin'—
An' fur the young one thet wus sent
   I took tew steddy savin'.
Jest cast yer eye on thet thar hill
   The sugar bush jest tetches,
An' round by Miller Jackson's mill—
   All round the farm stretches.

" 'Ain't got a mind tew giv thet land
   Tew any snip-snap feller
Thet don't know loam frum mud or sand,
   Or if corn's blue or yeller.
I've got a mind tew keep her yet.
   Last fall her cheese an' butter
Took prizes; sakes! I can't furget
   Her pretty pride an' flutter.

" Why, you be off! her little face
   Fur me's the only summer;
Her gone 'twould be a queer old place—
   The Lord smile down upon her!
All goes with her, the house an' lot—
   You'd like tew get 'em, very!

I'll give 'em when this maple bears
  A bouncin' ripe red cherry."

The farmer fixed his hat and specs
  And pursed his lips together;
The maple waved above his head
  Each gold and scarlet feather.
The teacher's honest heart sank down:
  How could his soul be merry?
He knew—though teaching in a town—
  No maple bears a cherry.

Soft blew the wind; the great old tree,
  Like Saul to David's singing,
Nodded its jewelled crown as he
  Swayed to the harp-strings' ringing.
A something rosy—not a leaf—
  Stirs up amid the branches:—
A miracle *may* send relief
  To lovers fond and anxious.

O rosy is the velvet cheek
  Of one 'mid red leaves sitting!
The sunbeams play at hide-and-seek
  With the needles in her knitting.
" O Pa!"—the farmer pricked his ears:
  Whence came that voice so merry?
The teacher's thoughtful visage clears—
  " The maple bears a Cherry!"

The farmer tilted back his hat:
  " Wal, gal, as I'm a human,
I'll allus hold as doctrine that
  Thar's nuthin' beats a woman!

THE ROWAN TREE

When crowned thet maple is with snow,
   An' Christmas bells are merry,
I'll let ye hev her, Jack—thet's so!
   Be sure yer good tew Cherry!"

THE ROWAN TREE.*

O WHEN the bonnie moon is fair,
   An' clear the loch like siller spread,
An' heather-sweet the gloamin' air,
   An' like a star thy flaxen head,
Why dost thou, Mary, make thy maen,
   An' lean thy white brow on thy knee?
Why drop thy tears on heath an' stane,
   Beneath the wavin' rowan tree?

There was a time when up the brae
   Thy foot, licht as the roebuck's, sprang;
Thy bonnie een ne'er turned away,
   Thy voice a gleesome welcome rang.
Thy lily hands why dost thou wring,
   Nor turn to smile an' gaze on me,
When straight as lavrock's skyward wing
   I seek the wavin' rowan tree?

There was a time thy leaf-soft cheek
   Against the brown o' mine was laid;
From 'neath thy lily-lids did break
   Sic love-licht looks, the mirky shade
O' nicht-fa', creepin' up the glen,
   Did pause, as if 'twere fain to flee

*Mountain ash.
301

Before some sudden sunrise, when
   We trysted 'neath the rowan tree.

There was a time when, as I played
   Wi' thy lang locks o' snooded gold,
Thy sma', saft fingers fondly stayed
   Clasped on my plaidie's rugged fold;
There was, my Mary, once a day
   Ilk hour—a honey-laden bee—
Slipped on the scented air away
   From us beneath the rowan tree.

Now, Mary, when the moon is high,
   Or when the gloamin's saft return,
I glide wi' thee the muirland by,
   I seek wi' thee the glimmerin' burn;
I touch thy locks, thy lips I press,
   Yet fast flow down thy tears for me,
E'en while thy white cheek I caress
   Beneath the wavin' rowan tree.

An' is thy heart, my Mary, sair?
   Tear-droukit a' thy locks o' gold?
An' paled thy roses red an' rare,
   For me beneath the kirkyard mold?
O Mary, sair is heart o' mine,
   For that* thy blue een canna see
My spirit keep fond tryst wi' thine,
   Beneath the wavin' rowan tree!

Oh, tears are saut an' love is long,
   An' dear love's sorrow for the dead;

* *For that*—because.
302

But love is true an' love is strong,
  An' love's a flame forever fed!
Sae, Mary, while thy dear, pure tear
  Rolls down sae swift for love o' me,
For love o' thee, unseen yet near,
  I meet thee by the rowan tree.

I'LL LAUCH TO SEE THE YEAR IN.

GIN I should live to seeventeen,
  Gin Jock should live to twenty,
Gin I be lucky wi' my wheel,
  Gin mackerel be plenty,
Gin Jock's auld kizzen gies a boat,
  Gin Auntie Jean gies gearin',
Gin Uncle Dauvit gies a goat,
  I'll lauch to see the year in.

Gin Minnie gies her braw white hen,
  Gin Daddie says, " God bless her!"
Gin plenishin' be spun by then,
  Gin Grannie gies the dresser,
Gin Dugald gies the oaken kist
  (He'll no' do that, I'm fearin'),
Gin rise the sun wi'out a mist,
  I'll lauch to see the year in.

Gin kindly win's the boaties blaw,
  Gin saft the auld waves wimple,
Gin ilka net a fu' draucht draw,
  Gin plenty shews a dimple,

Gin neebors canty are an' weel,
  Gin ilka thing looks cheerin',
Gin no ane hae an empty crool,
  I'll lauch to see the year in.

Gin loups the sea on New Year's Day,
  Gin shines the red sun rarely,
Gin ilka thing comes as I say,
  Gin nature smiles sae fairly,
Gin I get Jock an' Jock gets me,
  Gin baith get plenty gearin',
Gin no' a strae should fa' our way,
  We'll lauch to see the year in.

MY AIN BONNIE LASS O' THE GLEN.

Ae blink o' the bonnie new mune,
  Ay tinted* as sune as she's seen,
Wad licht me to Meg frae the toun,
  Tho' mony the braeside between;
Ae fuff o' the saftest o' win's,
  As willyart it kisses the thorn,
Wad blaw me o'er knaggies an' linns
  To Meg by the side o' the burn!

My daddie's a laird wi' a ha';
  My mither had kin at the court;
I maunna gang wooin' ava',
  Or ony sic frolicsome sport.
Gin I'd wed, there's a winklot kept bye,
  Wi' bodles an' gear i' her loof—

*Tinted—lost.

MY AIN BONNIE LASS O' THE GLEN

Gin ony tak her an' her kye,
    He'll glunsh* at himsel' for a coof.

My daddie's nae doyt, tho' he's auld,
    The winklot is pawkie an' gleg;
When the lammies are pit i' the fauld,
    They're fear'd that I'm aff to my Meg.
My mither sits spinnin'—ae blink
    O' a smile in her kind, bonnie ee;
She's minded o' mony a link
    She, stowlins, aft took ower the lea

To meet wi' my daddie himsel',
    Tentie jinkin' by lea an' by shaw;
She fu's up his pipe then hersel',
    That I may steal cannie awa'.
O leeze me o' gowany swaird,
    An' the blink o' the bonnie new mune!
An' the cowt stown out o' the yaird
    That trots like a burnie in June!

My Meg she is waitin' abeigh—
    Ilk spunkie that flits through the fen
Wad jealously lead me astray
    Frae my ain bonnie lass o' the glen.
My forbears may groan i' the mools,
    My daddie look dour an' fu' din;
Wee Love is the callant wha rules,
    An' my Meg is the wifie I'll win.

Glunsh—frown.

ISABELLA VALANCY CRAWFORD

A HUNGRY DAY.

I MIND him well, he was a quare ould chap,
   Come like meself from swate ould Erin's sod;
He hired me wanst to help his harvest in—
   The crops was fine that summer, praised be God!

He found us, Rosie, Mickie, an' meself,
   Just landed in the emigration shed;
Meself was tyin' on their bits of clothes;
   Their mother—rest her tender sowl!—was dead.

It's not meself can say of what she died:
   But 'twas the year the praties felt the rain,
An' rotted in the soil; an' just to dhraw
   The breath of life was one long hungry pain.

If we wor haythens in a furrin land,
   Not in a country grand in Christian pride,
Faith, then a man might have the face to say
   'Twas of stharvation me poor Sheila died.

But whin the parish docthor come at last,
   Whin death was like a sun-burst in her eyes—
They looked straight into Heaven—an' her ears
   Wor deaf to the poor childher's hungry cries,

He touched the bones stretched on the mouldy sthraw:
   " She's gone! " he says, and drew a solemn frown;
" I fear, my man, she's dead."   " Of what?" says I.
   He coughed, and says, " She's let her system down!"

306

A HUNGRY DAY

" An' that's God's truth ! " says I, an' felt about
    To touch her dawney hand, for all looked dark ;
An' in me hunger-bleached, shmall-beatin' heart,
    I felt the kindlin' of a burnin' spark.

" O by me sowl, that is the holy truth !
    There's Rosie's cheek has kept a dimple still,
An' Mickie's eyes are bright—the craythur there
    Died that the weeny ones might eat their fill."

An' whin they spread the daisies thick an' white
    Above her head that wanst lay on me breast,
I had no tears, but took the childher's hands,
    An' says, " We'll lave the mother to her rest."

An' och ! the sod was green that summer's day,
    An' rainbows crossed the low hills, blue an' fair ;
But black an' foul the blighted furrows stretched,
    An' sent their cruel poison through the air.

An' all was quiet—on the sunny sides
    Of hedge an' ditch the stharvin' craythurs lay,
An' thim as lacked the rint from empty walls
    Of little cabins wapin' turned away.

God's curse lay heavy on the poor ould sod,
    An' whin upon her increase His right hand
Fell with'ringly, there samed no bit of blue
    For Hope to shine through on the sthricken land.

No facthory chimblys shmoked agin the sky,
    No mines yawned on the hills so full an' rich ;
A man whose praties failed had nought to do
    But fold his hands an' die down in a ditch.

A flame rose up widin me feeble heart,
  Whin, passin' through me cabin's hingeless dure,
I saw the mark of Sheila's coffin in
  The grey dust on the empty earthen flure.

I lifted Rosie's face betwixt me hands;
  Says I, " Me girleen, you an' Mick an' me
Must lave the green ould sod an' look for food
  In thim strange countries far beyant the sea."

An' so it chanced, whin landed on the sthreet,
  Ould Dolan, rowlin' a quare ould shay,
Came there to hire a man to save his wheat,
  An' hired meself and Mickie by the day.

" An' bring the girleen, Pat," he says, an' looked
  At Rosie, lanin' up agin me knee;
" The wife will be right plaised to see the child,
  The weeney shamrock from beyant the sea.

" We've got a tidy place, the saints be praised!
  As nice a farm as ever brogan trod.
A hundred acres—us as never owned
  Land big enough to make a lark a sod."

" Bedad," says I, " I heerd them over there
  Tell how the goold was lyin' in the sthreet,
An' guineas in the very mud that sthuck
  To the ould brogans on a poor man's feet."

" Begorra, Pat," says Dolan, " may ould Nick
  Fly off wid thim rapscallions, schaming rogues,
An' sind thim thrampin' purgatory's flure
  Wid red hot guineas in their polished brogues! "

308

A HUNGRY DAY

" Och, thin," says I, "meself agrees to that ! "
 Ould Dolan smiled wid eyes so bright an' grey;
Says he, " Kape up yer heart; I never knew
 Since I come out a single hungry day.

" But thin I left the crowded city sthreets—
 Th'are men galore to toil in thim an' die;
Meself wint wid me axe to cut a home
 In the green woods beneath the clear, swate sky.

" I did that same; an' God be praised this day !
 Plenty sits smilin' by me own dear dure;
An' in them years I never wanst have seen
 A famished child creep tremblin' on me flure."

I listened to ould Dolan's honest words:
 That's twenty years ago this very spring,
An' Mick is married, an' me Rosie wears
 A swateheart's little shinin' goulden ring.

'Twould make yer heart lape just to take a look
 At the green fields upon me own big farm;
An' God be praised! all men may have the same
 That owns an axe an' has a strong right arm !

Index of Titles

Select Bibliography

Queen's University, Kingston. Library *A Catalogue of Canadian manuscripts collected by Lorne Pierce and Presented to Queen's University*. Toronto, Ryerson 1946. Isabella Valancy Crawford: pp. 100-4

Old Spookses Pass, Malcolm's Katie and Other Poems Toronto, James Bain 1884, 224 p.

The Collected Poems of Isabella Valancy Crawford, edited by J.W. Garvin Toronto, William Briggs 1905. 309 p.

Bessai, Frank 'The Ambivalence of Love in the Poetry of Isabella Valancy Crawford,' in *Queen's Quarterly* 77:404-18 Winter 1970

Burpee, L.J. *A Little Book of Canadian Essays*. Toronto, Musson 1909. pp. 1-16

Garvin, John W. 'Who's Who in Canadian Literature: Isabella Valancy Crawford,' in *Canadian Bookman*, 9:131-3 May 1927

Hale, Katherine *Isabella Valancy Crawford*. Toronto, Ryerson 1923. 125 p. (Makers of Canadian Literature Series)

Ower, John B. 'Isabella Valancy Crawford, the Cause,' in *Canadian Literature*, 34:54-62 Autumn 1967

Reaney, James 'Isabella Valancy Crawford,' in *Our Living Tradition*, Second and Third Series, ed. Robert L. McDougall. Toronto, published in association with Carleton University by University of Toronto Press 1959. pp. 268-86

'Seranus' [Mrs J.W.F. Harrison] 'Isabella Valancy Crawford,' in *The Week*, 4:202-3 Feb. 24, 1887